Lonely planet

EPIC
ROAD TRIPS
of the
AMERICAS

Explore the Americas' most thrilling driving adventures

CONTENTS

INTRODUCTION

"There was nowhere to go but everywhere, so just keep on rolling under the stars." So wrote Jack Kerouac in April 1951, as he formulated his ideas for *On the Road* – the classic Beat generation novel about road-tripping across the North American continent. That early draft was typed as a single, gigantic paragraph on a 120-foot scroll of tracing paper. It was produced in a small apartment on West Twentieth Street in Manhattan, and for countless imaginative readers would unleash the inspiration to drive far and wide into places unknown.

Where might "everywhere" be defined as in the pages of *Epic Road Trips of the Americas*? Chapters here carry you through North America, Central America, South America and the Caribbean. Traveling to the furthest extent west, to Hawai'i, the Big Island, writer Adam Karlin relates how "it is entirely feasible to drive from a beach to a desert to a rainforest to a snowfield, all in the space of about 90 minutes." To the furthest north, Adam Weymouth approaches the settlement of Chicken, Alaska, where a caribou herd 40,000 strong passes by on their annual migration, leaving "their prints in the dust of the roadside, like a series of quotation marks leading off to the distant hills." To the furthest east, Regis St Louis drives a coastal road in Brazil, meeting a band that plays *batucada* – a blend of African-influenced samba and Caribbean beats – on the streets of Salvador: "Three rows of percussionists weave hypnotic rhythms on oversized drums striped in red, yellow and green." And to the furthest south, Amanda Canning drives though some of Chilean Patagonia's most dramatic landscapes to reach Torres del Paine National Park, where "a puma turns and casts me a long look, his yellow eyes locked on to mine, then pads off, slinking over the hill in half-hearted pursuit of llama-like guanaco. I sit and wonder at the chance of it all."

The 50 main road trips you'll find described here are hugely diverse in their themes, as well as their locations. Natural wonders include Mexican deserts strewn with giant *cardón* cacti and shimmering Bolivian salt pans; fall foliage blazing gold, orange and red in the White Mountains of New Hampshire and turquoise waters lapping pink sands on the island of Eleuthera in the Bahamas. Seeking the best locally produced food and (at least, at overnight stops) drink forms further motivation to hit the road, tastes ranging from tomatoey "Western-style" BBQ in North Carolina to fragrant heritage pinots in Oregon's Willamette Valley.

There are road trips that connect a vision for the future with a considerate present. Elaine Glusac tackles Colorado's Top of the Rockies Scenic Byway in an electric vehicle, enjoying a pioneering drive over high-altitude passes – with stop-offs at gold rush ghost towns and bohemian backwaters, recently threaded together by a charger network that makes access by EV possible. On a parallel EV road trip, setting out from Vancouver for British Columbia's Kootenay Rockies, Carolyn B Heller weaves an eco-conscious route between quirky outdoor art and creative plant-based meals.

This book gives new reasons to get out there and explore further. Whoever you are – young or more mature; a solo traveller, or with a group of friends or family to bring along – and whether you have just a weekend to spare, a couple of weeks, or a hope to span continents over several months, you'll find encouragement here to revisit the unique freedom a road trip allows.

HOW TO USE THIS BOOK

The main stories in each chapter feature first-hand accounts of inspiring road trips based in that region. Each includes a factbox to start the planning of a drive – when is the best time of year, how to get there, where to stay. But beyond that, these stories should spark yet more ideas. We've started that process with the 'more like this' section following each story, which offers further ideas along a similar theme, not necessarily in the same country. In the contents pages all drives are color-coded according to difficulty, which takes into account not just how long, remote and challenging they are but also the logistics and local conditions. The index collects together different types of road trip for a variety of interests.

Clockwise, from left: BBQ served in Ayden, North Carolina; "vanlife" adventures in Colorado; cruising the coastline of Baja California, Mexico.

Opening spread, clockwise from left: the Glass Window Bridge on the island of Eleuthera, Bahamas; Joshua Tree National Park, California; a colorful facade in Granada, Nicaragua; salt fish balls with souse in Grenada; the Golden Skybridge, British Columbia. Previous pages: Ruta 23 in Patagonia

NORTH AMERICA

ACROSS THE GREAT DIVIDE: VAIL TO ASPEN

Elaine Glusac tackles Colorado's Top of the Rockies Scenic Byway in an electric vehicle, taking a pioneering eco-conscious drive up and over the Continental Divide.

Breathtaking doesn't begin to describe the Top of the Rockies Scenic Byway, which follows a high-country road at 10,000 oxygen-depleted feet (3048m). The region has long been a summer destination, beginning with the nomadic Southern Ute, who came to the alpine meadows to hunt game. But it was the gold and silver strikes beginning in 1860, and the later railroad boom to access the mines, that made this improbable stretch of road possible. It hugs chiseled granite ledges, vaults over plunging canyons, slaloms between lakes and fills windshields with vast panoramas. Vail and Aspen bookend the heart of the route, with a best-of-the-West mix of dizzying mountain passes, ghost towns and bohemian backwaters between them.

Among the many scenic roads that draw travelers to Colorado, the Top of the Rockies invites electric vehicle drivers to leave the interstate – where charging stations are most commonly found – and explore the wild. The state, which aims to decarbonize its power grid by 2040, has made electrifying its roadways,

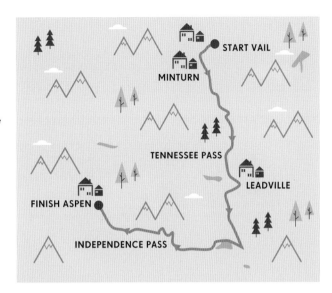

> *"The Leaf burns battery strength on a 3000ft gain peaking at Independence Pass, which crosses the Continental Divide in rubbernecking splendor"*

including mountain byways made for leisurely road-tripping, an emissions-free priority.

Snow still clots some high-elevation hiking trails when I set out from Vail on a warm and sunny June day, in a Nissan Leaf with 250 miles (402km) of charge, plenty to handle this 115-mile (185km) drive. But accelerating uphill and at altitude tends to eat battery life, making the one-to-one comparison misleading. Fortunately, the route's charging stations are no more than 50 miles (80km) apart, starting in amply electrified Vail, which was modeled on an ersatz Alpine village. As the intriguing Colorado Snowsports Museum here tells it, the architecture pays homage to the US Army's 10th Mountain Division, who trained nearby to fight in the Italian Alps in World War II. Some of them later returned to found modern skiing in the United States, building the sorts of ski towns the men had seen in Europe.

Vail's balconied condos and designer boutiques are just a few miles from the official start of the byway, which heads due south from I-70 on Hwy 24, dropping into modest Minturn. The reverse image of Vail, laidback Minturn strings along beside the Eagle River, which rambles southward, glinting in the morning sun as a fly fisherman casts for trout. Since its founding in the late 1800s as a railroad town, Minturn has been well known for its rowdy moments – including annual barstool races in which contestants strap skis to furniture – but this morning I join the flannel-clad locals and their dogs at Sunrise Minturn for lattes and breakfast burritos.

The Top of the Rockies rewards a slow roll, and I stop frequently to take it slower. A few miles down the road at Red Cliff, a former mining camp named for the surrounding red quartzite, the road bridges a dramatic gorge carved by the Eagle River, and the 13,200ft-high (4023m) Notch Mountain streaked in snow winks in and out of view at each bend in the road.

A scattering of ruined barracks are all that remain of legendary Camp Hale, where the 10th Mountain Division trained in a broad valley, now a National Historic Site on the roadside. Plaques detail the outfit and the layout of more than 1000 buildings that nature – including a family of gophers, buzzing broad-billed hummingbirds and watchful kestrels – is actively reclaiming.

At the 10,424ft (3177m) Tennessee Pass, announced with a turnout and a war memorial, I trade cell-phone photos with a motorcyclist, before continuing seven miles south to Leadville, a former boom town that originally inspired the construction of roads throughout the area.

Around 1880, Leadville's silver mines attracted some 30,000 residents, whose brief but profound prosperity is reflected in the grand homes and an opera house still to be found here. Now this funky town of less than 3000 attracts enough road-trippers to its 70 square blocks of Victorian architecture to support a lively mix of gift shops, galleries, roadhouse restaurants and residential museums. I get a private tour of the 1877 Tabor House, once belonging to town magnate Horace Tabor, from an enthusiastic docent who turns out to be its curator, and join the hoodie crowd who trek to shop at the Melanzana outdoor clothing store, which makes its apparel on site.

Just before the whisper of a village known as Granite, the byway forks north on Hwy 82 toward Independence Pass. Distracted by the view, I miss my route the first time around and find myself on another scenic byway, passing a parade of 14ers: mountains over 14,000ft (4267m) tall. The summits here are known as the Collegiate Peaks, each named after a prestigious university, from Harvard to Princeton.

Course corrected, I pause at Twin Lakes to walk a minute of the Colorado Trail, a 500-mile-long (804km) path that crosses eight mountain ranges between Denver and Durango. The route skirts the south side of the lakes at the base of Mount Elbert, leading to a former resort area-turned-ghost town named Interlaken, home to an ornate cupola-topped cabin built by the original developer.

The Leaf is burning battery strength on the next stretch, a 3000ft (914m) gain, peaking at 12,095ft (3686m) Independence Pass, which crosses the Continental Divide in rubbernecking splendor shared by bicyclists who've come the 20 miles from Aspen to test their legs through hairpin turns and rock-hugging passages with sheer drop-offs. The final stretch of highway introduces another ghost town, Independence, where I wander between the former general store and rough-hewn cabins of the abandoned 19th-century mining settlement.

Closed from roughly November through May, Independence Pass serves as the seasonal back door to the glitzy Roaring Fork Valley. Aspen itself is mostly associated with the pricey Gucci shops and art galleries that fill the handsome Victorians – a cue that, yes, this too was originally a mining town – all contained in roughly 100 walkable blocks. But Aspen is also known for its progressive environmental policies – the town buses are electric or powered by alternative fuels, for example – and the influential nonprofit Aspen Institute is devoted to tackling global problems including climate change, making it a fitting place to end an emissions-free alpine road trip.

EV RENTALS

Renting an electric vehicle will be your first summit. The major US car rental companies claim to have EV inventory, but they are still rare. Check directly with the car rental outlets at the Eagle County Regional Airport near Vail; Hertz, Dollar and Thrifty have announced plans to add EVs. Additionally, the peer-to-peer platform Turo, known as the Airbnb of cars, is a good source for finding electric cars (turo.com).

Opposite: a high altitude switchback on Independence Pass. Previous pages: Mount Elbert and Mount Cosgriff loom over Twin Lakes

DIRECTIONS

Start // Vail
Finish // Aspen
Distance // 115 miles (185km)
Getting there // Vail and Aspen have airports, but for more options and lower prices, fly into Denver International Airport. From Denver, Vail is a two-hour drive, while Aspen is four.
When to drive // Because Independence Pass is closed from November through May, you can only drive the full route in summer and fall. Though pine trees dominate, there are plenty of aspens that make the byway a great fall color tour.
Where to stay // Gravity Haus Vail brings contemporary flair to the Bavarian-ish village (gravityhaus.com). In Aspen, the Hotel Jerome fashionably updates the historic 1889 address, which remains the town's social hub (aubergeresorts.com/hoteljerome).

*Opposite, from top: skirting the shores
of Lake Tahoe, California; a miniature
electric vehicle in Hamilton, Bermuda*

MORE LIKE THIS
SCENIC ROAD TRIPS BY EV

THE CASCADE LOOP, WASHINGTON

The 440-mile (708km) Cascade Loop
strings together nine distinct regions where
the topography changes at least every two
hours; EV drivers will find frequent charging
stations. Named for the Northwest's
volcanic mountain range, the circular
route leaves Everett, just north of Seattle,
along the Puget Sound, turning east to
farmland and arty towns like Snohomish
before ascending to the namesake plunge
at Wallace Falls State Park en route to
4061ft (1238m) Stevens Pass. Next, the
Bavarian village of Leavenworth offers
kitschy fun (there's a museum with the
world's largest collection of nutcrackers),
and the Wenatchee and Columbia Rivers
meet in a valley filled with apple orchards
and wineries. The North Cascades will
tempt you out of your car and onto trails
headed for glacier-fed lakes. Finish up
driving – and beachcombing – the length
of laidback Whidbey Island.
Start/Finish // Everett
Distance // 440 miles (708 km)

BERMUDA

A set of limestone islands in the North
Atlantic totaling just 21 sq miles (54
sq km), Bermuda prohibits full-size car
rentals. Most visitors tend to rent scooters
to get around to the famous pink-sand
beaches of the British Overseas Territory.
But several rental agencies offer mini
electric cars, such as the Italian two-
seater Tazzari and a shrunken Hummer.
With speed limits at 22mph (35kph), you
won't get anywhere fast, but, then, you're
never going far between stops. Leaving
the capital of Hamilton, drive to the
17th-century settlement of St. George's on
the East End of the island, the picture of
colonial Britain in its tidy architecture and
cobblestone lanes. As you swing back to
follow the West End's hooking peninsula
en route to the Royal Navy Dockyard – a
former naval base that now houses shops
and restaurants – stop at Church Bay
Park to snorkel with Technicolor fish and
beachcomb the rosy strand of Horseshoe
Bay Beach.
Start/Finish // Hamilton
Distance // 55 miles (88 km)

LAKE TAHOE, CALIFORNIA

Nearly 60 fast chargers line the route to
Lake Tahoe, allowing for emissions-free
trips to the popular mountain resort. Start
out in Monterey on the rugged central
coast, home to the conservation-focused
Monterey Bay Aquarium, and skirt the
Silicon Valley sprawl on the way east
to Sacramento, the state capital with a
reputation for farm-to-table fare supplied
by surrounding growers. Take Hwy 50
through California Gold Rush country,
stopping to refresh with a quick dip at Lake
Natoma in Folsom, then continuing to the
wineries that cluster in the Sierra Nevada
foothills, offering tastings with mountain
views (Boeger Winery in Placerville is
particularly scenic). In the El Dorado
National Forest, hike to Horsetail Falls,
which wind forcefully down a granite rock
face, before arriving in South Lake Tahoe,
gateway to one of the deepest lakes in
North America.
Start // Monterey
Finish // South Lake Tahoe
Distance // 290 miles (467km)

ALLIGATORS, ART DECO AND THE OVERSEAS HIGHWAY

On this trip, Adam Karlin explores Miami, the Everglades, and the Florida Keys: a South Florida cocktail of weirdness, beauty and, of course, alligators.

I'm not saying all Florida stories involve alligators. I'm just saying this one has at least three.

But they come later, after I leave Miami, a city where the weirdness of the Sunshine State is baked into a patina of pastel, all overlaid with hot pink neon. I begin at the Vizcaya, an Italianate Renaissance-style wedding cake of a mansion built by James Deering, the Maine-born heir to an agricultural equipment fortune.

For me, the Vizcaya encapsulates Miami's illusion, opulence, folly and future; it's over the top, beautiful and innovative, yet also ill-positioned – its European furniture and art rotted away in the Florida humidity not long after the mansion was completed. When Deering died the Vizcaya passed on to nieces who couldn't maintain it; they, in turn, sold the property to the city of Miami, which operates the building as a museum, as well as a photo backdrop for a thousand weddings and *quinceañeras*.

From the Vizcaya I drive to Coral Gables, a posh neighborhood lined with banyan trees and (slightly) smaller versions of Vizcaya-esque Mediterranean mansions. For lunch I eat an excellent bagel at Coral Bagels, largely staffed and patronized by "Jewbans," an only-in-South Florida marriage of Jews and Cuban Americans.

Miami in particular, and South Florida in general, is a place of exiles; indeed, this city may have the largest variety of Spanish accents collected in one municipality. Many people come here seeking freedom and success, and some eventually find it.

I drive over the A1A causeway, arching across the straits of Biscayne Bay, the sky as turquoise as the waters below. The causeway connects Miami proper to Miami Beach, a separate city that at least initially eschewed South Florida's relentless drive for new development with historical preservation. In this case, what

has been preserved is a vision of the future, at least from the early 20th century: the hotels of South Beach's Art Deco district.

Painted in tropical pastels and adorned with terrazzo flooring, neon signage and architectural elements meant to evoke sea travel, Aztec temples and even space flight, these buildings were saved from destruction in the 1980s. They subsequently attracted an international slew of designers and tastemakers, some of whom were also drawn by South Beach's reputation as a gay-friendly slice of paradise. Then came the photoshoots, the models, the hip-hop videos – and now, me, strolling up Ocean Drive in the electric shadow of a dozen neon marquees.

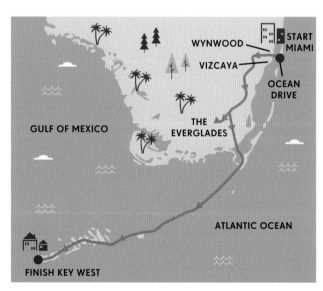

> *"I look at my guide, who seems unperturbed – the alligator is just sunning, she says"*

EVERGLADES CITY

Head west from Miami on the Tamiami Trail and you'll find a whole new Everglades. You'll pass Native American land, as well as mile after mile of flooded forests that feel more conventionally swampy than the wet prairie near Homestead. Keep driving and you'll get to Everglades City, a so-laid-back-it's-sleeping fishing village where the seafood is fresh and you can rent a kayak to explore the Ten Thousand Islands, a series of mangrove barrier islands.

From left: scenes from the Everglades swamp; a conch fritter stand in Key West; the Overseas Highway. Previous page: a 1950s Ford Thunderbird parked in Art Deco Miami Beach

I watch the mass snapping of selfies as the bold and beautiful of Latin America and Europe descend onto this beach for an international party. Amidst such glamour, I retire to a small Cuban cafe, needing the steadying support of eggs and a *cortadito* (an espresso shot and steamed milk). This is, frankly, a bad idea, seeing as it is now night and Cuban coffee makes me want to do anything but sleep.

I drive back to mainland Miami and the streets of Wynwood, which have rapidly gentrified into an adult playground filled with street art, graffiti murals, food halls and bars that are a hair more indie than the nightlife scene in South Beach. I walk around Wynwood for the better part of the night, eating sushi and drinking cocktails that roughly cost the down payment on a house, fueled by *cortadito* and the extreme FOMO of knowing yet another amazing bar is around the corner.

I run into my first alligator the very next morning at, appropriately enough, the area where Miami's trailing edge fades into the

Everglades. The gator is chilling between a canal and the shoulder of the road, not moving for love nor money on a Sunday morning; maybe it let loose in Wynwood the night before, too.

Then I drive south, toward Homestead, and listen to the Spanish language radio slip from Cuban to Mexican music, reflecting the demographics of this largely agricultural area. I snag fresh orange juice from the Robert is Here fruit stand, and continue into Everglades National Park.

South Florida is full of beauty – people, buildings and beaches – but the soft horizons of the River of Grass, a mix of flooded prairie and wooded swamp, never cease to outpace all of the above. I head out with a tour on a "wet walk" into a flower-laden dome formed by cypress trees. Within the dome, the pale morning sunlight illuminates a scene that is ridiculously sublime: orchid blooms, deep rushes of dark water and twisting vegetation.

Also: there's an alligator, grinning on a log. Alligators have millions of years of evolutionary comparative advantage in

wetlands. They were built for the swamp. As I stand there, knee deep in the muck, I think on how I was not. I look at my guide, who seems unperturbed – the alligator is just sunning, she says – and try to soak up her nonchalance the same way the gator is soaking up the light.

From here I make my longest drive of this trip on to the Florida Keys, the archipelago that stretches like a sandy necklace into the Gulf of Mexico. The Keys, long since populated by misfits, artists and independence seekers, can be considered, in terms of eccentricity, more "Florida" than Florida proper. It takes about three hours of driving along the Overseas Highway and its multiple causeways and mangrove islands to cross the Keys. At one point, I stop and stretch on Big Pine Key, one of the larger Keys, and there, in a freshwater slough, I spot the eyes of (you guessed it) a gator, winking back at me.

Taking this as a sign, I press on to Key West, a knuckle of rainbow-colored Caribbean colonial architecture, peppered with LGBTQ+-friendly bars, excellent (if pricey) fine dining and Bahamian, Cuban and Polish markets (the last serving a large Eastern European work-visa population). I watch the sun set over Florida Bay from Mallory Square, a famed gathering spot for street performers, while fire-eaters eat and buskers busk, and for a moment, the off-kilter world of South Florida manages a strange, surreal balance.

DIRECTIONS

Start // Miami
Finish // Key West
Distance // 210 miles (340km)
Getting there // Miami International Airport is one of the busiest in the country, but you can also fly into Fort Lauderdale-Hollywood International Airport, only 30 miles (48km) north. Car rental is easy at either. Get a Sun Pass with your rental; these allow quick navigation of toll roads.

When to drive // Florida is famed for its warm, sunny weather, and both the warmth and the sun characterize the climate of South Florida. You'll find cheaper rates and more heat in the summer, but this is also hurricane season. The shoulder seasons of mid-October through November and March through May offer a good balance of lower prices and consistent weather.

Opposite, from top: Bisbee, Arizona;
Frank Pepe Pizzeria Napoletana, New
Haven, Connecticut

MORE LIKE THIS
OFFBEAT AMERICA

PHOENIX TO THE BORDER

The red Arizona desert is home to a ton of character – and characters. In Phoenix, stroll through Roosevelt Row, especially on a First Friday arts walk, to see the creativity that brews in the desert heat. Don't leave town without grabbing cocktails at temples to midcentury neon cool like the Womack or Rips. Drive south to Tucson, a town that truly feels like the place where the United States and Mexico begin to blend into one another. The culinary evidence is the Sonoran dog, a hot dog topped with onions, tomatoes, salsa verde and pinto beans. It's hard to beat the backyard ambience of El Sinaloense Hot Dog Cart. Now head further south to Bisbee, a gorgeous border town where hippies and cowboys rub shoulders and grab beers together amidst Wild West architecture.
Start // Phoenix, Arizona
Finish // Bisbee, Arizona
Length // 210 miles (340km)

CONNECTICUT TO RHODE ISLAND

Two of the smallest states in the country pack in a lot of idiosyncrasies. Drive along the Connecticut coast and you'll soon hit New Haven, a town that balances salty portside grit with Yale, one of the nation's most prestigious universities. Head to Wooster St for an apizza (a nod to the Neapolitan dialect), New Haven's coal-fired take on pizza. Roll on east to New London, where cadets from the Coast Guard Academy rub shoulders with Caribbean immigrants, preppie yacht kids and old-school Italian American fishers. Head onward to Providence, a town where decades-old Portuguese restaurants share the block with eateries from northwest China. Stroll by the Athenaeum, a library that looks like it's a lost wing of Hogwarts, and keep an eye out for the cemeteries that inspired the 20th-century horror icon, HP Lovecraft.
Start // New Haven, Connecticut
Finish // Providence, Rhode Island
Length // 110 miles (180km)

BIRMINGHAM TO CLARKSDALE

Start in Birmingham, Alabama, and head straight to the Sloss Furnaces, a former steel facility that is now a sort of Gothic temple to a lost industrial age. After poking around the rusted ruins, grab dinner at Rodney Scott's, eat barbeque that will make a believer out of an atheist, and have a drink at the Garage, a cross between a garden supply store and a dive bar. Now leave town and drive northwest into Alabama hill country and Dismal Canyon, which is anything but. Rather, this wooded gorge is known for being lit with thousands of glowworms come nighttime. Head 120 miles (193km) west to Oxford, Mississippi, and walk the forest trails that surround the home of William Faulkner, before going to the Mississippi Delta and Clarksdale, where the blues endure amidst the expansive cotton fields.
Start // Birmingham, Alabama
Finish // Clarksdale, Mississippi
Length // 290 miles (470km)

BITE INTO NORTH CAROLINA'S BBQ TRAIL

Emily Matchar takes a journey deep into North Carolina's beloved BBQ culture, from tomatoey "Western style" in the Appalachians to vinegary "Eastern style" on the coastal plains.

In North Carolina, BBQ culture brings out the kinds of passions and rivalries we normally reserve for college basketball. We're born Carolina fans or Duke fans, and must stay that way until we return to dust. Likewise, depending on our hometowns, we're committed to lifelong Eastern- or Western-style BBQ partisanship.

Eastern style means a whole hog, slow roasted over woodsmoke, then shredded and tossed in a tangy vinegar sauce. Western style is just the pork shoulder, also shredded, but with a sauce that includes ketchup. It's sometimes also known as Lexington or Piedmont style.

Full disclosure: I began this trip a lifelong Eastern-style partisan. I grew up in North Carolina's Triangle area, slightly on the eastern side of the BBQ divide. No gloopy red sauce for me, thanks!

Fuller disclosure: I was raised a Duke fan, but switched sides after marrying my Carolina grad husband. My brother still hasn't forgiven me, but I'm not sorry. Go Heels!

So, I figured I should at least give Western style a fair try. Maybe it wasn't as sickly sweet as I imagined. After all, Carolina rules and Duke drools, right?

Thus begins the epic North Carolina BBQ Trail road trip. Following a map of top BBQ joints from the North Carolina BBQ Society, I plan to start in the east and move west. My only goals? Eat as much pork as possible and remain open-minded.

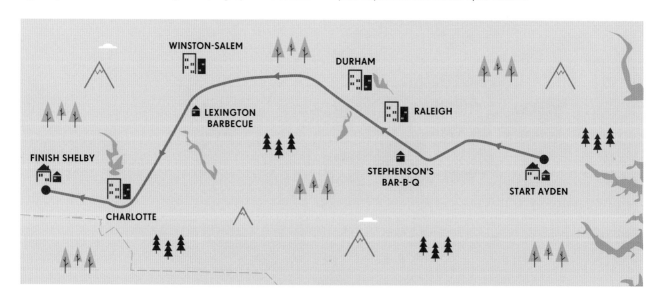

I launch my journey in the drowsy town of Ayden, in North Carolina's Inner Banks, whose biggest event is the annual Collard Festival. Yet it's become a pilgrimage site for BBQ connoisseurs because of one place: the Skylight Inn.

As I pull up in the sun-dazzled parking lot, I have to smile. The otherwise no-frills brick building wears a replica of the US Capitol Rotunda on its roof like a hat, giving it the kitschy air of a roadside attraction. But inside it looks just like any other local BBQ joint I've ever seen: tiled floor, '70s-era wood-look Formica tables, diner bottles of ketchup and mustard. I read the menu off an old-fashioned letterboard above the counter and order a BBQ tray with slaw and cornbread. Through the kitchen service window I watch a cook chop a pile of steaming pork into bits so fast his hand is a blur. Everything smells of sweet woodsmoke and cooking oil.

My BBQ tray looks like any other: a pile of meat in a waxed paper tray, a scoop of slaw, a slab of cornbread. But then I take a bite and – oh! – this is not any ordinary roadside BBQ. This is something higher, grander. Slippery ribbons of tender inner meat mix with crisp crackling bits from the outside of the hog ('cue lovers sometimes call this "the white" and "the brown"). It's smoky from its hours spent over a woodfire, and bright from the vinegar sauce, with a deep, savory porkiness.

No wonder people have been coming here since 1947. Loyal locals still call it "Pete Jones' place," for its original pitmaster, though he passed more than 15 years ago.

Leaving Ayden, I drive west through the Sandhills, which, despite its name, is a flattish region of poor soil and sparse pines. I cross into southern Wake County, where old tobacco farms now mingle with prefab Dutch Colonial-style houses. It's hot and sunny, and the wind streaming through my open window smells of cut grass. At the side of rural Hwy 50 lies Stephenson's Bar-B-Q, a long barn-shaped building across a cracked asphalt parking lot.

Stephenson's is known for having the smokiest BBQ around – they roast the meat for seven hours before leaving it over the smoking coals overnight. Biting into a dripping pork sandwich on a soft white roll, I can see why people have been coming here since 1958. I finish by spooning up a bowl of hot Brunswick stew, a classic North Carolina side dish of stewed beans, veggies and meat (usually chicken, though in days past it was squirrel).

Eastern for the win, right?

Not so fast. I cross the Piedmont region, the hills growing larger, the pines thicker. I skirt the exurban sprawl of the Triangle and the Triad and pull into Lexington, a former textile town that bills itself as the Barbecue Capital of the World. Fighting words.

Even in a BBQ-crazed town and a BBQ-crazed state, Lexington BBQ (Honey Monk's, to locals) stands out. The unassuming white bungalow makes all sorts of national lists, and pops up in glossy magazines and on the Food Network. I am prepared to be disappointed, even scornful. After all, I've crossed the state's dividing line – I am now in Western-style territory.

At first glance, my tray of chopped BBQ looks pretty similar to the others I've had, just slightly... redder. Both the meat and the slaw have a slightly rosy glow thanks to ketchup. But, taking a bite, I see it's not gloopy or cloying. Its slight sweetness balances nicely with the oiliness of the meat and the tang of vinegar.

Later that day, I continue on into the foothills of the ancient Appalachian Mountains. As I go further west, the air grows cooler, the sky a darker blue and there's a hint of autumn in the early September breeze. I stop in the town of Shelby, where Red Bridges Barbecue Lodge has been serving chopped, minced or sliced pork slathered in a brick-red sauce since 1953. The spot is classic Americana: neon sign, turquoise vinyl booths, gravelly voiced waitresses who call you "hon." And the 'cue? Well, it's good – all crispy brown cracklings and sweet-tangy sauce.

So, am I Team Western Style now? At the end of the day, I think my only loyalty lies with pork cooked long and low and smoky. The sauces? They're both good. It's like choosing between the beach and the mountains. Lucky for me, North Carolina has both. Which is why, as they say, if North Carolina wasn't God's favorite state, then why did he make the sky Carolina blue?

BARBECUE HISTORY

Food historians believe that barbecue is a Caribbean cooking tradition, where meat was cooked over indirect heat for long periods of time and dressed in citrus juice. The Spanish introduced pigs to the New World, and pork barbecue was born. Enslaved people spread the tradition across the South and vinegar came to replace citrus, the tanginess disguising marginal cuts of meat. Over time, what was once a necessity grew into an art form.

"It's smoky from its hours spent over a woodfire, and bright from the vinegar sauce, with a deep, savory porkiness"

Clockwise, from opposite left: pulled pork is prepared at the Skylight Inn, Ayden, North Carolina; find Western-style BBQ in Lexington, NC. Previous page: the BBQ & Chicken Combo served at the Skylight Inn

DIRECTIONS

Start // Ayden
Finish // Shelby
Distance // 300 miles (483km)
Getting there // Avoid any Eastern-Western debate by flying into the middle: Raleigh-Durham International Airport and Charlotte Douglass International Airport are both within an hour of several BBQ trail stops.
Where to stay // You can hit many stops on the eastern end of the BBQ Trail as day trips from popular beach towns like Morehead City; many of the western stops are near the scenic mountain town of Asheville.
More info // The North Carolina BBQ Society maintains the official BBQ Trail map and site (www.ncbbqsociety.com). The Southern Foodways Alliance is an excellent resource for the history of BBQ (www.southernfoodways.org).

MORE LIKE THIS
FOODIE ROAD TRIPS

THE KENTUCKY FRIED CHICKEN TRAIL

It's no coincidence that the fast-food behemoth KFC originated in the Bluegrass State. Kentucky has a long tradition of excellent fried chicken, which Colonel Sanders (yes, he was a real person) simply capitalized on. Start your tour de chicken at the Sanders Cafe in Corbin, where Harland Sanders began hawking his secret-recipe chicken during the Great Depression. From here, cross the Daniel Boone National Forest and through the limestone hills to the Beaumont Inn, a gracious brick building with white columns, whose restaurant serves a heritage-breed fried chicken from an old family recipe. Then head into the genteel horse-raising city of Lexington for the classic golden-fried drumsticks at Parkette Drive-In. Zigzag west through bluegrass meadows to Shelbyville, where Claudia Sanders Dinner House was founded by the Colonel's wife – she made a mean fried chicken too!

Start // Corbin
Finish // Shelbyville
Distance // 170 miles (274 km)

THE WISCONSIN CHEESE TRAIL

The Dairy State produces more than one-fourth of all the cheese eaten in the United States, so, if you're a cheesehead, why not go straight to the source? A tour of Wisconsin's southwestern area cheesemakers is an easy day or overnight trip. Start at Fromagination in the capital, Madison, which stocks local artisan cheeses like gouda-style goat milk Evalon and a smooth, nutty Moody Blue. From here, drive into lush Green County for a tour of the Swiss-style cheesemaker, Emmi Roth Käse. Lunch at Baumgartner's Cheese Store and Tavern – try the limburger and mustard on rye! Then double back north to rural Sauk County, where Carr Valley Cheese has been producing sharp cheddars for four generations. Head back to Madison for dinner at the Old Fashioned, a retro supper club with Wisconsin classics like cheese curds and bratwurst.

Start/Finish // Madison
Distance // 190 mi (306 km)

NEW MEXICO'S GREEN CHILE TRAIL

Late summer in New Mexico means chile-roasting season, the air perfumed with the smoky scent. Start in Hatch, home to the annual Hatch Chile Festival, and pick up a *ristra* (wreath of dried chiles), then stop at Sparky's for a green chile cheeseburger. Look for the enormous statue of Uncle Sam holding a green chile. Heading north through the golden landscape, hit Big Jim Farms in Albuquerque to pick your own heritage green chiles. Then it's on to the silvery high desert of northern New Mexico. In Santa Fe, head to Kakawa Chocolate House, which follows the pre-Columbian tradition of mixing chile and chocolate – try the green chile chocolate caramels or the chocolate-dipped *chile de arbol*. On Saturdays, don't miss the Santa Fe Farmers Market for chiles of all sizes and shapes.

Start // Hatch
Finish // Santa Fe
Distance // 250 mi (402 km)

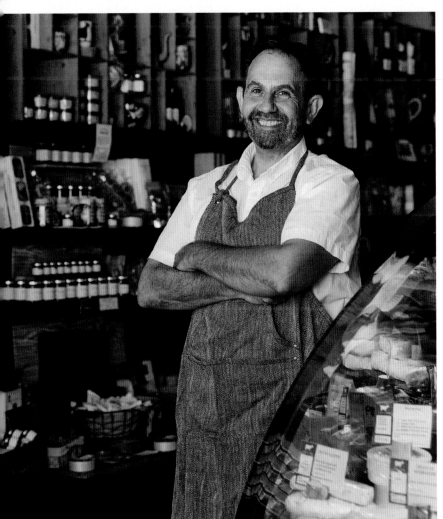

Clockwise, from top: green chiles roasting; Sanders Cafe in Corbin, Kentucky; Ken Monteleone, the owner of Fromagination cheese shop in Madison, Wisconsin

IN SEARCH OF THE OLDEST TREES

The Pacific Marine Circle Route travels through old-growth forests at the wilder end of Vancouver Island – woods, as Carolyn B Heller found, where there may be bears.

Some of North America's oldest trees live in British Columbia, and many of these giants stand tall on Vancouver Island, on Canada's Pacific coast. In search of big trees, I've decided to road-trip the Pacific Marine Circle Route, a 180-mile (290km) loop that meanders from the city of Victoria through the forests on the island's southern end.

I begin my solo adventure leaving Victoria on Hwy 1, which climbs above the Saanich Inlet as it turns north. To find my first wooded attraction, I detour onto Shawnigan Lake Rd. Skirting the lake's west shore, I come to the Kinsol Trestle, the largest of eight timber bridges that carried island trains throughout the early 20th century. I walk across the bridge, which is supported by a crisscrossing scaffold of wooden beams, high above the valley. At 145ft (44m) tall, Kinsol remains among the world's tallest freestanding trestles.

After my short hike, I head back to Hwy 1 along the vineyard-lined roads of the Cowichan Valley, where more than a dozen wineries, cideries and distilleries welcome visitors. Without a designated driver, though, I pass on the wine tasting, stopping instead in the village of Cowichan Bay.

The bay is as smooth as a mirror on this sunny autumn morning, with sailboats bobbing at the wooden docks. I peek into the tiny harbor-front Wild Coast Perfumery, which formulates its scents from local ingredients. Sniffing fragrances made from Douglas fir essence, juniper berry oil and cedar leaf tincture, gives me an aromatic introduction to the local forests.

I make another sweet-smelling stop at Westholme Tea Company, on a wooded road north of Duncan, where in 2010, owners Margit Nellemann and Victor Vesely established Canada's first commercial tea-growing business. Here you can rest a while to sample some of the green and white oolong teas that they grow, served in ceramics that Nellemann crafts.

From Duncan, I turn west onto Hwy 18. The road is more wooded, and it's in the woods that I find my day's final destination: the Farm Table Inn. This cedar and stone chalet has two guest rooms; mine has rustic wood furnishings and a puffy duvet.

In the dining room overlooking the forest, owners Evelyn Koops and George Gates tell me that they live onsite, raising chickens that I'll meet free-ranging around the property. The chickens will provide eggs for my breakfast the next morning, but tonight I dine on Pacific halibut in caper sauce, bannock with herb butter, curried cauliflower,

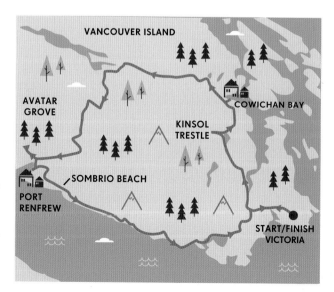

DEFENDING THE FOREST

In 2021, the forests of Vancouver Island became the site of the largest act of civil disobedience in Canadian history. During months of demonstrations, police officers arrested more than 1100 protesters attempting to stop old-growth logging on the site known as Fairy Creek, or Ada'itsx, on the traditional territory of the Pacheedaht First Nation. Mammoth old-growth yellow cedars are among the many trees at risk of being logged. The debates and protests continue.

"I've hiked along the ocean and into the woods, enjoyed good local food and seen not just massive trees but a hungry black bear"

Clockwise, from opposite: the Kinsol Trestle Bridge; a trail near the Cowichan River; evergreens at the edge of Sombrio Beach. Previous page: a gnarled giant western red cedar in Avatar Grove

and an assortment of roasted vegetables – beets, squash, carrots – from local farms. A dollop of chocolate mousse adds a sweet finish to my road-trip day.

The next morning, I follow the quiet sandy shore of Lake Cowichan and turn south toward Port Renfrew, where things start getting a little wilder. The road winds through the woods, narrowing yet further at a series of one-lane bridges. The forest gets denser, too, and soon, my vehicle seems to be the only one on the road.

I pull over at a sign for the Harris Creek Spruce and set out on foot. Walking along a short, forested trail, I spy my first really big tree. This is an enormous Sitka spruce, its massive trunk mossy and spotted with the morning sun.

Further south, I turn off onto a rutted, bumpy dirt road that travels deeper into the woods. I'm looking for a section of old-growth rainforest on the traditional territory of the Pacheedaht First Nation. The Pacheedaht call this area T'l'oqwxwat, which is known in English as Avatar Grove.

The road bisects the grove into two sections. I hike into the forest of the Upper Grove, where a sign on the boardwalk trail points toward "Canada's gnarliest tree." And it's an impressive one – an enormous red cedar with bizarre twists of wood wrapped like an alien growth around its hefty trunk.

Retracing my route and crossing into the Lower Grove, I find more gnarly trees among the skinnier pines. While they're not as huge as the famous gnarly cedar, similar quirky burls surround their trunks.

I could stay for hours in these fanciful forests, but I press on to the town of Port Renfrew. The fog is rolling in as I pull up to the Wild Renfrew resort, which has romantic log cabins directly on the Pacific, as well as a more modest but comfortable lodge up the hill, where

I'll be spending the night. At the lively Renfrew Pub, crowded with hockey fans, I eat a grilled salmon sandwich slathered with piquant wasabi mayo.

Back in my car the next morning, I follow Hwy 14 along the island's south coast. The road ducks in and out of the forest, peeking out from cliffs above the ocean before looping back into the woods.

I decide to pull off for a better view of the Pacific and stop above Sombrio Beach, where a short trail between the evergreens slopes toward the ocean. Just above the sand, I come to a campsite.

Three people stand in front of their tents, staring toward the bushes a few feet away. When I call, "Good morning," they pivot and stare at me. I shift uncomfortably, wondering what I might have interrupted here.

One of the men holds a finger to his lips, then points toward the shrubbery. "There's a black bear right there," he whispers.

I turn and see the bear, his head just visible above the greenery. He's stood up on his hind legs, grabbing berries from the bushes with both paws.

Startled, I babble, "I was just trying to walk to the beach," as I back away, the Pacific shore suddenly unimportant. Hustling back up the trail, I glance around nervously. I'm hoping that the bear doesn't have a buddy waiting in the woods.

All is quiet as I return to my car and continue toward the city. On this wild Vancouver Island road trip, I've hiked along the ocean and into the woods, enjoyed good local food and seen not just massive trees but a hungry black bear. It's surely time to head for home.

DIRECTIONS

Start/Finish // Victoria
Distance // 180 miles (290 km)
Getting there // BC Ferries from British Columbia's mainland dock at Swartz Bay Terminal, 19 miles (30 km) north of downtown Victoria. From the United States, Black Ball Ferry Line operates a car ferry from Port Angeles, Washington.
When to drive // Year-round, although the rainforest is least rainy between May and October.
Where to stay and eat // Farm Table Inn (www.farmtableinn. ca), Wild Renfrew (wildrenfrew.com)
Local tips // Beaches line the island's south coast, from Port Renfrew to Victoria. Check locally for bear warnings and try not to hike alone.
More info // Tourism Cowichan (www.tourismcowichan.com), Tourism Vancouver Island (vancouverisland.travel)

Opposite, from top: the fallen Dyerville
Giant in Humboldt Redwoods State
Park, California; Mount Revelstoke
National Park, British Columbia

MORE LIKE THIS
THE BIGGEST TREES

MOUNT REVELSTOKE NATIONAL PARK, BRITISH COLUMBIA

If you're road tripping the Trans-Canada Hwy across British Columbia between the Pacific coast and the Canadian Rockies, stop to check out the massive trees in Mount Revelstoke National Park. The park is located outside the mountain town of Revelstoke, popular with skiers and snowboarders in winter and hikers during the warmer months. Switchback up the 16-mile (26km) Meadows in the Sky Parkway into forests of hemlock and cedar with expansive views across the Columbia River Valley, but to find the biggest trees, pull off Hwy 1 for a short hike on the Giant Cedars Boardwalk Trail, where some of the old-growth trees are more than 500 years old.
Start// Vancouver
Finish // Calgary
Distance // 668 miles (1075 km)

OLYMPIC PENINSULA, WASHINGTON

You can find plenty of big trees on a road trip around Washington's Olympic Peninsula, particularly within the boundaries of Olympic National Park. In the park's 1 million plus acres (400,000 hectares) of wilderness, you can hike into the mountains, wander along the coast and explore the old-growth temperate rainforests. Head for the lowlands of the Sol Duc or Elwha Valleys for groves of Douglas fir and western hemlock. Deeper in the park, moss-covered Sitka spruce and western hemlock stand tall amidst the ferns and lichens in the jungle-like Hoh Rain Forest and Quinault Area. And if you'd like to add some vampire lore to your rainforest adventures, stop in the town of Forks, the setting for Stephenie Meyer's *Twilight* novels, where teen Bella Swan falls for an ever-so-handsome vampire.
Start/Finish // Seattle
Distance // 480 miles (770 km)

REDWOOD FORESTS, CALIFORNIA

One of North America's most famous "big tree" road trips takes you into the redwood forests of Northern California. Less than an hour's drive from San Francisco, you can get an introduction to the state's old-growth coastal redwoods at Muir Woods National Monument, but true tree lovers should continue north on Hwy 101 to visit Humboldt Redwoods State Park, where you can drive through the woods on the famous 31-mile (50km) Avenue of the Giants. Further north, the Redwood National and State Parks consist of four linked wilderness areas that are home to some of the world's tallest trees, growing in the Coast Range outside the Humboldt County towns of Eureka and Arcata. Return to the Bay Area along Hwy 1 to pair your tree tour with striking Pacific scenery.
Start/Finish // San Francisco
Distance // 675 miles (1085 km)

CONTINENTAL AMBITIONS

On a driving adventure across the breadth of America, Regis St Louis follows backroads past Appalachian peaks, gypsum deserts and wildlife-filled wetlands – with surprises along the way.

"Nothing behind me, everything ahead of me, as ever so on the road." So wrote Jack Kerouac in his roving masterpiece *On the Road* (1957). As I shift into fifth gear, it's hard not to think of the life-lusting wanderer while speeding across the George Washington Bridge, the towering skyscrapers of Manhattan receding in the distance. Before me stretches a vast continent packed with natural wonders – too many to cram into a single lifetime, let alone a one-month road trip. And yet, the untold possibility of the route ahead leaves me buzzing with excitement.

Low-rise mountains grow higher as I roll through Pennsylvania and into Virginia. Off the interstate, two-lane roads meander past rutted farmlands and oak and hickory forests. Late in the day I pull into Floyd, a tiny one-stoplight town tucked into the foothills of the Blue Ridge Mountains. A farmers' supply store and a barber shop flank the streets near the Floyd Country Store, the epicenter of the community here. Inside, the shelves are lined with all the essentials for modern-day homesteading: rolling pins, denim shirts, eco-friendly soaps.

Tonight is the Friday Night Jamboree, and a small stage is filling up with musicians while people of all ages take seats on folding chairs. A sign near the soda fountain reads: "Granny's Rules: no

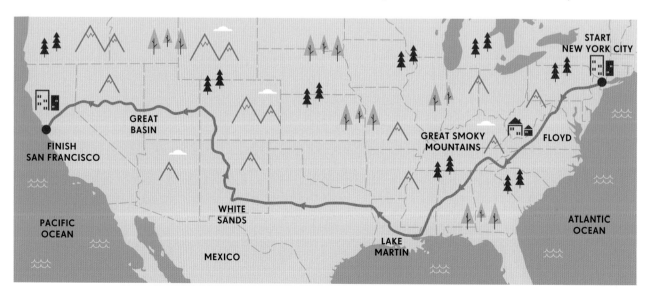

"Before me stretches a vast continent packed with natural wonders"

smokin', no cussin' and no drinkin'." Rapid-fire fingerpicking on a banjo spills over the audience, then a fiddle player and a guitarist join in. As the tempo picks up, the crowd takes to the dance floor. Amid the bobbing heads, a young man wearing a John Deere hat and shiny white clogs pounds out deft rhythms on the wooden boards. Later comes a slow-paced waltz and even a round of square dancing. When stepping out for fresh air, I notice a group of musicians playing in the parking lot across the street, and I hear the twang of a banjo further off. Bluegrass seems the heart and soul of this town, and that night I drift off to sleep with old-time ballads bouncing around my head.

Misty, low-lying fog clings to the darkened valleys as I set out the next morning. On the two-lane Blue Ridge Parkway, gentle curves roll past some of the world's oldest mountains. The full grandeur of the Appalachians unfurls when I reach the Thunder Struck Ridge Overlook. The deeply corrugated ridges of the Great Smoky Mountains stretch off to the horizon, and in the morning sun the grizzled summits seem cloaked in a blueish haze. Later, I hike along silvery streams through old-growth forests to the Ramsey Cascades, an impressive 100ft (30m) waterfall in a remote corner of the national park.

Heading deeper into the South, I stop in Atlanta to see Ebenezer Baptist Church, where Martin Luther King Jr inspired countless lives during his years as a co-pastor. Just up the road stands the two-story Queen Anne home where the peace

advocate was born, and the tomb where he and Coretta Scott King lie buried. Even on a weekday, a wide range of visitors – black and white, young and old – linger around the memorial fountain surrounded by the words of this giant of the American Civil Rights movement.

In Louisiana, the drive over the Atchafalaya Basin takes me on an elevated highway across the nation's largest river swamp. Dark-plumed anhingas dry their wings on the bare branches of bald cypress trees, while fishermen cast for bluegill from flatboats beneath the low-lying clouds. Just past Breaux Bridge, a Cajun guide named Butch takes me on a boat tour across the tea-colored waters of Lake Martin. His spotting skills are astonishing, as he points out bald eagles, black-crowned night herons, snowy egrets... "and there's a roseate spoonbill," he says, as a brilliant flash of hot pink catches my eye. "Some people around here like to call them Cajun flamingos." We slow while nearing a fallen tupelo tree, which is straddled by a large alligator – the first of dozens we see.

After traversing the dusty plains of Texas, I enter the blinding landscape of White Sands National Park in New Mexico. I follow a 16-mile (26km) scenic drive beside dune fields glittering like freshly fallen snow, then take a slow going walk across the Alkali Flat. I pass families sledding down the steep slopes, before reaching a vast expanse of nothing but gypsum in every direction.

Turning north, I cross the sunbaked expanses of northwestern New Mexico and follow the curves of the Animas River all the way

SYNCHRONICITY

One of the most bewitching sights of the Smokies is the *Photinus carolinus*, better known as the synchronous firefly. This insect is famed for its dazzling display of bioluminescence, where thousands of hovering insects flash in perfect harmony. Although the light display is related to mating, scientists aren't sure why the fireflies synchronize their blinking. The event happens for about two weeks sometime between late May and late June.

From opposite left: exploring Arches National Park; a restored steam locomotive of the Durango and Silverton Narrow Gauge Railroad; the Appalachians, viewed from the Blue Ridge Parkway. Previous page: crossing the Rockies in Colorado

DIRECTIONS

Start // New York City
Finish // San Francisco
Distance // 4500 miles (7242km)
Getting there // Three airports near New York (JFK, LGA and EWR) receive flights from pretty much everywhere.
When to drive // Travel in spring (April and May) for milder weather and fewer crowds. Autumn (late September through October) spreads fiery colors, though Rocky Mountain passes see snow from October through April.
Where to stay // The friendly Hotel Floyd (www.hotelfloyd. com) puts you in the heart of the Blue Ridge town. In Cajun Country, the Blue Moon Guesthouse (www.bluemoonpresents. com) is a traveler's favorite with live-music sessions (zydeco) in the backyard. Devils Garden Campground lies deep within Arches National Park (www.recreation.gov).

to Durango, Colorado. The peaks of the Rockies surround me as I continue past the old mining town of Silverton and onto Hwy 550 (aka the Million Dollar Hwy), where tight curves seem a hair's breadth from plunging drop-offs into the valley below.

The snowclad mountains transform into a Martian landscape of red-rock buttes when I reach Utah. In Arches National Park, the formations known as the Fiery Furnace glow with an otherworldly light beneath the setting sun.

Days later I find myself in a remote corner of Nevada, once again awestruck while taking in a view across subalpine forest to a 13,000ft (3962m) peak. I feel there's somehow nothing left to see, until I go hiking in the Great Basin National Park. On a trail beneath Wheeler Peak, I walk amidst the oldest living trees on the planet. Smooth of bark and twisted by the wind into sinewy, sculptural shapes, bristlecone pines have been standing here since before builders laid the cornerstone for the Great Pyramid of Giza. The oldest specimens have lived almost 5000 years, surviving freezing temperatures, deep snowfall and gale-force winds.

I can't shake the quiet, brooding presence of these weathered sentinels, even as I roll beneath the vermilion towers of the Golden Gate Bridge toward San Francisco. The United States is a land of grand cities and iconic national parks, but as my journey draws to an end, it's the unsung sights – the Appalachian towns and southern swamps, awe-inspiring pulpits and ancient trees – that leave me longing to return.

MORE LIKE THIS
GRAND NORTH AMERICAN JOURNEYS

ALONG THE EASTERN SEABOARD

Driving from Maine to Miami, you'll explore coastal enclaves and metropolitan centers packed with intrigue. This 15-state journey begins near the island-dotted waterfront in Portland, followed by walks in the cobblestone lanes of Boston's Beacon Hill. Tour the gilded mansions of Newport, Rhode Island, before heading into a thicket of big city culture in New York, Philadelphia and Washington, DC. In Virginia, follow the coast out to Chincoteague Island, where wild ponies still roam, then continue along the barrier islands of the Outer Banks. Watch the landscape change as you reach Savannah, its parks full of live oak trees dripping with Spanish moss. In Florida, wander back a few centuries in St Augustine, founded in 1565. Traveling the length of the Sunshine State, you'll finally arrive in the capital of Latin America – aka Miami.

Start // Portland, Maine
Finish // Miami, Florida
Distance // 1950 miles (3138km)

TRACING THE CONTINENTAL DIVIDE

The Continental Divide runs along the high peaks of the Rockies, determining whether water flows west to the Pacific or east to the Atlantic. Start off in Glacier National Park with a hike up Triple Divide Peak, where water flows in three directions (Hudson Bay, the Pacific, the Gulf of Mexico). From there wind your way southeast to Rawlins, Wyoming, one of the rare towns that sits right on the Divide. Prepare for astonishing vistas in Colorado, especially as you near Grays Peak, the Divide's highest point at 14,278ft (4352m). Your engine will appreciate the gentler elevations as you travel through the Plains of San Agustin in New Mexico. End the trip with a walk up Big Hatchet Peak, with lofty views across the desert, near the edge of Mexico.

Start // Glacier National Park, Montana
Finish // Big Hatchet Peak, New Mexico
Distance // 2010 miles (3235km)

TRANS-CANADA HIGHWAY

The journey across the world's second-largest nation takes you through six time zones. Start on the edge of the Pacific, driving up Vancouver Island before ferrying over to the mainland. The mountain-backed Fraser River will be your guide as you continue across much of British Columbia. The views only get better as you drive amid towering peaks on the edge of Glacier and Banff National Parks. Roll through prairies full of corn and cattle, and glimpse wind-sculpted hoodoos in the Canadian Badlands. The biggest of the Great Lakes comes into view as you skirt Lake Superior, before journeying past Ottawa, Montréal and Québec City. The final leg ends as this trip began, with a scenic ferry ride – this time across Cabot Strait – and a grand finish in St John's, the most easterly city in North America.

Start // Victoria
Finish // St John's
Distance // 5030 miles (8095km)

Clockwise, from left: Assateague Light, off the coast of the Virginia Eastern Shore; Beacon Hill, Boston; the Thompson River, seen from the Trans-Canada Highway in British Columbia

NEW MEXICO'S RESERVATION ROUTE

Simon Moya-Smith zips through Indian Country and the Land of Enchantment, in search of marijuana edibles, oils and ointments on the other side of the border with Colorado.

Rae is behind the wheel now, swerving in and out of traffic as I scribble notes on a coffee-stained stationary pad from Mexico.

It's 4pm, and a brutal sun pierces the eyeballs as we zip west. We just left Santa Fe, New Mexico, the epicentrum of seriously rich, wide-brim-hatted, turquoise-clad white well-to-dos in the Southwest. We're on our way to get good weed edibles that alleviate the pain and torment of debilitating diseases like arthritis. Right. At the time of writing, recreational weed is still illegal in the Land of Enchantment. But for those living in the northern part of the state, close to Colorado, all that's required is to hop the border and load up on the goods for family who desperately need them – so that's the focus of this journey, to get Mom the lotions and Grandpa the potions.

We're on I-25 and have just rolled in to the Pueblo of Sandia Village reservation. There are 23 Indian reservations in New Mexico, and before we get to our destination we'll pass through

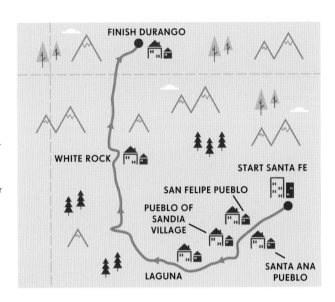

*"We have our
own languages,
laws and even
presidents"*

five more: San Felipe, Santa Ana Pueblo, Laguna Pueblo, Acoma Pueblo and the Navajo Nation, the latter being one of the largest in the country. There are no gas stations on the Navajo Nation between Thoreau and Farmington. No cell service either, which means if you run out of gas it's the buzzards for you.

Our destination is Durango, Colorado, where recreational weed dispensaries pepper the main drag. We have about three more hours to go. Of course, it's important to be careful when driving through rez after rez – random rez pups, roadkill, road rage and running out of Red Bull are all things to avoid. Keep the tank full of gas and an eye out for potholes and whatever creature will inevitably decide to test its fate and dart in front of you, sending you into a death swerve. I recall once clipping the tail of one

deer and the nose of another in the dead of night in northern Minnesota. I somehow managed to cut through the negative space between them, barely avoiding my own early end.

At Albuquerque we merge onto I-40; all the way to Thoreau, some 100 miles west, are shuttered frybread stands, even blockades and checkpoints at the entrance of almost every reservation. At one time, Indigenous families living on the rez could make stacks of cash on a Saturday afternoon selling authentic Native jewelry and fluffy frybread to highway-goers who'd make the pit stop for a bite or a beaded bracelet, but not right now.

We've booked a room at the Strater Hotel in downtown Durango, which is marketed as a Wild West–style joint.

"We're Indigenous," I say to Rae, who's Eskimo from Alaska.

"Do you think they'll let us in? Or perhaps they'll put us straight to work, taking photos in headdresses with the white guests." She doesn't respond, just keeps listening to the audio book I've been rude enough to interrupt.

OK. This is casino country, and the brightly lit joints have names like Black Mesa, Route 66, Dancing Eagle and Sky City... just to list four of the 21. As separate sovereign nations, we get to do things like that – establish small or massive casinos and resorts, because when you drive onto a rez you've legally left the United States. We have our own languages, laws and even presidents. Every Native enrolled with a nation or tribe has a dual citizenship, myself included, and it doesn't matter if we were born in places like Dallas, Denver or Detroit. We are the first ones, the original peoples, who get to say things like, "Human history began on this continent with us" – because it did.

For a minute there, I get a ping on my phone alerting me to an email and a pang telling me I got a text. But in an instant the four bars go back to nothing. A second of cell service. "What a tease!" I shout to Rae, interrupting the audio book for the twelfth time.

We're in the Navajo Nation now, the largest of the trek. Gorgeous, beautiful country, but no running water in most parts, so families have to haul gallons to their homes with water tanks in the back of pickup trucks. There is no wasted water in the desert. And if you see a bat flying sideways, get the hell inside. It probably drank water from a well, which was likely contaminated by non-Native corporate drillers out this way.

We're still on the rez. It's nearing night now. Almost to Farmington. A weird thing slithers in the distance, but we can't make it out. A massive semi passes us in a DO NOT PASS section on the highway. I'm about to comment, but refrain. I've interrupted the audio book for the last time.

As the sun sets we pull into Durango, where the hotel has sat since 1887, or something like that. There's a connected saloon on the corner. Two women are dressed in mid-shin, ruffled skirts and petticoats, as cowboys in scarfs sit at the bar. "Two Indians walk into a saloon..." I chuckle to Rae as we waltz in.

We stay for a few nights at the haunted hotel, don't see a single ghost, but do square up to a few glaring cowboys to pass the time. This is the Wild West after all, and some blue-eyed mustachioed types here still don't like Indians in their cowtown. Eventually, we grab the high-voltage edibles and the cream with THC, and bail for browner places.

We're back in New Mexico now, back on the Laguna Pueblo rez, mourning again the defunct frybread stand. The brutal sun is behind us this time as we travel east, off this rez and zapping by the next.

The moral to this story is to always buy local when you're on the rez. And watch out for cowboys with massive mustaches in Wild West saloons in the Rockies, especially if you're Native.

CHRISTMAS STYLE

In New Mexico, "Christmas style" has nothing to do with holiday decorations: it is instead essential dining lingo. In the land of roasted Hatch chiles, Christmas style simply means you'd like a combination of red and green chile sauces smothering your order of huevos rancheros, enchiladas or medium-rare steak. New Mexico is so renowned for its chiles that state legislators even added a pair on the license plate.

Clockwise, from opposite left: Sky City Casino Hotel is owned by the Acoma Pueblo; jewelry for sale along the I-40; chiles drying; New Mexico's Bisti/De-Na-Zin Wilderness. Previous pages: dwellings of the Acoma Pueblo

DIRECTIONS

Start // Santa Fe, New Mexico
Finish // Durango, Colorado
Distance // 327 miles (526km)
Getting there // There's a small airport in Santa Fe, but the Albuquerque International Sunport serves more destinations. Rent a car in Albuquerque or hop on the Rail Runner Express train to Santa Fe.
When to drive // Roads can be treacherous after a winter storm, but are still worth driving to see the gorgeous San Juan range outside Durango, especially during the holidays.
Where to stay // In Albuquerque, try the Hotel Chaco (www.hotelchaco.com). In Durango, the antique-filled Strater Hotel (strater.com) is rumored to be haunted.
Detours // Chaco Culture National Historic Park is the ancestral home of the Pueblo people, with 9th-century ruins.

Opposite, from top: hiking in
the Badlands, South Dakota;
an Oglala Lakota dancer

MORE LIKE THIS
RESERVATION DRIVES

PINE RIDGE RESERVATION, SOUTH DAKOTA

Home to the Oglala Lakota Nation, Pine Ridge Reservation has some of the most beautiful landscapes in the Western US. On the northern end of the rez lies the Badlands: steep valleys, spires of piercing rock formations and a dry, rugged terrain under an ocean of big blue sky. The Lakota named it the Badlands, or maco sica, due to the lack of water and the difficulty of travel here on foot or by horse. While summer temperatures can easily surpass 100°F (37.8°C), the Pine Ridge rez is absolutely worth a visit for the Oglala Days celebration, also called the Oglala Lakota Nation Wacipi and Fair, which takes place in July and August. There, you can enjoy traditional foods, dancing, drumming and authentic Oglala Lakota jewelry and wares on sale.
Start // Badlands National Park
Finish // Allen
Distance // 42 miles (67km)

SHINNECOCK RESERVATION, LONG ISLAND, NEW YORK

While land theft and the forced removal of Indigenous peoples has resulted in most reservations being located in the West, several were established on the East Coast. One of those is the Shinnecock Reservation near the southeastern tip of Long Island, located next door to the wealth and pomp of the Hamptons. A 2½-hour drive from Brooklyn, the Shinnecock Reservation hosts a massive powwow every summer, right off the sandy shores of the Atlantic. Folks come from as far as New Jersey and just across the Long Island Sound from Connecticut to partake in music, dance and food that predates the European arrival by thousands of years. Get out of the hustle and bustle of the city to enjoy an ancient culture, language and people.
Start // Brooklyn
Finish // Shinnecock Reservation
Distance // 88 miles (141km)

NATIVE VILLAGE OF UNALAKLEET, ALASKA

Unlike Indigenous communities in the continental US and Canada, Alaska Natives – while recognized by the government as separate sovereign nations – do not live on reservations or reserves. Instead they live in villages, one of which is the small coastal community of Unalakleet. This is accessible only by plane, boat, snowmobile or dogsled, and visitors occasionally drop in to hunt and fish. While Alaska in January can reach a mercury-shattering -40°F (-37.8°C), temperatures in July are a pleasant 70°F (21.1°C). Traditional cuisine is based on whale, seal, king crab, salmon, moose and caribou. The village is considered a hub for the surrounding people, including the Yupik, Inupiaq, Siberian Yupik, Cupiq and the Athabaskan Nation, which can provide rich cultural exposure for those willing to travel so far north.
Start // Anchorage
Finish // Unalakleet
Distance // 391 miles (629km)

OREGON'S UNSUNG BOOZE TRAIL

Road trips are thirsty work. Anita Isalska embarks on an alternative Oregon Trail from pinot noir country to Bend's brewpubs, finishing at the cowboy bars of Pendleton.

Oregon beckons to hikers, rafters and campers. Its natural splendor also lures idlers, like me. I'm eager to see the state's vast plains and alpine peaks, but intent on viewing them through a tipsy haze.

That's why I'm plotting a route across Oregon via wineries, microbreweries and boozy saloons. Together with my husband, Matt, I'll quaff my way from the northwest coast to the eastern prairies.

We're setting out from Cannon Beach, where we've downed espresso to fortify us for the road ahead. Aboard our trusty Subaru, we quickly leave the crowds behind. The eastbound Hwy 26 curves sinuously through Ponderosa pines, and for miles we see nothing but forested foothills and rolling farmland. But after an hour, trim rows of vines start to appear. We're approaching the Willamette Valley, the most celebrated wine region in the Pacific Northwest.

More than 500 vineyards thrive here, many of them cultivating pinot noir. These notoriously fickle grapes are right at home in Oregon's climate, where the generous rainfall and mild temperatures cajole them to ripen and flourish, producing a wine that is light, spicy and beautifully brick-red.

Pulling off Hwy 18, I nudge the accelerator, coaxing the car uphill to Coeur de Terre Vineyard. Finally at rest, Matt and I both sigh with satisfaction as we fling open the doors to an absurdly picturesque scene. The chalet-style tasting room overlooks vineyards that tumble downhill. Purplish grapes hang from the vines in pear-shaped clusters. We eye up a spot on the pine deck, and settle into wooden chairs for a wine tasting.

The co-owner of Coeur de Terre, Lisa Neal, scurries out to pour fragrant pinots into a sextet of tasting glasses. I savor each variety's different notes, from raspberry to warming spice. Ordering

a full glass of my favorite heritage pinot, I gently remind Matt that it's now his turn to drive.

Fortunately, we're only a few minutes away from McMinnville, our stop for the night. In the morning, we fling open the curtains to see 19th-century buildings housing wine bars and restaurants. But the road beckons, and soon enough we're driving past meadows and fire-scarred forests to our next destination, Bend.

An hour in, Hwy 20 begins to undulate through the rugged foothills of the Cascade Mountains. Volcanic peaks, like Three Fingered Jack (7844ft/2391m) and Mt Washington (7795ft/2376m), point to a cloudless sky. After another two hours, the road levels out

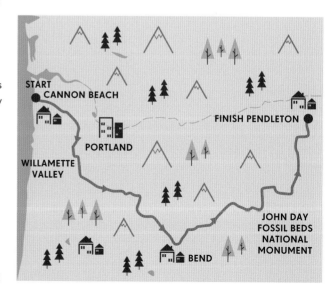

COWBOY ROUND-UP

Pendleton's motto is "let 'er buck." And if there's one time to see that happen, it's during the annual round-up (www. pendletonroundup. com), where cowboys and cowgirls have cavorted since 1910. Folks don their finest ten-gallon hats to cheer hoof-kicking acrobatics, watch military displays and join casual whiskey-swillin' hootenannies. It's also a Native American cultural highlight: local Umatilla, Cayuse and Walla Walla people set up hundreds of teepees, showcase millennia-old dance traditions and sell ornate beadwork.

and we arrive at Bend, an old logging town that has reinvented itself for outdoor adventurers.

But exertion isn't mandatory. Stepping out of the car, we see dozens of people in rafts bobbing down the Deschutes River, cans of IPA in hand. A little further east is Bend Brewing Company, spilling out into a beer garden shaded by lodgepole pines. Folks are raising tropical IPAs and coffee porters, while their dogs snooze away under the picnic tables.

Bend Brewing Company is one of dozens of breweries, each trying to out-innovate the others with unexpected flavors, low-ABV ales, gluten-free options, CBD beers – you name it.

Before settling into the beer scene, we decide to stretch our legs. We grab rental bikes, pootle beside the river and complete our loop back in downtown Bend, where we join dozens of Lycra-clad drinkers at Deschutes Brewery. Moments later, Matt has a dark cherry ale in hand, while I sip a gluten-free IPA with the aroma of bitter orange. As the hours pass, only the chill of twilight ushers us to our hotel for the night.

When our alarms buzz us blearily awake, we drive east toward our final destination: the cowboy bars of Pendleton. We zoom along the Ochoco Highway, and the Cascades' tall peaks and pine forests recede into the distance. They're soon replaced by wide plains dotted with sagebrush and juniper, lit gold by the noon sun.

When we take Hwy 19 north, the landscape abruptly changes again. We've reached the John Day Fossil Beds National Monument, where coral-pink hills are streaked with crimson and ochre. I ease off the gas pedal so we can marvel at this rainbow-colored landscape, and finally pull over by the Blue Basin trailhead. Even on this short walk, we can experience John Day's confounding color palette, from vivid red ash to hills flecked with mint-green clay. It feels utterly remote – in fact, the complete lack of cell service is making it difficult to arrange the evening's pub crawl in Pendleton...

After two more hours heading along Hwy 395, my phone finally

"Ordering a full glass of my favorite heritage pinot, I gently remind Matt that it's his turn to drive"

trills back to life with a message from our host, Josh. He says he's excited to show us around Pendleton, and eager for us to try the town's namesake whiskey.

After parking beside our mildewy motel, we head downtown. Pendleton is a curious place, an unexpected hive of nightlife in Umatilla County's sea of wheat fields.

"There's a dive bar I've been meaning to try," grins Josh, leading us to the Packard Tavern. There are a few whoops as we file inside, and the bartender immediately strides over.

"Beers?" she intones. Turns out, this is more of a command than a question.

"I was hoping for whiskey," corrects Josh.

"Whiskey?" The bartender's eyes flash in amusement, and her darkly penciled eyebrows shoot upward. "This ain't no cocktail bar. Listen, I'mma help you guys out."

We follow the bartender outside, where she directs us to the Rainbow Cafe, a treasury of hard liquor. Inside, bison heads gaze blankly from the walls, and neon Bud Light signs crackle above the bar. Amber bottles glint, from local corn whiskey and huckleberry vodka to wheat whiskey made right here in Umatilla County.

We order the latter, perching on leatherette stools to watch the patron pour four-finger-thick serves of whiskey. The scent is sweet, like butterscotch, and after one smoky sip, I feel a warm contentment unfolding inside me. Night is falling, but here in the Rainbow Cafe, lights twinkle and whiskey glasses clink merrily – a refuge from Oregon's winding roads and boundless plains.

Clockwise, from above: pinot noir grapes being harvested in the Willamette Valley; Deschutes Brewery & Public House in Bend; cowboys at the Pendleton Round-up. Previous page: the Coeur de Terre Vineyard

DIRECTIONS

Start // Cannon Beach
Finish // Pendleton
Distance // 507 miles (816km)
Getting there // Arrive by train or plane in Portland. If renting a car in Portland, you can skip Cannon Beach and head straight to McMinnville.
When to drive // May to October avoids challenging winter road conditions and unpredictable spring weather.
Where to stay // Bend has family-friendly apartments and chain hotels, while McMinnville has stylish boutique stays; our choice is the Atticus (atticushotel.com). Pickings are slimmer out east, but you'll find some charismatic B&Bs, like Pendleton House (www.pendletonhousebnb.com).
Best detour // Native American history is on show at the Tamástslikt Cultural Institute, 8 miles (13km) east of Pendleton.

*Opposite: at SLO Brew The Rock,
in San Luis Obispo, California*

MORE LIKE THIS
TASTING ROUTES

CALIFORNIA'S COASTAL BEER TRAIL

Quaff lagers, ales and chocolatey porters along this boozy twist to California's iconic Hwy 1. Begin by bar-hopping Santa Rosa, California's burgeoning microbrew capital (don't miss the Belgian-inspired beers at Russian River Brewing). Stray south to San Francisco, making time for creamy coffee porter at Standard Deviant and crisp lagers at neighborly Anchor Brewing. Take coastal Hwy 1 for cliffside views en route to San Luis Obispo, where stalwart SLO Brew has been pouring honey-blonde ales since the '80s. Next up is the City of Angels: German pilsners and English-style ales at Monkish Brewing will slake your thirst, and you can stop at buzzing Bruery Terreux in Anaheim on your way east. Steer south to Belching Beaver for peanut-butter stout and mango-flavored IPAs before finishing in surfy San Diego, where a bevvy more microbreweries await.

Start // Santa Rosa
Finish // San Diego
Distance // 650 miles (1046km)

TENNESSEE'S WHISKEY LOOP

Seek out Tennessee's richest, oakiest whiskies on a grand circuit of this Southern state. Warm up at the honky-tonk bars of Nashville, where you can sip award-winning bourbon at historic Nelson's Green Brier Distillery. Next, head east to Brushy Mountain Distillery to glug apple pie moonshine, made within the forbidding walls of a former penitentiary, then continue to downtown Knoxville for standout malt whiskey at PostModern Spirits. Heading on east, amber liquors await at small-batch Bootleggers Distillery. Meanwhile at Ole Smoky Barn, you can toe-tap to bluegrass while swirling a snifter of salty watermelon or caramel apple whiskey. If your driver is still sober, head southwest to Chattanooga, whose namesake whiskey distillery breaks up the trip to Lynchburg. Here, world-famous Jack Daniel's offers tours and knock-out tasting flights. Complete the loop by driving north to rustic Leiper's Fork Distillery before returning to Nashville.

Start/Finish // Nashville
Distance // 550 miles (885km)

QUÉBEC'S HARD CIDER ROUTE

Imagine French wine culture transported to North America's orchards, and you have Québec's hard cider scene: exacting, sophisticated and enormously varied. This fruity route weaves from Montréal to the romantic Île d'Orléans, via tasting rooms and *cidreries* galore; drive in autumn to see orchards at their blushing best. Start by driving south from Montréal to sleepy Hinchinbrooke, where Ferme Black Creek's English-style orchard produces brut, classic and maple varieties of cider. Next, head east to Domaine ValBrome, where you can relax in deck chairs for an outdoor tasting of sweet, dry and semi-sweet ciders. Better yet, pick your own apples northeast at Cidrerie Verger Bilodeau, also a producer of "ice cider," a punchier regional twist produced from frozen apples. Just remember to fill your trunk with apple mustard and apple butter before you leave.

Start // Montréal
Finish // Île d'Orléans
Distance // 323 miles (520km)

THE PACIFIC COAST HIGHWAY

Amanda Canning follows the trail of surfers and road-trippers while driving from San Francisco to LA, discovering cute seaside towns, wild scenery and awesome breaks en route.

The last wisps of early-morning fog are drifting around the reddish-orange girders of the Golden Gate Bridge, the iconic structure marking a fitting start to the trip I'm about to take. With the entire continent of North America to my left and the vast expanse of the Pacific to my right, I plan to drive Hwy 1 from San Francisco to Los Angeles, sticking to the coastal road as it twists and dips south.

As I leave the city behind, passing old motel signs that advertise "very quiet rooms," all other vehicles on the road seem to have one thing in common – surfboards, strapped to their roof racks. California's surf culture took off in the 1920s, when the boom in private car ownership allowed travelers to zip up and down the coast in search of the best surf breaks. Over the next 450 miles (725km), surfers will be a constant sight through my car's windshield – standing at the side of the road or sitting on their van's tailgate, staring at the waves and the wetsuit-clad riders already out at sea.

At Santa Cruz, I pull over to watch surfers of all ages, sizes and abilities tackle some particularly impressive waves as California brown pelicans wheel in the wind above. Beside me, a teenage boy tells his novice and clearly nervous young brother, "Surfing is like riding a huge skateboard, you'll see." They shuffle with their boards down to the shore and make their way into the ocean, and I continue into town, to join families and groups of friends eating tater twists and cotton candy on the wooden boardwalk fronting its beach.

The landscape gets wilder as the road winds south – contorted cypress trees grow out of the cliffs above small coves pockmarked with rock pools and littered with driftwood. Beyond them, sleek,

shiny harbor seals flop on surf-thrashed boulders poking out of the water. The smell of saltwater and seaweed hangs heavy in the air. Hwy 1 becomes more rollercoaster than road at this point – one moment it hugs the coast at beach level, the next it rises and the sea is suddenly a precipitous drop far below. Fifteen miles (24km) beyond the genteel resort town of Carmel, the human ingenuity in taming this landscape is revealed at one of California's most recognizable landmarks – Bixby Creek Bridge. Biker dudes on Harleys and young couples driving campers all pull over to take pictures of the bridge, which towers 280ft (85m) above a steep-sided canyon right on the edge of the Pacific.

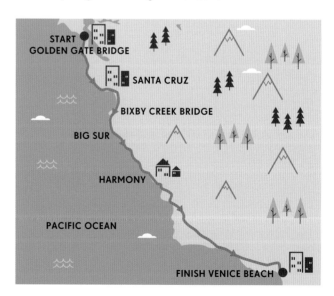

SURF'S UP

Santa Cruz is the place for a crash course in Californian surf culture. It has a great little surfing museum in a tiny lighthouse overlooking one of the town's best surf spots – Steamer Lane (www.cityofsantacruz.com). People gather here throughout the day to watch surfers catching breaks on the waves below. Call into the shop of legendary surfer Doug Haut and pick up T-shirts, caps and so on, and see how boards are shaped (www.hautsurfboards.com).

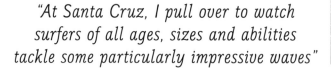

"At Santa Cruz, I pull over to watch surfers of all ages, sizes and abilities tackle some particularly impressive waves"

With the sun high in the sky and temperatures rapidly heading toward "baking," it's a relief to leave the coast for a bit and follow the road into the cool darkness of the pine and redwood forests just inland. I stop in the cute town of Big Sur for blueberry strudel; watched over by a bluebird intent on scooping up any crumbs, I spend time looking at the notices outside the coffeeshop. The ads for tie-dye workshops, yoga classes and wind chimes are a reminder that this stretch of coastline is as popular with California's original hippies as it is with surfers.

When Hwy 1 rejoins the coast, it squiggles and twists around a series of headlands, and the pace of the vehicles on the road slows to leisurely. With the sun bouncing off the Pacific and turning the pampas grass covering the low hills golden, it's hard not to stop at every roadside lookout point and gape at the views.

A colony of elephant seals is heaped up on the beach at Ragged Point. They lie prone, occasionally tossing sand over themselves with a flipper and showing noisy disapproval if a neighbor gets restless. Awkward bags of blubber on land, they

turn into slinky, hydrodynamic machines once they've heaved themselves into the water. Beyond their turf, the landscape changes again. It mellows and softens into a ripple of dry hills – the Spanish colonizers who built haciendas, ranches and churches here in the 18th and 19th centuries must have felt right at home. This is farming country, and it's tempting to pull over at every roadside stall for strawberries, mangoes, pineapples and oranges. At the tiny village of Harmony, many road-trippers turn into Harmony Cellars and sit on picnic tables outside with a plate of charcuterie and a glass of zinfandel. Many also choose this point to veer off Hwy 1 and head inland, drawn by the lure of the wineries and cellar doors of San Luis Obispo, a few miles east.

I continue my journey south, though, and spend some time driving parallel to the rail tracks that also trace this route. The shadowy outlines of the Channel Islands, a national marine sanctuary, are visible across the frothing, wind-whipped ocean. It's a thrill when the view is briefly obscured by the handsome blue-and-silver livery worn by the locomotive and carriages of

From left: local surfers wait for a break in Santa Cruz; McWay Falls spill onto the shore near Big Sur, off Hwy 1; coast redwoods. Previous page: the Bixby Creek Bridge

DIRECTIONS

the Pacific Surfliner, rattling past on its way to Los Angeles.

The train beats me to the City of Angels, but I'm not far behind. The multimillion-dollar beach houses of Malibu announce a decided change of pace – Hwy 1's natural attractions come to an end, replaced by equally diverting human creations. The meandering coastal road becomes a broad freeway lined with arrow-straight palm trees, and the RVs are replaced by sports cars and commuters zipping by on electric scooters. From here, the highway continues all the way to San Diego, 120 miles south (193km), but it's the end of the road for me. A journey that started at one icon ends at another: Venice Beach.

As bodybuilders do push-ups and shimmy up poles at Muscle Beach, and lifeguards in red shorts pack up their stations for the day, I rest on the sand and watch the sun sinking into the Pacific. It's an experience I almost certainly share with all those road-trippers still making their way along the coast; no matter where you are on Hwy 1, at the end of the day, you're guaranteed to pull over and gaze out to sea.

Start // San Francisco
Finish // Los Angeles
Distance // 457 miles (735km)
Getting there // Fly into San Francisco International Airport and out of Los Angeles International Airport.
When to drive // Fall is a great time to take the trip – it's still warm, getting hotter as you head south, and there's less traffic on the road.
Where to stay // In San Francisco, get inspiration for a road trip in Hotel Emblem, which has a literary theme and Beat Generation quotes on the walls; in LA, Hotel Erwin is steps from the beach and has a rooftop bar perfect for a sundowner.
More info // The tourist board (www.visitcalifornia.com) has plenty of info on road-tripping in the state.

MORE LIKE THIS
SURF-CENTRIC ROAD TRIPS

FLORIDA

Art Deco architecture, a thriving Cuban cultural scene and nonstop nightlife: Miami can be a tough place to leave. A trip north to Daytona Beach is the bait to get you out of the city. Starting on South Beach, where Miami's surfers gather when the swell is good, the road hugs a built-up stretch of shoreline where, nonetheless, golden sands, barreling breaks and pin-straight palm trees are never far from view. Away from the waves, there are plenty of distractions to justify a stop en route, including the Kennedy Space Center, the island sanctuary of Blowing Rocks Preserve and the Surfing Florida Museum in West Palm Beach. The journey's end should be celebrated by getting into the water; there are plenty of surf schools and board rental shops in Daytona Beach, and even more beach bars if you'd rather watch.
Start // Miami
Finish // Daytona
Distance // 262 miles (422km)

NORTH COAST, PUERTO RICO

Puerto Rico is the ideal surf destination, with warm water year-round, waves to suit all abilities and numerous surf schools and outfitters. A leisurely road trip from capital San Juan along the north coast to Rincón connects the dots between sandy beaches, coastal villages and seaside shacks ever ready to serve up a plate of crab or cod fritters. There are many places to stop and surf or swim along the route, but highlights include sheltered Crashboat Beach in Aguadilla and the beautiful golden sweeps of Middles and Jobos beaches to the northwest. Rincón is a great place to spend a few days at the end of the drive, with hippy vibes, perfect sunsets and plenty of bars to grab a cold beer. The laidback beach town hosts contests and a famous surf festival throughout the year.
Start // San Juan
Finish // Rincón
Distance // 93 miles (150km)

KAUA'I

It's difficult to know in which direction to look when driving stretches of Rte 56 between Lihu'e and Hanalei Bay: at the turquoise waters of the Pacific on one side or at the spectacular crinkled mountains on the other. The road between the two surf towns, each on a horseshoe bay, is only 30 miles (48km) long, but you could easily spend a couple of days beach-hopping along it. Away from the surf, diversions include the hiking trails through Nounou State Forest Reserve; the sculpture park and botanical gardens at Na Aina Kai; the seabird colonies at Kīlauea Point National Wildlife Refuge; Hanalei Valley Lookout, with views over taro fields and mountains; and the tidal rock pool at Queen's Bath. Hanalei Bay is an atmospheric place to spend a couple of days at the close to this road trip.
Start // Kalapaki Beach, Lihu'e
Finish // Hanalei Bay
Distance // 32 miles (51km)

Clockwise, from top: a surfer catches
air in Rincón, Puerto Rico; Hanalei
Bay on Kaua'i, Hawai'i; a lifeguard
tower on South Beach, Miami

ROUNDING QUÉBEC'S LA GASPÉSIE LOOP

Trailblazing fishermen and fleeing colonialists gave the Gaspésie its complex cultural character, but it was the dense forests, rich seas and prolific wildlife that drew Etain O'Carroll here.

Even if you speak French, the dialect spoken on the Gaspé Peninsula – or the Gaspésie as it is also known – is almost unintelligible. A throwback to 17th-century France with a colonial overtone, it bewilders visitors and sets locals apart, even from their Québécois neighbors. But then again, the Gaspé is a place apart. An isolated peninsula on the edge of the Americas, it is surrounded by exceptionally rich seas.

These seas attracted the attentions of Basque and Portuguese fishermen before the French arrived in 1534. Not long after, the precocious Gaspé became a cosmopolitan hub with settlers from France and the Channel Islands followed by the English, Scottish

and Irish. A roaring trade in fur and fish linked this isolated outpost to Europe, the Caribbean and South America, and a hybrid culture evolved combining the settlers' languages, traditions and music.

The looping Rte 132 skirts the perimeter of the now sparsely populated Gaspé. The seaboard is marked by striking rock formations, pebble beaches and dense forests that stop abruptly on the crest of rugged cliffs. Inland, it's remote and untouched, with wild rivers and forested mountains making it perfect for hiking, mountain biking, white-water rafting, fishing, skiing and snowshoeing.

This combination of heritage, nature and adventure is what makes the Gaspé so alluring. As you drive, you'll be constantly tempted to

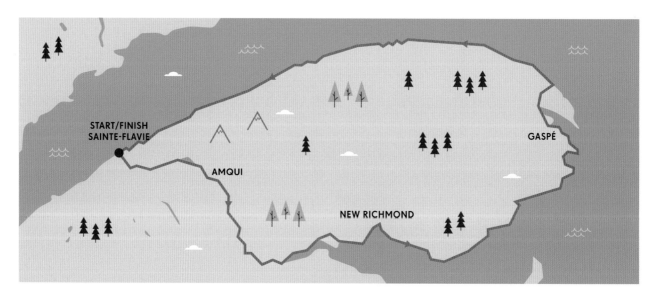

*"I am constantly tempted
to stop and hike, take
a boat trip, kayak, go
whale-watching or linger
over a long lunch"*

stop and hike, take a boat trip, hop in a kayak, go whale-watching or linger over long lunches of succulent lobster and smoky eel.

I start out gently with a tranquil drive east from Québec City, passing the charming villages of the Bas-St-Laurent. But by the time I make it to Ste-Flavie, things have become a little less genteel, a little more provincial and, with every passing mile, a lot more wild.

As I drive east the landscape becomes more rugged – windblown cottages cling to rocky headlands and striated cliffs tumble to the sea. Along the northern coast I spot Marcel Gagnon's army of rough wooden figures emerging from the water at Ste-Flavie and then the 133 turbines of one of Canada's largest wind farms at Cap-Chat.

I detour inland to the Parc National de la Gaspésie, a wild, densely forested place, home to some of Québec's highest peaks, and miles of glorious hiking trails. Alpine meadows and lush valleys give way to the fantastically named Chic-Choc and McGerrigle Mountains, which host the region's only herd of woodland caribou.

Back on the coast, sinewy cliffs round the head of the peninsula to Forillon National Park, where mountains plunge directly to the sea, forest blankets the slopes, whales bask in the water and harbor seals dot the rocks. At Grande-Grave beach there's a restored fishing village giving a glimpse of how late 19th-century settlers lived.

It was here, at the tip of the peninsula, that Breton explorer Jacques Cartier landed in the 16th century. The land was known to the Indigenous Mi'kmaq people as gespeg, meaning "end." Cartier knocked a wooden cross into the ground, claimed it for France and began a period of great upheaval. The history of the Mi'kmaq is poignantly illustrated at the Site d'Interprétation de la Culture Micmac de Gespeg where a reconstructed 17th-century village and summer camp offers a chance to learn about their culture.

I take the undulating road that winds on around craggy headland until I reach the pretty village of Percé, where the Rocher Percé (Pierced Rock) rises out of the sea. This huge hunk of limestone is the Gaspé's most famous landmark and has a colossal rock arch at one end. Beyond the rock is Île Bonaventure, North America's largest migratory bird refuge. More than 250,000 sea birds nest here, most of them raucous northern gannets.

The landscape changes as I round the head of the peninsula to Chaleur Bay. It's a region of picturesque villages and beaches set against a backdrop of red cliffs and forested mountains. The sheltered location drew a jumble of settlers, and local culture is a vibrant mix of influences held together by a shared love of the sea.

Herring, lobster and salmon fisheries keep the economy alive and a host of sites unveils the history of the fishermen. Further west, at Miguasha National Park, things go much further back. The cliffs here are rich with fossils, many dating from the Devonian period.

As the road turns inland back to Ste-Flavie it winds along the lush Matapédia Valley where covered bridges and heritage homes nestle in verdant forest surrounding lakes and salmon fisheries. Anglers come here in droves. It seems at every turn I'm reminded of the abundant natural resources on the Gaspé; it's easy to see why the peninsula attracted so many early settlers. I know I'll be back.

ACADIAN SONG AND DANCE

The Acadians were descendants of the French who settled on the eastern seaboard of Canada. They were exiled by the British in the 18th century, some fleeing as far south as Louisiana – the Cajuns – others taking refuge in New Brunswick and the Gaspé. Their language, culture and music evolved in a unique way. A great place to see it in action is the Théâtre de la Vieille Forge in Petite Vallée.

Opposite, from top: the restored 19th-century village at Grande-Grave; the sublime peninsula at Forillon National Park. Previous page: steer clear, literally, of the region's many moose; skirting the Gaspésie seaboard on Rte 132

DIRECTIONS

Start/Finish // Ste-Flavie
Distance // 550 miles (885km)
Getting there // Head east from Québec City along the southern shore of the St Lawrence River.
When to drive // Spring and autumn for bird watching; summer for live music and kayaking with whales; autumn for salmon fishing; winter for snow sports.
Good to know // Moose are common here and can do severe damage to your car. They're especially active at dawn and dusk in autumn. Black bears are also regularly seen; keep all smellables well away from your tent if you're camping.
Side trip // For a brush with the wilderness, head inland on Rte 299 through the Chic-Choc Mountains.
More info // www.tourisme-gaspesie.com

Opposite: following the route of the gold rush along the Yukon's Klondike Highway

MORE LIKE THIS
PIONEERING DRIVES

KLONDIKE HIGHWAY, YUKON

Climbing steeply out of Skagway, the Klondike Hwy rises over the infamous White Pass that proved the undoing of many would-be prospectors in the Klondike Gold Rush. It's a tough, lonely but breathtaking drive, following in their footsteps all the way to Dawson in the Yukon. The road passes through large tracts of wilderness where desolate mountains loom over steely lakes and abandoned roadhouses, cabins, dredges and tailings hark back to the glory days. There are few modern communities along the route. Places to stop include amiable Carcross with its historic general store and surreal sand dunes, Whitehorse, the thriving capital of the Yukon, and finally bohemian Dawson, a throwback to the gold rush era. False-fronted wooden houses line Dawson's dirt roads, colorful characters still pan for gold in the remaining claims and you can party the night away with dancing girls and honky-tonk tunes at Diamond Tooth Gertie's Gambling Hall.
Start // Skagway, Alaska
Finish // Dawson, Yukon
Distance // 444 miles (715km)

VIKING TRAIL, NEWFOUNDLAND

Tracing a historic route through one of the most remote corners of Canada, the Viking Trail links ancient burial grounds, the oldest European settlements in North America and relics of French and British occupation along a route lined with stunning scenery. Icebergs float majestically past monumental sea stacks, towering fjords are gouged out of some of the world's oldest mountains and salmon the size of small children leap up the rivers. It's an incredible drive along a windswept coast where wooded valleys give way to sheltered coves, ancient volcanic formations and landscapes scarred by colossal glaciers. En route you'll pass 5000-year-old burial grounds at Port au Choix, Unesco-protected fjords and, at the very tip of northwest Newfoundland, a Viking settlement established five centuries before Jacques Cartier or Christopher Columbus set foot in the Americas.
Start // Deer Lake
Finish // St Anthony
Distance // 304 miles (489km)

STEWART-CASSIAR HIGHWAY, BRITISH COLUMBIA

Cut out of the dense forest that surrounds the towering mountains of northern British Columbia, the Stewart-Cassiar Hwy was only completed in the 1970s. It joined the trails that gold prospectors, loggers and miners had used to explore the area and winds through some of the wildest and most isolated territory in BC. Driving the route offers pioneer history and First Nations culture aplenty, all set against a backdrop of magnificent lakes and icy peaks. Expect grizzly and black bears, caribou and moose, ghost towns and lava fields, and tiny, doggedly determined communities. Take a detour to the historic mining town of Stewart or to Gold Rush remnant Telegraph Creek and you'll get history by the bucket load, as well as further spectacular scenery.
Start // Kitwanga Junction
Finish // Watson Lake, Yukon
Distance // 450 miles (740km)

AROUND THE WHITE MOUNTAINS

For Amy Balfour, this loop through New Hampshire is a dramatic tug-of-war: majestic mountains lure her forward while gorges, waterfalls and one grand hotel demand immediate detours.

As a lifelong hiker, I find a drive through the White Mountains to be an exquisite form of torture. Just steps from the road, unfurling through the hardwood forest, is a network of trails that I will never have time to conquer. The trailheads are like mountain sirens, calling out promises of roaring streams, tumbling cascades, alpine huts, windswept summits and valley vistas that roll to the horizon. But there is no way that I can hike them all.

The Kancamagus Hwy (NH 112) ribbons west from the town of Conway, and is where my road trip begins. This 34.5-mile (55.5km) National Scenic Byway is beloved by leaf-peepers in autumn, when the foliage blazes yellow, gold, orange and red. But I prefer to drive "the Kanc" during the spring, when the Saco River, unleashed from the frozen winter, roars to life and the trees begin to shake off their chill. And the wildlife? Let's just say things are getting frisky out there.

My first stop is the US Forest Service ranger office, which is

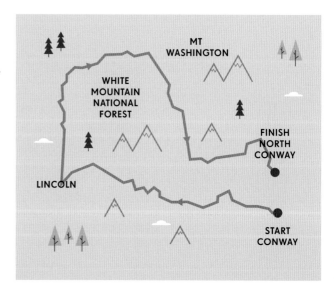

just to the west of town, where I pull in for a recreation parking pass (a total of $5 for the day), a list of roadside trails and a few minutes of chitchat with the ranger about the adventures that await ahead. From here, the byway rolls west into the White Mountain National Forest. This vast expanse of hardwoods and conifers soon surrounds me like a big green hug, its grip loosened only by the exuberant Swift River, which splashes alongside the road just beyond my window.

The byway was named after Kancamagus (the Fearless One), chief of the Pennacook Native American people who inhabited the area in the late 15th century. Though the Pennacook were largely peaceful, ongoing aggressions by the English drove the chieftain to bloody conflicts with the invaders. The Pennacook eventually scattered and Kancamagus moved north, but the thick forest here still feels wild, like a territorial outpost.

This elemental sense of wildness is on full display at the Rocky Gorge Scenic Area, where the Swift River drops through a corridor of granite. My favorite spot for photographs is the graceful footbridge a short walk east from the parking area. Look upstream at the tumbling waters then take your shot.

Like most hikers, I'm drawn to trails that end with a payoff,

a big "wow" that replenishes the spirit – or at least earns my physical burn. The 0.3-mile (0.5km) hike to Sabbaday Falls meets these criteria. The trail ends at a compact gorge waterfall, which powers through granite bedrock then cascades into lovely pools. The trail is an easy streamside stroll and wheelchair accessible.

From here the byway roller-coasters up to the Kancamagus Pass (elevation 2855ft/870m), where overlooks give panoramic mountain views. The road then drops into the town of Lincoln, where the White Mountains Visitor Center welcomes road trippers with coffee, a large fake moose and a forest ranger desk. Just beyond is North Woodstock and the Woodstock Inn, Station and Brewery; the patio here is my preferred spot for a post-drive sandwich and brew.

Steep mountains flank I-93, an easy-going interstate that flows north for eight scenic miles (13km) through Franconia Notch State Park. The roadside attractions here include the Flume Gorge, a cascade filled corridor of granite whose mossy walls reach heights of 90ft (27m). A few miles north, the Cannon Mountain Aerial Tramway whisks guests to a lofty viewpoint.

Just north, Hwy 3 rolls through the town of Twin Mountain then joins Hwy 302 for a spin through Bretton Woods, the photogenic centerpiece of the Presidential Range, the highest mountain range in the White Mountains. And while it's true that I brake for mountains, I slam to a surprised halt for the Mt Washington Hotel, a red-capped wonder shimmering at the base of Mt Washington. Yep, this beauty never fails to catch me off-guard when it bursts onto the horizon.

In 1944, the hotel hosted the Bretton Woods Conference, which created the World Bank and stabilized the global economy at the close of WWII. The world leaders in attendance hoped to avoid the devastating economic failures that followed WWI.

I like to wander the hallways off the lobby, where I stare at black-and-white photos of the property and wonder about the lives of long-ago guests and staff. For mid-trip inspiration, I stop a moment on the back veranda to soak up the impressive view of mighty Mt Washington, the tallest mountain in New England.

This stretch of Hwy 302 is also a conduit to adventure. In summer, the Mt Washington Cog Railway and its coal-fired steam locomotive carries passengers to the mountain's 6288ft (1916m) summit. Layer up for this chilly trip. Summit temperatures hover around 45°F (7°C) in summer, and it's windy up there.

South of the resort, you might find me dozing in an Adirondack chair on the front lawn of the Appalachian Mountain Club (AMC) Highland Center, which is a convenient launch pad to the trails crisscrossing the Presidential Range. Reasons to stop? Trail information, a hearty meal and an endless supply of adventure-loving guests. Also known as my people. The lodge-style dorm rooms are a convenient place to rest up and check your gear before tackling a hut-to-hut hike on the nearby Appalachian Trail.

Back on Hwy 302, you might glimpse the Conway Scenic Railroad Notch Train as it chugs into the depot just south of the Highland Center. The train begins its leafy journey in North Conway, a friendly mountain town packed tight with indie motels, cozy breakfast joints and outlet stores. My favorite last stop is the convivial Moat Mountain Smokehouse and Brewery, where the Czech-style lager, the ½lb burger and the spicy Cajun fries are always a good idea.

HUT-TO-HUT HIKING

The Appalachian Mountain Club (www.outdoors.org) runs eight overnight huts along the Appalachian Trail in the White Mountains. It's a day's hike between each dorm-style hut, in use for more than 125 years and complete with bunks, pillows and blankets. From summer to early autumn, a dinner and breakfast are included with your booking. A seasonal "croo" cooks the meals and shares info about the region.

"This vast expanse of hardwoods and conifers soon surrounds me like a big green hug"

From left: across Big Lake to Mount Washington; Crawford Depot serves the Conway Scenic Railroad Notch Train. Previous page: rainbow foliage runs the length of Kancamagus Hwy

DIRECTIONS

Start // Conway
Finish // North Conway
Distance // 92 miles (148km)
Getting there // Boston Logan International Airport is a 2½-hour drive from Conway.
When to drive // Autumn draws crowds for the colorful foliage display, which peaks between late September and mid-October. Summer is an idyllic time for hiking. Spring temperatures can be fickle, and many attractions are closed, but there may be lighter crowds.
What to bring // If you plan to hike, pack layers of noncotton clothing, a windbreaker or rain jacket, and sturdy shoes. You may want hiking poles for the steeper trails.
More info // www.visitwhitemountains.com

Opposite, clockwise from top:
cacti in the Sonoran Desert, Arizona;
a totem pole in Skidegate, Haida
Gwaii; a fiddle-maker at work in
Floyd, Virginia.

MORE LIKE THIS
HERITAGE DRIVES

CROOKED ROAD, VIRGINIA

During America's colonial era, European settlers in the Appalachian region began playing their fiddles alongside banjos brought over by enslaved Africans. The Bristol Radio Sessions brought this old-time mountain music to the masses in 1927. Today, the Crooked Road Heritage Music Trail celebrates old-time music and bluegrass, swinging past music jams, bluegrass museums and down-home restaurants on a journey through the Blue Ridge Mountains of southwestern Virginia. You'll find live music along the trail most nights of the week, with lively crowds dancing every Friday night at the Floyd Country Store. Signs along the route are emblazoned with banjos, and road-side exhibits give information and recordings of local musicians you can tune into on your car radio. Don't miss the Carter Family Fold, where Johnny Cash performed his very last live show.
Start // Rocky Mount
Finish // Breaks Interstate Park
Distance // 330 miles (531km)

HAIDA GWAII ADVENTURE, BRITISH COLUMBIA

Far-flung and isolated, the lush Haida Gwaii (Islands of Beauty) are steeped in superlatives – most stunning scenery, tastiest seafood and most accessible First Nations culture. This rugged northwestern archipelago maintains its pioneering spirit, but you'll be welcomed to what feels like the edge of the Earth with a warm, hearty greeting. You'll be arriving from mainland Prince Rupert on a BC Ferry, so arrange a hire car from Skidegate in advance. Check out the Haida Heritage Centre – a First Nations highlight – before a journey that sticks to Hwy 16 all the way to Rose Spit and the dense, treed Naikoon Provincial Park fronted by 60 miles of white sand beach. In between, stop at the Bottle and Jug Works at Tlell, the forest trail to the Yakoun River at Port Clements, and Masset, with its disused military base, First Nations' village and maritime museum.
Start // Skidegate
Finish // Rose Spit
Distance // 85 miles (137km)

WILD WEST, ARIZONA

There's no better place than central Arizona to celebrate your inner cowboy or cowgirl. From Wickenburg north to Sedona and Flagstaff, the hard-charging Hwy 89/89A rolls through a scrubby landscape of deserts and mountains that wears its Wild West history on its dusty sleeve. Cowboy museums and dude ranches will try to lure you from your car as you climb from the Sonoran Desert into the Weaver Mountains, home to Prescott and its rowdy Whiskey Row. Wyatt Earp and Doc Holliday drank here in the 1870s. The artsy charms of Jerome – a former mining town clinging to the side of a mountain – soon give way to the red rocks of Sedona, where Pink Jeep Tours (www.pinkjeeptours.com) tries to lasso up customers for rides over the red rocks. Lively Flagstaff channels the past at old hotels and an ever-rocking log cabin, better known as the Museum Club.
Start // Wickenburg
End // Flagstaff
Distance // 150 miles (241km)

BAJA CALIFORNIA: FROM TIP TO TOE AND BACK AGAIN

Epic desert scenery, punctuated by remote turquoise bays and centuries-old architecture, awaits Anna Kaminski on an intrepid drive through Baja California, Mexico.

Cabo San Lucas is exactly as I remember from fifteen years prior. It's late December and the town is filled with gringo revelers, here for Christmas vacation. By the marina, trinket sellers are holding impassive-looking iguanas, just in case passers-by want to have their photos taken with them. The iguanas are wearing tiny Santa hats.

I've been driving hell for leather since leaving Tijuana. Though Baja California's populous border city has shed some of its gritty image in recent years, reinventing itself as a fusion-dining and craft-beer destination, I still remember it as a seedy place from a long while back. I'm retracing an impulsive Greyhound bus journey I took as an 18-year-old backpacker, and adding a few stops to absorb Baja's desert scenery and other attractions.

After leaving Tijuana, I had breezed through the cruise-ship port of Ensenada, hurrying south along Rte 1, swinging inland amidst a blur of scrubland-covered hills and boojum trees. From there it was a more leisurely pace, and I stopped to admire crumbling, centuries-old Dominican missions in the colonial towns of Loreto and Mulegé, then strolled the old-world *malecón* (seafront promenade) of La Paz port, before finally arriving in Cabo San Lucas.

The next morning finds me on my inflatable kayak, paddling through placid blue waters to the south of Cabo's famous headland, past the sandy cove of Playa del Divorcio (Divorce Beach) and onward to the dramatic rock formations of Playa Los Amantes (Lovers' Beach). Amantes? Divorcio? How ironic that they're next to one another. Then I'm at Land's End, Baja's southernmost tip, watching as the first rays of the rising sun hit El Arco – a jagged stone arch – and give the sandstone a delicate pink hue.

A figure dressed in cowboy garb dangles from a noose next to the

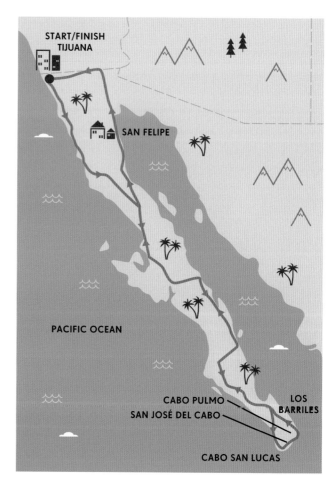

START/FINISH
TIJUANA

SAN FELIPE

PACIFIC OCEAN

CABO PULMO

SAN JOSÉ DEL CABO

LOS BARRILES

CABO SAN LUCAS

entrance of the Meson del Ahorcado (Hanged Man's Inn) in San José del Cabo, the more traditional town east of Cabo. When I was here fifteen years ago, it was an al fresco taco shack that impressed me with the sheer range of fresh salsas served alongside the *tacos de lengua, de carne asada, adobada...* The whole operation is indoors now, with every inch of the interior covered in vintage brass clocks and other antique bric-a-brac, but the tacos are still there, and the punchy, searingly flavorful salsas take my taste buds on a trip down nostalgia lane.

Leaving San José's brightly painted adobe houses behind, I detour from Rte 1 and take the road less traveled, skirting Baja Sur's eastern coast. The partially paved, occasionally bumpy drive carries me past blink-and-you'll-miss-them one-street villages and flotsam-strewn deserted beaches. My destination? Cabo Pulmo – little more than a scattering of thatched-roofed, earth-colored houses, a couple of taco shacks and a wide sweep of white-sand beach.

Cabo Pulmo is known for some of the best snorkeling and diving in Baja, so I overnight here, heading out in the morning with Cabo Pulmo Divers. Reaching our destination of El Bajo, we don our scuba tanks and backflip off the edge of the boat, sinking slowly down toward the vast reef. The marine activity among the corals is astounding: shoals of colorful reef fish dart about; we see a couple of grazing sea turtles, sinuous ribbons of moray eels and a school of jacks swirling themselves into a giant ball of rippling silver.

"We don our scuba tanks and backflip off the edge of the boat, sinking slowly down toward the vast reef"

I stop in Los Barriles that night, too exhausted from a day spent underwater and too sun-drunk to drive far. It's a breezy, palm-studded little town. Very breezy, in fact. Dozens of kitesurfers are visible out at sea, riding the crests of waves kicked up by the powerful westerly winds. But I'm more interested in the wildlife. Come dusk, the winds have somewhat abated and the shapes of mobula rays – small manta rays – are visible, performing acrobatic leaps high above the water. I watch their capering until it gets too dark to make out their shapes.

After a very early start from the Wild West–like coastal town of Santa Rosalía, I drive for five hours nonstop through the cactus-studded Desierto de Vizcaíno, its small dusty towns soporific in the heat. I stop for lunch at sticky-tabled Lonchería Nueva Chapala, just before the Chapala T-junction. Here, Rte 5 splits off from Rte 1 and barrels northeast toward Baja's east coast.

The practically deserted road reaches the vivid blue of the Sea of Cortés and skirts the coastline, and I find myself hemmed in between

CALIFORNIA GRAY WHALES

From mid-December to mid-April, pods of gray leviathans migrate from frigid Arctic reaches to the warmer waters of their favorite bays around Baja California. Pregnant females are partial to four sheltered bays in the Sea of Cortés – Laguna Ojo del Liebre, Laguna San Ignacio, Puerto San Carlos and Puerto López Mateos. There they give birth to their 1500lb (680kg) calves and help them build up strength for the arduous return journey.

Clockwise, from opposite left: the Adobe Guadalupe winery, off Hwy 1 near Ensenada; Hwy 1 heads into the desert south of Tijuana; a giant cardón cactus; a reef in Cabo Pulmo National Marine Park. Previous page: standup paddleboarding near La Paz

the water and the rugged mountains of Sierra de San Pedro Mártir. This is easily one of the most scenic stretches of my Baja journey.

The shrimping town of San Felipe is where hundreds of bikers from across the border converge every other year in April as part of the El Diablo run, to drink beer and carouse on the beach. A brief drive south of there, I take the Valle de Gigantes turnoff and stretch my legs in the desert among enormous *cardón* cacti, their multipronged arms reaching for the sky – they are five to six times as tall as me, and are the only large plants that can survive the intense heat here.

I pause at the San Felipe airstrip. I'm a massive James Bond fan, you see. From *Quantum of Solace*, you might remember an aerial dogfight scene. In that, Bond flew a 1939 Douglas DC-3A through scrubland-covered rocky canyons and over cactus-studded desert, pursued by a sleek and sinister SIAI-Marchetti SF.260TP flown by forces loyal to General Medrano, the exiled Bolivian dictator. That scene was shot right here in the Parque Nacional Sierra de San Pedro Mártir. With its engines failing, the DC-3A soared vertically above the desert, before Bond and fellow secret agent Camille Montes Rivero skydived to their escape.

My journey ends via a winding, eerily empty and allegedly haunted stretch of highway along the Rumorosa Pass – where a tanker chase scene from another Bond flick, *Licence to Kill*, was shot in 1988. The pass brings me right back toward my starting point, the border city of Tijuana.

DIRECTIONS

Start/Finish // Tijuana
Distance // 2107 miles (3391km)
Getting there // Fly into San Diego, California, and take the San Diego trolley to the Mexican border, or fly into Tijuana directly.
When to drive // You can road-trip across Baja any time of year, but mid-January to mid-March is best for whale-watching. March through April is when the desert blooms.
Car rental // It's cheaper to rent a car in Tijuana than north of the border in San Diego. If you're not planning to return the way you came, you'll pay a hefty one-way drop-off fee in Cabo San Lucas
Hot tip // Don't confuse the towns of Rosalito, El Rosario de Arriba and Santa Rosalía en route.

*Opposite, from top: Cerro Paranal
Observatory, in Chile's Atacama
Desert; the Alaska Range, seen
across Denali National Park*

MORE LIKE THIS
CINEMATIC DRIVES

QUANTUM OF SOLACE, CHILE

Home to a VLT (Very Large Telescope),
the gleaming, futuristic edifices of Cerro
Paranal Observatory sit on a hilltop in the
southern reaches of the Atacama Desert,
which has some of the clearest skies on
Earth. The observatory's Martian-like
landscape of ochre-colored plateaux, and
bare ridges and peaks, were featured in
the James Bond film *Quantum of Solace*.
In the movie, Cerro Paranal's ESO Hotel
– a squat, copper-colored building set into
the rock – doubles as Hotel Perla de las
Dunas. Bond infiltrates the hotel, captures
mastermind Dominic Greene and finally
leaves him stranded in the desert. Cerro
Paranal Observatory is normally open
for prebooked visitor tours on Saturdays,
and is a straightforward drive south of
the mining port of Antofagasta on the
Pan-American Hwy, then along a snaking
ribbon of pavement through red hills to
the summit.
Start/Finish // Antofagasta
Distance // 162 miles (260km)

INTO THE WILD, ALASKA

In a clearing in the midst of dense spruce
forest, by the banks of the turquoise-
colored Jack River, stands a rusty green
bus. It's the movie-set replica of the bus
where Chris McCandless, aka Alexander
Supertramp, spent the last months of his
life in the real-life story, *Into the Wild*. The
actual bus stood west of the one-street
town of Healy, some 50 miles (80km)
further north, and became a focal point
for fans until its removal in 2020, after at
least two people were swept away by the
Teklanika River while trying to reach it. From
Anchorage, the supremely scenic Parks
Hwy winds north to Healy, with views of
the snowcapped peaks of Denali National
Park to your west. Watch out for caribou
wandering onto the road and be prepared
for adverse driving conditions in the
coldest months.
Start/Finish // Anchorage
Distance // 498 miles (801km)

THE MOTORCYCLE DIARIES, ARGENTINA

In 1952, 23-year-old Che Guevara
embarked on a motorcycle journey
across Argentina with his biochemist
friend Alberto, on the back of a 1939
500cc Norton, nicknamed *La Poderosa*
(The Mighty One). Their adventures,
immortalized in Guevara's book, *The
Motorcycle Diaries*, formed the basis for
the namesake 2004 movie. From Neuquén,
the scenic Rte 237 cuts south, following
the Limay River. Just north of the compact
service town of Piedra del Águila (Eagle
Rock), a narrow dirt-and-gravel track and
a rickety-looking bridge lead you east
across the river. Further south is where the
pair tinkered with *La Poderosa* against the
backdrop of snowy peaks and the intense
blue of Nahuel Huapi Lake. From here, Rte
40 leads to San Martín de Los Andes. The
pair's journey can be retraced at any time
of the year.
Start // Neuquén
Finish // San Martín de Los Andes
Distance // 270 miles (435km)

DRIVING IN A
WINTER WONDERLAND

*Orla Thomas drives between Vermont's tiny towns and vast forests in winter, discovering
endless seasonal pit stops and a thriving counterculture along scenic Route 100.*

Woodstock's buildings are so uniformly pristine that walking among them is like strolling through a Hollywood set. Historic clapboard properties feature picket fences whiter than the snow, behind which children frolic under new falling flakes. Lacquered front doors are hung with wreaths of holly and through huge windows I spy charming Christmas decorations: fireplace stockings, ornament-laden trees. Even if your visit doesn't coincide with Woodstock's annual Wassail festivities – a weekend of feasting, caroling and general merriment that culminates in a costumed parade – the town delivers seasonal good cheer in abundance.

A 15-minute drive away in Quechee Gorge, Simon Pearce's store could pass for Santa's workshop. In the basement is a turbine-powered glassblowing studio fueled by the Ottauquechee River, which rushes past just outside. Here, young artisans create pieces that wouldn't look out of place on an elvish production line – evergreens rendered in glass, and tree ornaments including candy canes, rocking horses and colored baubles. Vermont has a long-standing appreciation for the handmade; this part of the state is also home to ShackletonThomas, run by furniture-maker Charles Shackleton and potter Miranda Thomas.

Pulling up at their workshop in a repurposed mill just outside Woodstock, I find Miranda painting a stylized rabbit onto a ceramic bowl. "The natural world informs our work," she says. "Vermont is a place of leaves and trees. People who live or visit here make that a part of their lives." ShackletonThomas' philosophy is that handmade objects possess a "fourth dimension" – a soulful quality, which manufactured items lack. I run my fingers over a milky-blue mug. "People are very receptive to what we do here,"

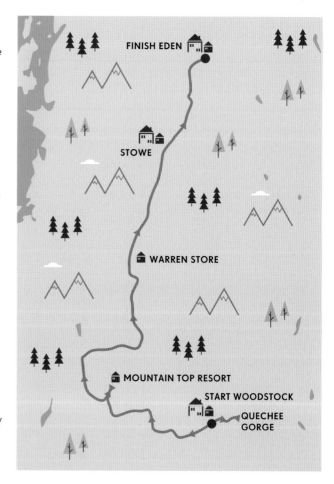

says Miranda. "There's a bit of a counterculture in Vermont."

This "small is beautiful" ideology is also apparent in Vermont's food scene. Symbolically, the state capital, Montpelier, is the only one in the United States without a McDonald's. Instead, farm-to-table restaurants make the most of Vermont's abundance. Its best-known products are maple syrup – over 50 percent of the nation's sweetener is produced here – and Ben & Jerry's ice cream. There are more artisanal cheesemakers and craft breweries per capita here than anywhere else in the US, and their products feature with pride on local menus.

Like the Mountain Top Resort in Chittenden, where I stop for a grilled cheese made with local Cabot cheddar. Just outside the tavern is a sledding hill, where kids take turns careening down the slope. The sled, thought to have been the first vehicle used by humans, predates cars by several millennia. Later came the horse-drawn sleigh – offered up for rides here and every bit as romantic as those featured in my road-trip read, Laura Ingalls Wilder's *Little House in the Big Woods*. Wrapped in blankets, I glide across the snow to a soundtrack of jingling harness bells.

Soon it's time to return to my modern ride and join the scenic Rte 100. Heading north on Vermont's celebrated road, I pass farms

"People like to support their local businesses. It's a community thing"

and fields, the odd tumbledown barn and wooden houses with mini snowplows parked in their drives. In accordance with local zoning laws, no building is taller than 125ft (38m), and billboards have been banned since 1968. Even the pitstops are photogenic – at quaint Warren Store I pick up coffee, whoopee pie and a jar of local peanut butter. Hugging the Green Mountain National Forest, Rte 100 takes in more trees than people: maple, birch, elm and ash alongside great swathes of evergreen firs and spruces, boughs heavy with snow.

This reliable powder brings an annual influx to Vermont's ski towns, of which Stowe is perhaps the prettiest, its white church spire poking from the snow to give it the look of an iced cake. Stowe is also a place of pilgrimage for another reason: it's home to one of America's most sought-after beers. An India pale ale consistently voted one of the world's best, Alchemist's Heady Topper is rarely available outside the state. Today, co-founder Jen Kimmich is helping out with curbside sales. "We do make great

TAKE COVER

Vermont has over 100 covered bridges, the highest concentration anywhere in the world. Built mostly between 1820 and 1940, these wooden structures were covered to protect them from the elements: the state's climate means an uncovered wooden bridge would only stay safe for around 15 years. There are several in the town of Woodstock, while Emily's Bridge in Stowe is said to be haunted by a jilted lover's ghost.

beer," she says with a modest shrug. "We used to sell from a smaller brewpub, but it caused traffic jams down Rte 100."

Jen is amused by the furor surrounding their signature brew. "People like to support their local businesses, as well as enjoying produce grown on their doorstep. It's a community thing." The Alchemist's idea of community is inclusive. A rainbow sign in their window reads: "Hate has no business here. We stand with our LGBTQ+ community members. We stand with Muslims, refugees and immigrants in our community. All are welcome."

Whether newly arrived or long settled, Vermonters have space to carve out their own version of paradise in the least-populated US state after Wyoming. Jim Blair found his in the far north, in the aptly named village of Eden – a remote corner hidden along backroads coated ever more deeply with snow. I find Jim looking a little like Santa in his red coat, and surrounded by the large pack of Alaskan huskies he keeps for dog-sledding. "These guys are family and friends to me. Dogs are just like people wearing fur coats," he says. "Each animal has its place in the hierarchy, but you could say I'm top dog."

I sleep soundly in one of Jim's wooden cabins under a patchwork quilt, rising at dawn for an early outing with the dogs. Once in their harness, the huskies begin to howl – a chorus that only stops when they set off. "I think of it as singing," says Jim. "They're joyful because they love to run." The sound-dampening effect of the snow makes the journey through forest preternaturally quiet, the only noises those of canine exertion and Jim's calls. "I learned early on that the dogs aren't happy chained," he says. Jim's empathy is heartfelt – unsuited to a life shackled to a desk, his need for freedom, for days spent roaming the hills, is as real as that of his animals. It is a thread that unites many who live here – a certain independence of spirit that's distinctively Vermont.

Clockwise, from opposite left: Jim Blair and his sled dogs; a flight of beers in Stowe; Middle Covered Bridge in Woodstock; painting pottery at Shackleton Thomas' workshop, near Woodstock. Previous page: taking a horse-drawn sleigh ride

DIRECTIONS

Start // Woodstock
Finish // Eden
Distance // 140 miles (225km)
Getting there // Lebanon Municipal Airport in New Hampshire is the closest to Woodstock, but more flights go into Burlington, 90 miles (145km) northwest, and Boston, 140 miles (225km) southeast. Car rentals can be made from all – book a 4WD to help with winter conditions.
When to drive // Woodstock's Wassail takes place in early December, when the snow arrives – it lasts through March.
What to pack // Bring thermal base layers, a warm jacket, hat, boots and gloves.
Where to stay // 506 on the River Inn (www.ontheriverwoodstock.com), Moose Meadow Lodge (www.moosemeadowlodge.net).

*Opposite, from top: Delicate Arch
in Arches National Park, Utah;
Exit Glacier, seen from the Harding
Icefield Trail, Alaska*

MORE LIKE THIS
WINTER DRIVES

ARCHES NATIONAL PARK, UTAH

The archetypal image of Utah is of sun-scorched red rocks, but Arches is equally enchanting in winter, when visitors can escape both scorching heat and the crowds. After checking driving conditions at the Visitor Center, head for the Windows, where you can see some of the Park's largest arches occasionally dusted with snow between November and March. Take half an hour to walk beneath either Double Arch or North Window. Next swing by Balanced Rock for the super-easy 10-minute loop trail, then head to Delicate Arch Viewpoint to see the park's most famous formation. Stop by Wolfe Ranch to get a feel for the life of early homesteaders before finishing up in Devil's Garden, an inspiring landscape of wafer-thin arches and soaring spires.
Start // Arches National Park Visitor Center
Finish // Devil's Garden Trailhead
Distance // 27 miles (44km)

SEWARD HIGHWAY, ALASKA

In Alaska's dark and snowy winter months, the adventure begins as soon as you leave the state's biggest city. Rent an SUV, crank up the 1980s hit *Anchorage* and make the most of the daylight as you pass between the sweeping shorelines of Turnagain Arm and the snowcapped Chugach Mountains. The town of Whittier makes for an intriguing detour – almost its entire population of 300-odd people lives in a single high-rise block – before returning to the scenic byway for phase two of the drive: the Kenai Peninsula. Famed as a playground for adventurers, even those who don't explore its trails will leave mesmerized. The road ends at the harbor town of Seward, where you can celebrate with a meal in the charmingly old-fashioned downtown before driving on to get a glimpse of Exit Glacier, 15 miles (24km) away.
Start // Anchorage
Finish // Exit Glacier, near Seward
Distance // 161 miles (260km)

LAKE DISTRICT, ARGENTINA

During the Argentine winter of June through August, visitors can expect to find the country's Lake District dusted with snow, making it a particularly beautiful time to drive the Ruta de los Siete Lagos. First, overnight in a wooden chalet in Bariloche – the region's largest town – where you can check local road conditions. Head north and you'll soon pass Lake Nahuel Huapi, which gives its name to the surrounding national park. The route's official gateway is the resort of Villa la Angostura, where the scenery steps up a gear – Lago Espejo (Mirror Lake) shimmers on a still day. Keep your eyes peeled for deer as you follow the RN40 into San Martín de los Andes, a hub for outdoor adventure and close to the ski slopes of Cerro Chapelco.
Start // Bariloche (formally San Carlos de Bariloche)
End // San Martín de los Andes
Distance // 120 miles (190km)

WINE AND SURF IN LONG ISLAND

Regis St Louis drives east of New York City, finding Long Island's wildlife reserves, barrier islands and vineyards to be a world removed from the concrete jungle.

Long Island grapples with some complicated stereotypes: it's sometimes labeled as the land of blue-collar brawlers and city-loathing commuters, and at other times as a place of lavish mansions and out-of-touch plutocrats. In truth, the United States' longest island outside of Alaska is all this and more. It is both densely populated and dotted with wide expanses of farmland, home to postmodern villas fronting glorious beaches as well as seaside ports dating back to the 17th century.

New York City also occupies a piece of Long Island – Brooklyn and Queens anchor its western end – while being a world away. Though I'd lived in Brooklyn for many years, I had never set out to explore this realm of contradictions lying just beyond the concrete-laden horizon. And so, one late September morning, I hit the road with a rather nebulous goal: to experience as many facets of Long Island as I can possibly cram into a week-long trip.

Clinging as much as possible to the ocean, I forego a faster drive along the big LIE (Long Island Expressway) and turn onto the Belt Parkway, a scenic if busy six-lane road that hugs the shoreline, taking me under the Verrazzano-Narrows Bridge and past the deep blue expanse of Gravesend Bay.

It's still early in the day when I arrive at the Jamaica Bay Wildlife Refuge. Incongruously wedged between JFK airport and

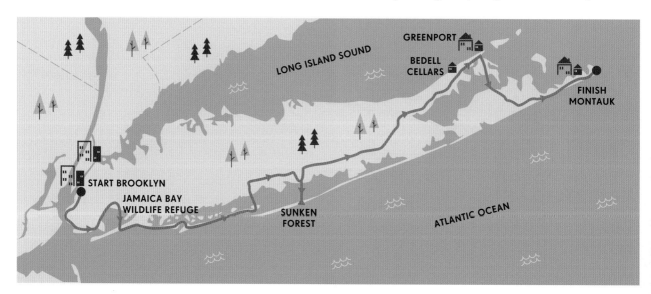

the beachside neighborhoods of outer Queens, the protected wetland encompasses salt marshes, freshwater ponds, open bay and islands in one of the most important bird sanctuaries in the Northeast. Planes roar overhead as I walk the trail around West Pond, hoping to catch a glimpse of some of the 330 bird species that have been spotted here. Out on the mudflats, sandpipers, plovers and other shore birds are feeding on small prey when a falcon soars past, causing them to scatter. "You should've been here yesterday," a man carrying binoculars says. "There were a surprising number of raptors, even an American kestrel and a Cooper's hawk."

From Jamaica Bay, I drive across the sturdy, 1930s-era Marine Parkway Bridge to Far Rockaway, a neighborhood that clings to a slender peninsula that's been a popular seaside retreat since the mid-19th century. I turn east and follow the edge of the ocean, as salty breezes gust through my window. Within a few miles, I've officially left NYC, as I cross from Queens into Nassau County and zip past Long Beach and on to Jones Beach, a remarkably undeveloped stretch of sand.

At Sayville, I leave the car behind and catch a ferry to Fire Island, a 50-mile-long (80km) barrier island that links various communities. Its year-round population of 250 swells in the summer, particularly in Cherry Grove and the Pines, famed destinations for LGBTQ+ visitors. It's a 30-minute boat ride across the Great South Bay, though I feel I've somehow teleported into

the tropics after I arrive on the dock and kick off my shoes to better walk the sandy lanes. I pass architectural confections like the bayfront Belvedere Guest House for Men, which is modeled on a Venetian palace, as well as relics from the past – the boarded-up Carrington House is where Truman Capote allegedly wrote *Breakfast at Tiffany's*.

West of Cherry Grove, I find my way into the Sunken Forest. Protected by sand dunes, this enchantingly named reserve hides a rare maritime holly forest. Sassafras, juneberry, holly and other hardwoods are the forest's old-growth species, some of which are over 300 years old. Above me, branches in the canopy stretch out in a mazelike web, growing horizontally to compete for the scarce resources on offer.

After catching the ferry back, I get behind the wheel to make my way deeper into Long Island. I stop at the town of Riverhead, which lies near the mouth of the Peconic Estuary. From here, the island branches into two separate peninsulas: North Fork and South Fork. I drive along Riverhead's photogenic Main Street, past ice cream parlors, diners and a 1930s movie theater before meeting up with Rte 25, which takes me into North Fork. Fragments of the city disappear amid vineyards, orchards and nature preserves. Sometimes compared to Napa Valley, North Fork, with its 40-odd wineries, is a tiny slice of wine country plunked down on the edge of the Long Island Sound.

I pull off the road at Bedell Cellars, a small family-run estate that produces outstanding rosés, malbecs and viogniers. On a spacious terrace overlooking the grapevines, I join two travelers from Maryland over tasting flights.

It's clearly harvest season, and roadside stands are packed with bushels overflowing with shiny red apples alongside rows of gaudy pumpkins, bright yellow squash and baskets of sunflowers – not to mention homemade jams and pies. At road's end, I reach Greenport, a waterfront town first settled in 1682. Once a major fishing port and whaling hub, the settlement still has some working fishing boats. As I stroll along the harbor, past grassy squares, an antique carousel and the compact lanes of downtown, I once again feel as though I'm slipping through a wormhole, this time into maritime New England.

From Greenport, I take the vehicle ferry across to Shelter Island – sometimes described as the pearl between the pincer-like claws of North and South Fork – then take yet another ferry to North Haven and continue east. I run out of road near Montauk, a former Native American settlement named after the Algonquian-speaking Montaukett tribe. The town has seen its share of hardships over the years, including shipwrecks, Revolutionary War skirmishes and devastating hurricanes, though these days it's famed for its dune-backed beaches and powerful waves.

On my final day, I rise for an early walk along Ditch Plains Beach and feel as though I've reached the edge of the continent. My apartment lies a mere 120 miles (193km) from where I'm standing, but as the sky slowly lightens from indigo to the faintest of blues, I don't recall ever having seen such a magnificent sunrise in Brooklyn.

> "I feel I've teleported into the tropics, and kick off my shoes to walk the sandy lanes"

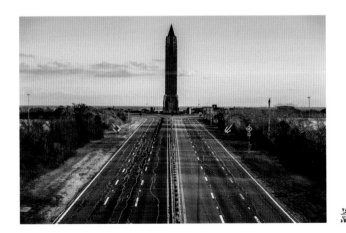

MONTAUK POINT LIGHTHOUSE

The fourth-oldest active lighthouse in the US was commissioned by George Washington and built in 1796. It's a narrow, quasi-claustrophobia-inducing climb to the top, but the reward is worth the effort: 360-degree views take in Block Island and the Connecticut shoreline on clear days. The lighthouse stands near the point where the slave ship *La Amistad* first came ashore in 1839, prior to the famous trial in New Haven.

Clockwise, from opposite: Point O' Woods on Fire island; Montauk Point Lighthouse; the Jones Beach water tower. Previous page, from top: surfers head to Rockaway Beach, Queens; the Ocean Parkway passes Zachs Bay

DIRECTIONS

Start // Brooklyn
Finish // Montauk
Distance // 172 miles (277km)
Getting there // JFK, in the southwest corner of Long Island, is the busiest airport in NYC.
When to drive // Peak times are June through September. Go a month before or after for warm weather and fewer crowds.
Where to stay // The Sound View Greenport (www.soundviewgreenport.com) is a creatively redesigned 1935 motor inn perched on the waterfront.
Where to eat // Legendary seafood shack Clam Bar at Napeague (www.clambarhamptons.com), near Montauk.
Detours // Tour the Pollock-Krasner House, East Hampton, where Jackson Pollock and Lee Krasner lived and painted.
More info // www.discoverlongisland.com

Opposite, clockwise from top left: a vineyard at harvest time in Palisade, Colorado; Taughannock Falls in the Finger Lakes region of upstate New York; Luckenbach, Texas

MORE LIKE THIS
UNDER-THE-RADAR WINE ROUTES

VINEYARDS AND PEAKS, COLORADO

The western slope of the Rockies hides some of the biggest surprises in Colorado, including fertile farmland and red-rock canyons. Lying at the confluence of the Colorado and the Gunnison Rivers, Grand Junction makes a fine gateway to the region. It's a short drive from there along the Colorado River to Palisade, which is famed for its many orchards and vineyards. You can stop in tasting rooms and load up on fresh fruit in season, before continuing up to the Grand Mesa, the world's largest flattop mountain. It's a winding drive to the summit, with scenic viewpoints above the valley far below. Up top, you can take in the aspen forests or mountain bike legendary singletrack. Looping west, Colorado National Monument has majestic rock formations best experienced on a hike across the canyon floor.
Start // Grand Junction
Finish // Colorado National Monument
Distance // 135 miles (217km)

WINE IN THE WILD WEST

Cowboys, cacti and... cabernet? True, Texas isn't the first word that springs to mind when talking about varietals, but wine has been made in the Lone Star state since the 1650s. The epicenter of viticultural action is Hill Country, home to over 100 wineries and vineyards that stretch across 9 million acres (3.6 million hectares). From Fredericksburg, head east along Hwy 290 (aka the Wine Road), stopping at properties like Signor Vineyards, where you can sip sangiovese beneath live oak trees. After loading up on bottles for the trip home, stop in Luckenbach, where you can catch live music in a barn-like dancehall, get your fill of presidential lore in Johnson City and see impressive caverns near Boerne. End the trip by overnighting in a dude ranch in Bandera, a town full of Western bars and honky-tonk clubs.
Start // Fredericksburg
Finish // Bandera
Distance // 130 miles (209km)

VINES AND VISTAS IN THE EMPIRE STATE

With its cool climate and short growing season, New York's Finger Lakes region is not unlike Germany's Rhine Valley, and is similarly strong in off-dry whites such as riesling. Ithaca is a handy gateway to the region, and is home to Cornell University, botanical gardens and gorges. It's a short drive to the 215ft (66m) cascade in Taughannock Falls State Park. Continuing north, you'll follow the densely forested shore of Cayuga Lake up to waterfront Sheldrake Point Winery and the picturesque town of Seneca Falls, from where the women's suffrage movement was launched in 1848. Over in sparkling Seneca Lake, you'll find the pioneering Hermann J Wiemer Vineyard. The last stop is in tiny Dresden, where you can follow a walking trail along a rushing river past waterfalls en route to Keuka Lake.
Start // Ithaca
Finish // Dresden
Distance // 96 miles (155km)

LUCKENBACH TEXAS
REE DANCE FRI
SARAH GAYLE MEECH 1PM SAT

HISTORY LESSONS ON THE NATCHEZ TRACE

Emily Matchar drives between antebellum inns, Native American burial mounds and Civil War battle sites on this 444-mile historic trail from Nashville to Natchez.

My passenger says it's weird that Americans eat biscuits for breakfasts. "Isn't that, like, bad for your teeth?" he asks.

Greg is a 23-year-old Australian backpacker, and there are lots of things he doesn't understand about the United States. Drive-through ATMs. Cereal with marshmallows in it. Tipping.

I met him at a hostel in Nashville, and when he asked if he could join me for a stretch of my own road trip – the Natchez Trace Parkway from Tennessee to Mississippi – I said sure, why not? This is the America you don't get to see when you're hopping from big city to big city.

Now we're headed south out of Nashville toward the Loveless Cafe, an iconic breakfast spot at the north end of the Trace. Their biscuits are said to be the best in Tennessee.

"American biscuits are like what you call scones, but better," I tell Greg. "You'll see."

We pull up to the little white house with a covered porch and an enormous neon sign. Lon and Annie Loveless opened this spot in 1951, serving hungry travelers on old Hwy 100. Greg and I sit down at a little table with a red-and-white checked tablecloth, and 10 minutes later we're chowing down on a pile of hot fluffy biscuits smeared with butter and jam.

"See?" I ask.

Greg does see.

After breakfast, I pull back on the road. Now we're officially on the 444-mile (715km) stretch of National Scenic Byway designated as the Natchez Trace. The road follows what was once a Native American footpath, later used by merchants, traders of enslaved people and frontiersmen.

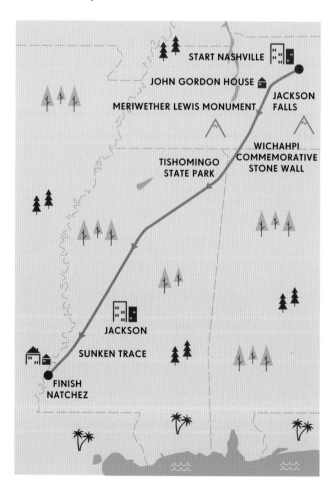

START NASHVILLE

JOHN GORDON HOUSE

MERIWETHER LEWIS MONUMENT

JACKSON FALLS

WICHAHPI COMMEMORATIVE STONE WALL

TISHOMINGO STATE PARK

JACKSON

SUNKEN TRACE

FINISH NATCHEZ

KAINTUCKS

Before steamboats, boatmen floated goods down the Ohio and Mississippi Rivers to market at Natchez and New Orleans. These boatmen were known as "Kaintucks" – though only some of them actually came from Kentucky. Once they'd delivered their goods, they'd dismantle their flatboats and sell them for lumber. Then they'd walk home via the Natchez Trace, sleeping in rustic inns called "stands." The journey took about 35 days. In 1810, some 10,000 Kaintucks traveled the Trace.

Clockwise, from above: view from the Natchez Trace Parkway Bridge, near Nashville; biscuits at the Loveless Motel and Cafe; carved stone owls at the Wichahpi Commemorative Stone Wall. Previous page: the Sunken Trace

After the neon and noise of Nashville, the road is blessedly peaceful. There are no restaurants, gas stations, motels or strip malls along this route, just miles of smooth two-lane country road. It's early summer, and the tree canopy is so dense it feels like driving through a green tunnel. Cyclists in blaze orange sail by; this entire parkway is a designated bicycle route. Greg fiddles with the radio dial.

We pass Birdsong Hollow and Water Valley, plush green basins quilted with farm fields and dotted with darker green stands of trees. About 45 minutes in, I pull up at a tall brick house with boards over its windows. It stands lonesomely at the far edge of a large lawn.

"Haunted house?" Greg asks.

"Sort of."

This is the former home of John Gordon, who operated the nearby Duck River ferry in the early 1800s. Ferries were once a crucial part of trade on the Natchez, since it wasn't feasible to build bridges so far out in the wilderness. Today Gordon's house is a historic site; a short walk takes us to the banks of the Duck River, now a placid stream shining in the summer sun.

A few miles down the road we stop again, this time at the Baker Bluff overlook, where we gaze across an arcadian landscape of rolling green hills dotted with barns and fat white cows. From here, a quick hike leads to Jackson Falls, a cascade tumbling over mossy shale into a clear cold pool.

We're not on the road half an hour before we stop again, this time at a memorial park dedicated to Meriwether Lewis.

"Who?" asks Greg.

"You know, the 'Lewis' in the Lewis and Clark expedition."

"What?"

"He was an explorer," I say, and decide to leave it at that. It's been a while since my last US history class.

The site is actually Lewis' grave. Aged 35, he died at a rural inn at this location in October 1809 and was buried nearby. His death was deemed a suicide – he was saddled by debt and addled by alcohol – though his family always believed it was a murder. In the early 2000s, some 200 of his descendants unsuccessfully petitioned the National Park Service to have his body exhumed and reexamined. So, Lewis rests where he died, beneath a broken stone column symbolizing a life cut short. Nearby is a replica of the log cabin inn, Grinder's Stand, built during the Depression.

It's in a slightly mournful spirit that Greg and I get back in the car and continue south. A little more than an hour later we enter Alabama; the Trace cuts through a tiny corner of the state. But within this tiny corner is a fascinating site: the Wichahpi Commemorative Stone Wall. Alabaman Tom Hendrix hand-built the wall to honor his great-great grandmother, Te-lah-nay, a member of the local Yuchi Nation, who was displaced from her land during the Trail of Tears.

Native displacement is a recurring theme along the trail. Across the border in Mississippi, Tishomingo State Park is named for the Chickasaw chief who fought alongside US troops in several battles and was rewarded with eviction from his ancestral lands. He died along the Trail of Tears. The air inside the park feels like a cool breath exhaled from the creeks and rivers. There are ferny hills, moss-slippery rocks and a desperately charming wooden footbridge.

Greg has lost his camera.

"Maybe I left it in Nashville?" he says, hopefully.

The air grows sultrier the further we drive. We pass cypress swamps, Confederate graves and millennia-old Native burial mounds. Greg tries the assortment of all-American road trip snacks I've brought for the occasion: Slim Jims, Flamin' Hot Cheetos, Moon Pies, Chick-O-Sticks, Cow Tales.

"These are spicy!" Greg says accusingly, holding the bag of Cheetos at arm's length.

"It says 'Flamin' Hot' right on the bag," I tell him.

He grumbles, licking orange dust off his fingers.

We're almost to Natchez when we stop at a site that seems to encompass the entire spirit of the trail. Known as the Sunken Trace, it's a portion of the old footpath used by so many people over the years that the ground has eroded away, leaving a mini ravine. Standing inside, it's impossible not to imagine the travelers who have come before: soldiers, settlers, Native hunters, Mississippi boatmen. And now me, and Greg-from-Australia, adding our footprints to the ancient dirt.

"It's impossible not to imagine the travelers who have come before"

DIRECTIONS

Start // Nashville, Tennessee
End // Natchez, Mississippi
Distance // 444 miles (715km)
Getting there // Nashville has an international airport, with a good selection of car rental agencies. From Natchez, there are major airports in Jackson (Mississippi) and Baton Rouge (Louisiana), both about 1½ hours' drive away.
When to drive // Summer can be oppressively hot and humid; any other time of year is fine, though spring means wildflowers and fall brings russet-hued vistas.
Where to stay // While you can drive the entire trace in one (very) long day, there are three NPS campsites along the way.
More info // The NPS website is full of info, and has links to lists of dining and accommodations outside the Trace itself (www.nps.gov/natr).

MORE LIKE THIS
OTHER NATIONAL SCENIC BYWAYS

NORTHWEST PASSAGE SCENIC BYWAY, IDAHO

This 202-mile (325km) journey through north-central Idaho follows the route taken by Lewis and Clark on their journey to the Pacific. Beginning in Lewiston, you'll trace the serpentine contours of the Clearwater River Canyon. Hillsides are thick with firs, the sky blue as denim. You'll pass the camp where Lewis and Clark stopped to build canoes in 1805, helped by the local Nez Perce people. Look out for the Heart of the Monster, a rock formation central to the Nez Perce creation story. At Kooskia, keep left to continue on through Nez Perce lands toward Lolo Pass, high in the Bitterroot Mountains on the border with Montana. Along the way, make ample stops to pick wild blackberries, fish for steelhead (license and permit required) and explore hidden hot springs.
Start // Lewiston
Finish // Lolo Pass
Distance // 202 miles (325km)

NORTH SHORE SCENIC DRIVE, MINNESOTA

You'll pass no fewer than eight state parks on this 154-mile (248km) route along Lake Superior's northern shore. In the summer, it's a glorious journey of waterfall hikes, fish shacks, cherry pie and icy lake swims. Begin by gawping at Duluth's historic Aerial Lift Bridge over the Duluth Ship Canal, whose span rises vertically to let boats pass. Next up is the tidy brick Two Harbors Lighthouse, Minnesota's oldest. Search for agates along Flood Bay, see the cascades at Gooseberry Falls and take the billionth photo of the Split Rock Lighthouse. Look out for both a black and a pink beach (really! Although it's pink rocks, not sand). Sugarloaf Cove offers ancient lava formations, Lutsen Mountains has a gondola to ride and the terminus of Grand Portage is home to the aptly named High Falls.
Start // Duluth
Finish // Grand Portage
Distance // 154 miles (248km)

HELLS CANYON SCENIC BYWAY, OREGON

This 208-mile (335km) byway wraps around the Wallowa Mountains of northeast Oregon in a horseshoe shape. From La Grande, a major stop on the Oregon Trail, you'll drive through ranchlands and along the bends of the Wallowa River. Pause in artsy Joseph for a coffee and local gallery tour, then check out the icy depths of glacial Wallowa Lake. In summer, ride the tramway to the summit of Mt Howard. Brace yourself for your first view of Hells Canyon at the Hells Canyon Overlook. Gawp at the massive furrow in the earth – this is North America's deepest canyon. Climb back in your car, the snow-capped Wallowas in your mirrors, and stop outside Baker City for the National Historic Oregon Trail Interpretive Center, to learn about the pioneers who came this way before you.
Start // La Grande
Finish // Baker City
Distance // 208 miles (335km)

*Clockwise, from top: the Clearwater
River Canyon, Idaho; Split Rock
Lighthouse, Minnesota; Joseph, Oregon*

GOING TO THE SUN

*Becky Ohlsen finds herself holding her breath as she ascends this
thin ribbon of road at the edge of a vast glacial valley in Montana.*

There are only a few locations on Earth I've been that really must be seen to be believed, and Glacier National Park is one of them. Photographs may hint at its glory, but even the very best shots are unable to capture the sheer scale of the place, the jagged gray peaks and the steep angle of the valley walls.

In a site like this, I can almost feel the earth move – it's easy to imagine a time when ancient masses of ice carved out a path, leaving behind an utterly changed landscape. And if that's not enough, two words: grizzly bears.

Among the best ways to see and appreciate the park is by driving the Going-to-the-Sun Road. It's a narrow, edge-clinging ribbon of pavement, the kind of road that makes me feel as if I'm in an IMAX cinema, getting a vivid, wide-screen view of the world. It also makes me feel very small and, occasionally, a little nervous. Limited access heightens the road's appeal: it's covered in snow most of the year, and is only fully open from late June or early July to mid-October, after maintenance crews have cleared the snow and repaired any seasonal damage. Completed in 1933, Going-to-the-Sun is the only paved road that crosses the park. That means traffic is heavy, and maintenance work is more or less constant, so plan on taking it slow.

You can drive the road in either direction, or both, of course, but the scenery has the biggest impact if you go from west to east. I duly make my start in West Glacier, a small community

built around the various ways of exploring the park; if you're up for more adventure, this is a good place to ask about guides, hiking trails, snowshoeing tours, river rafting, fly-fishing or whatever else you're into. I had made sure I fueled up first – there are no gas stations along the way.

For many people, a brilliant drive along a beautiful route creates a certain momentum that can be difficult to resist.

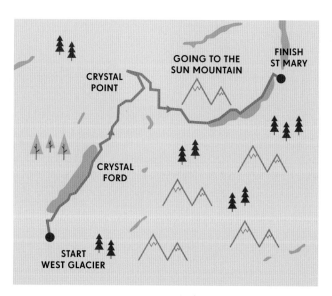

Swept up in the rhythm of the drive, you may find that you are reluctant to stop. But trust me: on this particular road, the stops are half the fun. Fortunately, there are numerous pullouts along the road, and I will make full use of them, pausing for a photo or just to drink in the awesome views.

Heading east, I feel like I've only just started when I am compelled to pull over. I'm in tiny Apgar, a village right on the the edge of gorgeous Lake McDonald, the largest lake in the park. The view is sublime – a glass-like lake sweeps before me to the whitecapped mountain peaks that cluster together at the opposite end of the lake. (For most of the winter, this is as far along the road as cars are able to proceed.) Also in the village are a permit office and visitor center, campgrounds, a motel, gift shop and cafe.

Back on the road, I soon reach the McDonald Creek Overlook, another worthy stop. The creek changes personalities according to the season; in summer, it's gentle and tidily contained between its wide, rocky banks, but in early spring the force of the water is strong enough to make the viewing platform I'm standing on tremble.

My next stop is Avalanche Creek; by now I'm ready to get out and stretch my legs. Two excellent trails start here: a 1-mile (1.6km) wheelchair-accessible boardwalk loop called the Trail of the Cedars, which takes you through the only grove of cedars in the park, and a longer 4.2-mile (6.8km) round-trip hike to Avalanche Lake. The lake is a treat to see: a blast of bright turquoise surrounded by steep rocky walls.

AN ENGINEERING MARVEL

Early plans included 15 switchbacks along the road, snaking tightly back and forth up the valley to Logan Pass. But a team of engineers continued to study the area, eventually deciding they could use the current route instead. This meant the road would blend almost seamlessly into its surroundings. If you tire of gazing at the landscape, ponder for a moment the amount of work that went (and still goes) into building a road in a place like this.

Clockwise, from above: brown bears make the park their home; humans can do likewise in Lake McDonald Lodge; the rapids at Logan Pass. Previous page, from top: Grinnell Lake; a mini-tunnel on Going-to-the-Sun

Once back in my car, I find myself on the Loop: a section of the road that's shaped a little like a bobby pin. Drifting along its gentle switchback I cannot help but admire the people who dreamed up, planned and constructed this road. A trail here leads to Granite Park Chalet, a superbly situated wooden lodge built by the Great Northern Railway in 1914. It's now a National Historic Landmark.

Just beyond The Loop there's a chance to see two examples of the impressive engineering that made the Going-to-the-Sun Road a reality. First is the Weeping Wall. As a result of the construction process, several rivulets of water now stream down the hillside above the road, sometimes drenching westbound vehicles in a chilly glacial spray. A little further on are the Triple Arches; together they form an elegant solution to the problem of several gaps in the rock base supporting the road.

If every trip has an ultimate destination, for me that destination is Logan Pass. It's the highest point along the route and a good turning-around spot if you're short on time.

A number of short hiking trails start from the parking lot, on both sides of the road. Venturing out on one of these will earn you some of the most wondrous views in the park, although even the views from the parking lot are good.

Drivers who continue eastward along the road will find still more hiking trails from Siyeh Bend, as well as even more ominous craggy mountaintops and a distant view of Blackfoot and Jackson Glacier. See these while you can; glaciers throughout the park have been steadily shrinking.

Toward the end of the road I make sure to stop at the St Mary Falls trailhead, a 2.4-mile (4km) round-trip hike that leads to the namesake falls and lake – it's a fitting way to end such a spectacular drive.

"Rivulets of water stream down the hillside, sometimes drenching westbound vehicles in a chilly glacial spray"

DIRECTIONS

Start // West Glacier
Finish // St Mary
Distance // 50 miles (80.5km). It's a two-hour drive, but allow twice that for stops and hikes.
Getting there // Glacier Park International Airport has car rental outlets and is located just outside Kalispell, a 30-minute drive from West Glacier.
When to drive // The road is open late June or early July to mid-October, weather permitting. Check ahead (www.nps.gov/glac).
Where to stay // Lake McDonald Lodge (www.glaciernationalparklodges.com) is a historic Swiss chalet-style lodge with cabins, on the shore of the park's largest lake.
Park entrance fee // US$35 per car (good for seven days).

*Opposite: the sun rises over
Toroweap Point, Grand Canyon
National Park, Arizona*

MORE LIKE THIS
WESTERN LANDSCAPES

FOUR CORNERS CRUISE

This road trip is super-sized, covering the grandest views and biggest wows in the Southwest – from Vegas to Zion to the Grand Canyon and beyond. The timid should stay at home. Starting in Las Vegas, swing through the Valley of Fire State Park, then cruise through Arizona into Utah and Zion National Park, which offers what may be the best day hike in North America, before continuing on Hwy 89 to the clifftop view of the Colorado River at Horseshoe Bend, simultaneously beautiful and terrifying. Further on, the rugged buttes of Monument Valley look, from a distance, like the remains of a prehistoric fortress, red-gold ramparts protecting ancient secrets. But their sun-reflected beauty will lure you in. There are so many stunning sights on the remainder of this loop through five states back to the awesome Red Rock Canyon that it's hard to pick standouts, but a walk along the South Rim Trail will best reveal the Grand Canyon in all its magnificence.

Start // Las Vegas
Finish // Red Rock Canyon National Conservation Area
Distance // 1852 miles (2980km)

THE HOGBACK, UTAH

The drive south on Rte 12 from Torrey starts gently enough before climbing to a 9000ft (2750m) pass, frequently covered in snow. Despite that, it is a beautiful drive through the thick pine forests of the Dixie National Forest. But it really gets interesting after Boulder. There was a time when the only road that connected Boulder and Escalante in Utah was a trail called Hell's Backbone. True to its name, it was – and still is, if you care to tackle it – as nasty a piece of track as you'll find in the Old West. Eventually it became obvious that a better road was needed and work began on the stretch that would include the Hogback. A narrow, tarred road that clings precariously to the top of a razorback ridge, filled in occasionally with some soil, the Hogback is balanced between steep spills down to creeks and near-vertical canyons. There are few places to park, but stop when you can: the vistas are wonderful. And talking of wonderful, Escalante's Circle D restaurant has slow cooked BBQ to die for.

Start // Torrey
Finish // Escalante
Distance // 65 miles (112km)

FANTASTIC CANYON
VOYAGE, ARIZONA

This scenic route north to the Grand Canyon is a great all-rounder. It's pretty, it's wild and it embraces Arizona's rough and tumble history. Picturesque trails wind past sandstone buttes, ponderosa pines and canyon views. Wild West adventures include horseback rides, saloon crawls and standing atop a 1900ft (580m) mine shaft on a terrifying glass platform at Audrey Headframe Park. But the route's not stuck in the past. A burgeoning wine scene and ale trail add 21st-century sparkle. Tackle this drive in spring or autumn by starting in Wickenburg, which looks as you'd imagine it did in the 1890s, then heading on to Prescott and Jerome, a copper-mining town once known as the "wickedest in the West." Cottonwood has more contemporary delights via excellent food and wine, while the remainder of the drive toward the Grand Canyon offers riparian scenery, sandstone monoliths, red cliffs and expansive plateaus.

Start // Wickenburg
Finish // Grand Canyon Village
Distance // 285 miles (459km)

BIG SKIES IN
THE LONE STAR STATE

Regis St Louis dusts off his boots and hits the road in Texas, home of sunbaked deserts, chiseled mountains and enough culture to make a city slicker sigh.

"Texas is a state of mind. Texas is an obsession. Above all, Texas is a nation in every sense of the word." John Steinbeck wrote these incantatory words back in 1963 during a meandering road trip around the United States, but they ring no less true today. Texas pride runs deep, which is perhaps not surprising given its backstory – Texas was an independent republic for ten years after gaining its independence from Mexico in 1836. The state's colossal size – it's over twice as large as Germany – is also no exaggeration.

Driving from Louisiana, I am quickly reminded of Texan proportions when I encounter a sign reading "El Paso 857 [miles]," which is roughly the distance between Philadelphia and Jacksonville, Florida. Luckily, I am not heading to the westernmost reaches of Texas – at least not yet. Instead, I have more important concerns than ticking off highway miles. To paraphrase the wisdom of the ancients: "The journey of a thousand miles begins with one good meal." And I hope to find the perfect caloric start in Houston, a city with a dizzying restaurant scene, fueled in large part by its sizable immigrant population. I pull into Taste of Nigeria, a hub for the West African community, and lunch on vivid green *ewedu* (a traditional Yoruba soup made of jute leaves) followed by steaming hot *jollof* (a rice dish) topped with catfish and served with plantains. Low-volume Afrobeat plays overhead, and the stress of interstate driving slowly fades as I sip Nkulenu's Palm Wine.

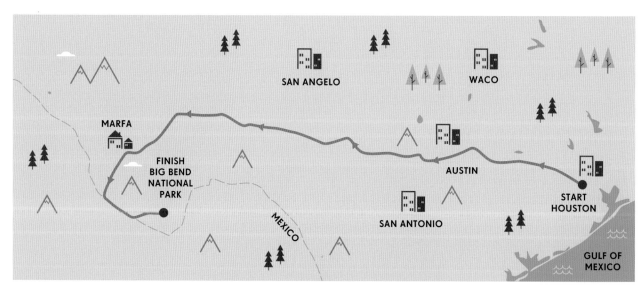

Later, I head to the Menil Collection, a 17,000-piece trove of artworks spread across five buildings in the leafy Montrose neighborhood. Rather than taking in the wide-ranging exhibitions, I go to the Rothko Chapel, a plain brick building that offers little clue as to the contents within. The doors close behind me, a hush descends and I find myself in an octagonal room of gray stucco walls with a central skylight casting diffuse light. Fourteen massive paintings adorn the walls. At first glance they seem an almost uniform black, but as I linger, shades and subtleties appear, and the quiet power of these works begins to resonate. I end up spending far longer than intended, and depart feeling sad that Mark Rothko, who spent the last six years of his life working on this chapel, did not live to see its completion in 1971.

The next morning, the flatlands spread before me as I pass through one-horse towns with jolly names like Prairie View, Ledbetter and Giddings. The sun is blazing overhead by the time I roll into Austin. I seek refuge in the expanse of Barton Springs Pool. Fed by natural springs, with a temperature always hovering around 68°F (20°C), the waters make me gasp as I jump in. Delightfully chilled, I warm up on the grass under a century-old pecan tree and watch Austinites enjoying a lazy afternoon. Later I stroll to Barton Creek, a gurgling, boulder-strewn waterway that courses past old-growth stands of juniper and cedar. A few waders are out cooling off in the creek, including a woman holding a long pink leash attached to a Shetland pony. "He loves the water!" she tells me as he bites at the trickling stream like an oversized puppy.

That evening, I join the crowd gathered on the south side of the Congress Avenue Bridge. The attraction: the twilight exodus of Mexican free-tailed bats as they fly off to hunt. Ever since the 1980s a huge colony of these winged mammals have roosted in the nooks and crannies beneath the bridge. Just after sunset, a dozen or so emerge, followed by a few others, until finally a great flapping tidal wave gushes past. Tens of thousands fill the sky, as America's largest urban population of bats (some 1.5 million at times) appears en masse.

The landscape grows more parched as I motor west, with the sea of desert scrub broken by rock formations that emerge like ghostly sails from the desert. With a speed limit of 80mph (129km/h), I streak across the sunbaked plains beneath the widest skies I've ever seen.

It's high noon when I roll into Marfa, a dusty low-rise town that could easily pass for a Western filmset — an attribute well known to Hollywood location scouts. I park near the Hotel Paisano, a weathered Spanish-colonial building where James Dean and other celebrities stayed while filming *Giant* back in 1958. Nearby stands the Presidio County Courthouse, with a dome topped by the Goddess of Justice. In one hand she holds a sword and in the other... well, nothing at all. According to legend, back in the late 1800s, a gun-slinging cowboy shot the scales out of her hand with a rifle, saying, "There is no justice in Presidio County."

Despite its Wild West bravado, Marfa has a sensitive side, too. On the outskirts of town, the Chinati Foundation transformed an abandoned army base into a renowned collection of large-scale art installations. I join a guided tour, taking in giant balls of

"I streak across the sunbaked plains beneath the widest skies I've ever seen"

MARFA LIGHTS

Near the Chinati Mountains, mysterious orbs of light suddenly appear then disappear over the desert landscape. Whether ghosts, alien spacecraft or some obscure atmospheric phenomenon, the lights have mystified onlookers for well over a century. The cowboy who first reported them in 1883 thought they were Apache signal fires, while more recent eyewitnesses claim they are distant car lights. The viewing area is 9 miles (14.5km) east of Marfa on Hwy 90.

Clockwise, from opposite left: Mule Ears Peaks, Big Bend National Park; bats over Congress Avenue Bridge in Austin; Rothko Chapel in Houston. Previous page: wranglers on horseback overlook the Dixie Dude Ranch in Bandera; an endless road beneath a wide sky in Big Bend National Park

DIRECTIONS

Start // Houston
Finish // Big Bend National Park
Distance // 798 miles (1284km)
Getting there // Houston's George Bush Intercontinental Airport serves destinations around the world.
When to drive // Wildflowers and warm days accompany March to May. Expect stifling heat from June to August.
Where to stay // Austin's Hotel San José (www.sanjosehotel. com) is a stylish 1930s motel. At El Cosmico (www.elcosmico. com) in Marfa you can sleep in a converted travel trailer, tipi, safari tent or yurt. Book well ahead for a room in Big Bend's Chisos Mountains Lodge (www.chisosmountainslodge.com).
Detours // At the McDonald Observatory, north of Marfa, peer through telescopes at some of the world's clearest skies.
More info // www.traveltexas.com, www.nps.gov/bibe

mashed-up painted steel, sculptures of eerily glowing florescent-tubes and massive concrete boxes in the wind-whipped grasslands. Several visitors are transfixed. Another wears a disgusted look that calls to mind the writer Charles Bukowski's feelings on aesthetics: "Great art is horseshit, buy tacos."

The next day, I continue south along hauntingly barren terrain that grows more mountainous as I near the Mexican border. With low chiseled peaks on one side and the Chihuahua Desert on the other, I follow the serpentine curves of the Rio Grande all the way to Big Bend National Park.

It's late afternoon when I reach a viewpoint overlooking a grand sweep of the Chisos Mountains, which soar like islands in the sky above the desert floor. As the sun hangs low in the sky, 500-million-year-old cliffs glow with a golden light, and I feel as though I'm peering back through the eons when Texas was neither a place on the map nor even an idea, but rather a vast landscape of infinite possibility.

MORE LIKE THIS
RUGGED NORTH AMERICAN LANDSCAPES

CANYONS AND MOUNTAINS, CHIHUAHUA

Across the border from west Texas, Chihuahua is both the largest state in Mexico and home to some of its most impressive natural wonders. Beginning in its eponymous capital city, get a taste of Norteño character in historic buildings like Pancho Villa's former 48-room mansion, now a revolutionary war museum. North of there, adobe ruins of the 800-year-old site of Paquimé shed light on the region's ancient past. In Creel, you can experience Indigenous cultures on guided visits to Rarámuri communities. Nearby, you'll find big adventures in the Barrancas del Cobre – a system of canyons six times larger than the Grand Canyon. Ride ziplines above plunging chasms in Divisadero, swim beneath Mexico's highest waterfall at the Cascada de Basaseachi and follow winding roads to the canyon floor for an overnight in the village of Batopilas.

Start // Chihuahua
Finish // Batopilas
Distance // 1100 miles (1770km)

BLUEGRASS TRAILS, KENTUCKY

A land of thundering racehorses, bourbon distilleries and verdant countryside, Kentucky makes a captivating setting for a rambling road trip. On a loop around the central and eastern parts of the state, you'll take in expansive stretches of wilderness, encompassing both highs (Appalachian summits) and lows (massive caverns). In Lexington, get your dose of city life exploring leafy Victorian neighbourhoods and craft breweries before heading south to Daniel Boone National Forest. Continuing southeast, you'll pass the rolling greenery of the Appalachian foothills en route to Black Mountain, Kentucky's highest peak. West of there, you can follow the Cumberland Parkway to Mammoth Cave, the world's largest known cave system – subterranean passageways span over 400 miles (644km). Looping north, stop for bourbon tours near Bardstown, then catch horse racing at Churchill Downs followed by ghost hunting in the Waverly Hills Sanatorium.

Start // Lexington
Finish // Louisville
Distance // 550 miles (885km)

ROAMING IN IDAHO

Overshadowed by the neighboring states of Montana and Washington, Idaho is one of the most underrated states in the West, and is home to rugged mountain ranges and nearly 4 million acres (1.6 million hectares) of wilderness. Start off in the parks-loving capital of Boise: trails take you up into the forested foothills, and you can immerse yourself in the city's Basque roots at restaurants downtown. The onward journey follows mountain waterways – like the meandering Snake River – across the state to the Teton Valley. There, amid jagged peaks, you'll find outstanding hiking, horseback riding and mountain biking, as well as skiing in winter. Looping back west, you can stop in Sun Valley for more outdoor adventures, then continue on to Stanley, a charming town of log cabins at the foot of the Sawtooth mountains.

Start // Boise
Finish // Stanley
Distance // 650 miles (1046km)

Clockwise, from top: a mountain biker enjoys one of the many trails just above downtown Boise, Idaho; Grays Arch, a natural rock formation in Daniel Boone National Forest, Kentucky; Shoshone Falls on the Snake River, Idaho

THE REAL #RVLIFE

Joel Balsam embarks on an RV odyssey from Memphis to San Diego – passing through the South, including the Lone Star State, then UFO country, before landing on the Pacific coast.

What shows up when you search for #RVlife or #vanlife on Instagram? Sparkling adventure chariots in front of wondrous mountain or desert backdrops? Happy families and impossibly hot couples?

The great American road trip has been romanticized since 1919, when Dwight D Eisenhower embarked on one before he became president. But it was never my dream. Although I travel a lot, my trips usually involve a rickety bus.

Road tripping across the United States was, however, a dream for my new partner, Stephanie. Her fondest memories of growing up were summers spent at a trailer park, and she'd passed the last two years driving across Canada in her 1987 Chevy RV. Now she had the US in her sights – a trip from Toronto through the South and on to California over four months. To be with her, I'd give #RVlife a try.

I fly into Memphis to meet Stephanie. When I arrive, she's already thick into it. Leaning up against her 18ft (5.5m) home on wheels, named "Stevie Lee," she looks like a total badass. I'm nervous as hell.

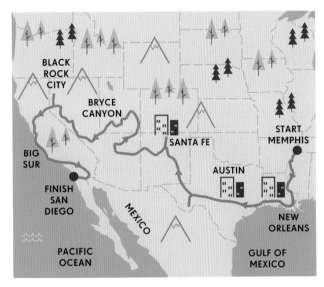

"The United States is filled with completely random and delightful roadside stops"

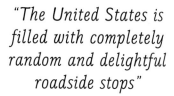

We drive to the Mississippi Delta. As Robert Johnson's guitar crackles through the RV's speakers, traces of Mississippi's poverty are reflected through the window. But there's also much to be cherished. There are BBQ joints with spicy tamales, rib tips and fried catfish. There's the almighty Mississippi River – you know, the one Sam Cooke sang about – and a resurgence of soul and blues initiated by devoted locals in Clarksdale. And of course, there's the wide-open road.

Then smoke starts billowing from the RV's hood. We pull over and a guy with a ZZ Top beard confirms our worst fear – the engine is blown, just a few days into our journey. Stephanie is devastated as she watches a tow truck haul ol' Stevie Lee to a mechanic in Yazoo City.

But Southern hospitality hears our cries. As the RV is in for repairs, we're invited to a gospel church, where we witness a baptism. We tuck into fried chicken with all the fixings and walk around Yazoo City's historic old town. None of this is in our plans, but it's amazing and we have that busted engine to thank.

On the road again about a week later, the point hits home that the United States is filled with completely random and delightful roadside stops. In Kentwood, Louisiana, we find the unofficial Britney Spears museum – with life-sized cardboard cutouts of the pop star, as well as her real childhood bedroom.

As a city guy, I'm absolutely thrilled when we cross the 24-mile (39km) Lake Pontchartrain Causeway to New Orleans. We hit up

Bacchanal, a wine bar that feels like a stranger's wedding reception, and share a fiery-hot shrimp po'boy at Parasol's. I declare the Big Easy my favorite US city, but it's not meant for RVs – urban areas are way too difficult to drive around and find suitable parking spaces.

In Acadiana, we take part in the ultimate food crawl – crawfish boils, hulking turkey legs, gas station boudin, the Tabasco hot sauce factory – and I continue to learn lessons about #RVlife. As we roll into a field to sleep under the moonlight, I come to realize that while I'm having so much fun, I'm also pretty lonely. Yes, I have Stephanie, but it isn't so easy to just go out for a beer with a friend, or to meet strangers the way I do on my other travels.

The RV must have read my thoughts, because a few days later as we're driving into Austin, Texas, it breaks down... again. We learn that the engine we'd gotten was a lemon and it will be a few weeks before we can have a new one installed under warranty.

Out of the blue, Stephanie gets a message from someone following our situation on Instagram, who invites us to park on her driveway until the RV is fixed. We become fast friends, swimming in Barton Springs and inhaling breakfast tacos. Then another stranger offers to pick us up for a mini-road trip to Big Bend National Park and over the Mexican border to cool off in crystal caves. It's as if Stevie Lee is telling us: "Yes, RVing can be lonely, but the people who help along the way make the trip."

Once we're underway again, New Mexico proves to be as out there as they say. We spend hours wandering around bizarre rock

CREOLE TRAIL RIDES

In the South's cowboy country, hooves click-clack and trucks blast zydeco on weekend trail rides, a decades-old Creole tradition that few outside these communities know about (blame revisionist history and Western films for that). Prepare your belly for spicy rabbit gumbo, turkey legs smothered in gravy, and plenty of cold beer – trail rides tend to turn into dance parties that last late into the night. Everyone's welcome, so long as you're respectful.

From opposite left: "Stevie Lee" in action; the Earthship Biotecture upcycled house, New Mexico; Joshua Tree National Park, California. Previous pages: the open road in the rearview; taking in views from the RV

formations in Carlsbad Caverns, visit Earthship Biotecture – an eco-friendly house of the future – and crawl through the "Dryer Portal" art installation at Meow Wolf in Santa Fe.

In the Southwest, we visit Antelope Canyon, Monument Valley, Bryce, Zion... all just, wow. As I scroll through my photos, I realize we've morphed into that idyllic adventure couple I'd been seeing on Instagram.

In Nevada, we somehow get some sleep in the Clown Motel (decorated with over 2000 clown dolls), before racing up to the Burning Man festival – and while that's a story in itself, I'll confirm that having an RV is the ideal way to do it.

With a month left, we cut over to California's storied Hwy 1, where we climb cliffs past squawking seals and stop for a folk show under fairy lights at Big Sur. Scared away by word of hostility toward RVers in Los Angeles, we join other outcasts in the Joshua Tree desert and "the last free place," the community of Slab City, before finally curving back down to San Diego.

As we put the RV into storage, I think again about the Instagram posts I'd looked through before the trip. Yep, there sure were views like that, and we had so many other photo-worthy moments of bliss. But Instagram leaves a lot out, too. The loneliness. The anxiety I felt when the RV broke down. And those incredible moments when strangers came to the rescue.

While those experiences aren't always seen as fit for social media, the real #RVlife is what's made this drive so epic.

DIRECTIONS

Start // Memphis, Tennessee
Finish // San Diego, California
Distance // 4800 miles (7725km)
Getting there // Memphis is a good starting point for the Delta and the South, but you can start your RV journey anywhere along this route.
When to drive // Go in spring or fall to avoid summer heat.
Where to stay // RV campgrounds with water and electricity hookups are plentiful. Free short-term camping is often permissible on BLM land and in Walmart parking lots.
Useful apps // iOverlander (www.ioverlander.com) shows crowdsourced places to camp for free and pump out or fill up propane tanks. Roadtrippers (roadtrippers.com) allows you to make a detailed plan for the route, but embracing spontaneity is what road trips like this are all about.

*Opposite: driving the Icefields Parkway
through Banff National Park, Alberta*

MORE LIKE THIS
RV ODYSSEYS

COAST TO COAST, CANADA

From Irish and Scottish vibes along the
Atlantic coast through *la belle province*
to the endless horizon of the prairies and
gaping Rocky Mountains, crossing Canada
is a rite of passage for many, and certainly
less trafficked than a similar US trip. Keep
an eye toward the sky for a glimpse of the
northern lights, which can appear when you
least expect. In the Canadian version of
Woodie Guthrie's *This Land is Your Land*,
coast to coast is considered to be from
Bonavista, Newfoundland, to Vancouver
Island, British Columbia – but you won't be
faulted if your cross-country trip begins in
Montreal or Toronto. Camping for up to 21
days is free on Crown Land for Canadian
citizens, but nonresidents will need to buy
a permit ahead of time.
Start // Bonavista
Finish // Tofino
Distance // 4350 miles (7000km)

THE PACIFIC COAST

Chris McCandless, America's most iconic
nomad of the last half-century and the
subject of Jon Krakauer's *Into the Wild*,
hitchhiked north to Alaska for a "new
and different sun." The desire to go north
and get off the grid remains irresistible to
many, and this Pacific coast route is easily
one of the continent's most frequented
long-distance road trips. There's just
something about sleeping next to crashing
waves that'll make you want to do it
again and again for weeks on end. Drive
with the window open (or top down) up
California's rugged Hwy 1 past gigantic
redwoods, stopping for espresso in Seattle
before heading up to British Columbia's
celebrated old-growth forests. When you
finally get to Alaska's stark tundra and the
ancient glaciers of Denali National Park,
pay your respects to the fallen nomad.
Start // San Diego, California
Finish // Denali National Park, Alaska
Distance // 4000 miles (6437km)

NEW YORK TO FLORIDA

Forgo flying direct with all the other
snowbirds, and instead take a leisurely
drive from NYC south to the Sunshine
State. The Atlantic coast is packed with
one historic site after another. There's
Independence Hall and the Betsy Ross
House in Philadelphia, the birthplace
of *The Star-Spangled Banner* in
Baltimore, DC's myriad monuments and
museums, Civil War history in Richmond,
pastel-colored 19th-century buildings
in Charleston, and a drive through
Savannah's Oak Tree Lane – which is
as pretty as they say. When you reach
Florida, give surfing a try in Jacksonville,
catch a NASCAR race on Daytona Beach
and then veer inland to spend some
quality time with the theme park of your
choice in Orlando. This drive's a perfect
one for the whole family.
Start // New York City
Finish // Miami, Florida
Distance // 1530 miles (2462km)

THROUGH NEW ENGLAND'S HAUNTED HISTORY

With moody scenery and grisly history, New England beckons to dark-hearted travelers. Anita Isalska hits the road in Massachusetts in search of myths, monsters and macabre souvenirs.

It's mid-November in Massachusetts and the Halloween pumpkins are starting to sag. Nights are closing in quickly, and fall foliage is darkening to blood-red. In short, conditions are perfect for a New England road trip.

Dark history drew me to Massachusetts, and I'm hungry to explore the region's savage beauty and grisly past. Together with my friend, Ali, I've spent the last couple days meeting Boston's old ghosts. In cemeteries like King's Chapel, 300-year-old tombs jut toothily from the ground. Even grassy Boston Common was formerly a public execution site. But there are many more unsettling mysteries to probe, so we're road tripping to literary tombs, old battlegrounds and sites likely to be forever linked to the Salem Witch Trials.

After picking up our rental car, it's a white-knuckle ride through Boston's impatient rush-hour deluge. Finally, the knot of highways releases us onto Rte 2 toward Concord. Stands of maroon-leafed oak trees guide our way, and soon we're cruising past the big blue expanse of the Mystic River (the name derives from "large estuary," or *missi-tuk*, in the Algonquian language, rather than any mystical associations).

We arrive in Concord, where the living are as present as the dead. This sleepy town is known for past battles and long-departed writers, and landmarks associated with the illustrious dead are everywhere.

We take a walk across Concord Battleground, whose tall grasses are lit gold by the afternoon sun. This is where the "shot heard round the world" rang out in 1775, marking the start of the Revolutionary War that claimed thousands of lives. We stroll on to Sleepy Hollow Cemetery, where *Little Women* writer Louisa May Alcott occupies her family plot, while transcendentalist Henry David Thoreau slumbers under a grand tomb.

Evening is starting to descend, so we jump back into the car and drive east to Salem. It's an easy zip along I-95; the road weaves between Quannapowitt and Suntaug Lakes and the views get lovelier as we approach Salem. New England's instantly recognizable colonial houses are all around, their ornate porticoes and steeply pitched roofs aptly resembling witches' hats.

The town is known for the 17th-century witch trials, but I'm more startled by the scale of Salem's souvenir industry. As soon as we step out of the car, we see stores brimming with demonic apparel.

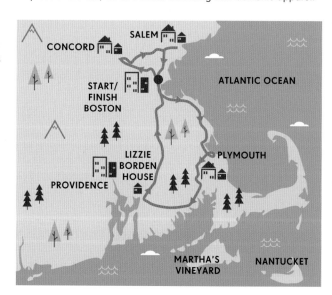

After joining a local history tour, our guide leads us through softly lit lanes, weaving together history and hearsay. On Essex St, we pause at Ropes Mansion, where the ghost of a screaming woman is said to appear. Further along we see the so-called Witch House, a well-preserved 17th-century building once owned by Jonathan Corwin, a judge in the infamous trials. Between February 1692 and May 1693, more than 200 people were accused of witchcraft and 20 were executed. But just as Ropes Mansion delivered no ghosts, the Witch Trials lack witches: the true evil was the collision of hysteria, unchecked Puritan morals and staggering legal negligence.

Feeling more chilled by human nature than the supernatural, Ali and I thank our guide and check in to the venerable Hawthorne Hotel. In the morning, we swap notes: the only disembodied voices I've heard are through the hotel's thin walls, while Ali's room on the reputedly haunted sixth floor has failed to deliver a single phantom. Secretly, we're relieved.

We leave Salem and join Rte 3A, the scenic road to Plymouth. We follow the shore of Massachusetts Bay, clanking across suspension bridges and flying through forests of white cedar and blushing chestnut oak.

After a couple of hours, we're trundling along tidy streets where American flags flutter from big columned porches. Plymouth is "America's Hometown": New England's founding colony was established here in 1620 by passengers on the *Mayflower*, whose 100ft (30m) replica (the *Mayflower II*) now sways by the shore.

On a day like today, when the air is crisp and there's a merry chatter of families snapping up *Mayflower* fridge magnets, Plymouth feels like a wholesome place, but its origins are grim. Only a slim percentage of the Native Wampanoag people survived two epidemics during the 1610s, likely introduced through earlier contact with Europeans. Meanwhile, the original English colonists were wholly unprepared for their first agonizing winter in the New World — nearly half of the 102 Pilgrims died.

No wonder Plymouth has more than its fair share of ghosts. We park near *Mayflower II* and walk to Burial Hill, a cemetery in use since the first colonists came ashore. Though the earliest wooden grave markers haven't survived, there are tombs with lichen-spattered inscriptions and weathered skull carvings that date back to the 1680s. Continuing downhill, we trip along North St to two of Plymouth's most haunted locales — but in the sunshine, Spooner House and Trask House look charmingly benign.

By sundown, Plymouth Bay is glittering with coppery light. We hasten back to the car and follow the southbound Tremont St, before cruising west along I-195. As twilight casts its ashy hue over the sky, pine forests fly past the window, and soon enough we're at our final

MANSIONS OF RHODE ISLAND

The smallest state in the US delivers both history and hauntings. The city of Newport is bejeweled with magnificent mansions that date to the Gilded Age. The finest is the Breakers, a sublime Italianate summer residence commissioned by Cornelius Vanderbilt II, whose family amassed incomprehensible wealth during the railroad boom. Local lore claims that Cornelius' wife Alice haunts the house, but the Breakers staff say the ghostly dame keeps to herself.

Clockwise, from top: a tombstone marks Authors Ridge in Sleepy Hollow Cemetery; the House of the Seven Gables Museum in Salem; Halloween pumpkins in Boston; a woman dressed as a witch at Salem's Halloween fair. Previous page: a cemetery in Salem

"For a group of people scrutinizing a 19th-century crime-scene photo, we're strangely upbeat"

stop: the Lizzie Borden House. A gruesome double-murder took place here in 1892, still recalled by local schoolchildren with the couplet: "Lizzie Borden took an axe / and gave her mother 40 whacks."

"It wasn't actually 40 whacks," explains our guide, Jack, with considerable glee. He rattles a laminated photograph and details the horrific attack. For a group of people scrutinizing a 19th-century crime-scene photo, we're strangely upbeat. As we stand in the florally themed historic house, now lovingly remodeled as a B&B, everyone is chatting animatedly about whether Lizzie Borden issued the fatal blows.

Whether we decide Lizzie is a hardened heroine or a maidenly axe-murderer, we're all here for the same thing: a sinister thrill. Emerging from a weekend of foul deeds and bloody injustices, I'm the one feeling a little monstrous — yet I'm already planning the next day's eerie itinerary. In a place so embroidered with mysteries, it's hard to resist the call of New England's dead.

DIRECTIONS

Start/Finish // Boston
Distance // 240 miles (386km)
Getting there // Boston is served by Logan International Airport, where you can rent a car. Alternatively, arrive by train and pick up your wheels downtown.
When to drive // Maximize spooky ambience by traveling in fall, but avoid Halloween week when prices and crowds surge in Salem.
Guided tours // History comes alive with expert guides. Book ahead at lizzie-borden.com and through www.salem.org.
Vegan eats // New England is famous for seafood, but you'll find surprisingly rich plant-based pickings. Don't miss Double Zero in Boston, Jodi Bee Bakes in Salem, and Diego's in Newport.

MORE LIKE THIS
GHOSTLY DRIVES

MACABRE SIGHTS OF THE MIDWEST

Ready to test your nerves? Begin in Shaker's Cigar Bar in Milwaukee, formerly a brothel run by Al, Frank and Ralph Capone, and later a haunt of serial killer Jeffrey Dahmer. On your way out of town, stop at the Forest Hill Cemetery, where stately tombs provide the repose for wealthy beer barons. Continue west to Cresco, Iowa, where a 1914 theater is rumored to be haunted by long-departed vaudeville performers, then meet more ghosts by driving southwest to Des Moines' sumptuous Jordan House. Still sleeping soundly? Venture to the Villisca Axe Murder House, the site of an unsolved brutal killing; the house still draws ghost whisperers. Finish up in Omaha, where you can try your luck in the Museum of Shadows, a collection of more than 3000 cursed objects (maybe skip the souvenirs...).

Start // Milwaukee, Wisconsin
Finish // Omaha, Nebraska
Distance // 620 miles (998km)

GEORGIA'S HAUNTED HOTELS

Sweet dreams... every stop on this route has a famously haunted hotel. From Atlanta, drive east to Augusta and stay overnight at the Partridge Inn (1836). The ghost of a heartbroken young woman is said to wander the halls in her never-worn wedding dress. (Curiously enough, the hotel is a popular wedding venue.) Drive south to Savannah and overnight at the Marshall House, a mid-19th-century former hospital where cantankerous ghosts slam doors. Further south, bed down at the Jekyll Island Club Resort where the odor of cigar smoke gives away the presence of a spectral J Pierpont Morgan. Before looping back to Atlanta, drive northwest to Americus and the Windsor Hotel. Tours of this 1892 property will regale you with tales of ghostly occupants, including a tragically murdered young girl and a former doorman still dutifully greeting guests.

Start/Finish // Atlanta
Distance // 705 miles (1135km)

OFFBEAT TEXAS

Sure, there's big skies and barbecue... but how about a road trip through some of Texas' most eccentric spots? Begin with curios in Dallas: the Adrian Flatt Collection assembles bronze hand statues cast from celebrities, presidents and athletes. Head west toward Fort Worth to visit the graves of Bonnie and Clyde, then detour north to Aurora. In 1897, a so-called UFO crash-landed here; local news reported the pilot as an alien, but the town still gave him a Christian burial at Aurora Cemetery. Continue southwest to Waxahachie to admire a grandiose gothic house modeled after spooky '60s sitcom *The Munsters*. Push south to Waco, home to a mammoth gravesite, whose ancient bones continue to puzzle paleontologists. Finish up in Austin, where you can meet an animatronic Lyndon B Johnson and watch bats fly out from beneath Congress Avenue Bridge.

Start // Dallas
Finish // Austin
Distance // 313 miles (504km)

Clockwise, from top: JP Morgan's Jekyll Island Club Resort, Georgia; Aurora Cemetery in Texas, site of a supposed alien's grave; Shaker's Cigar Bar, hangout of the Capones, Wisconsin

RECHARGING IN BRITISH COLUMBIA'S KOOTENAY ROCKIES

Road-tripping solo in an electric vehicle, Carolyn B Heller mixes hiking, creative outdoor art and imaginative plant-based meals into an emissions-free Canadian adventure.

I t's 6am on a late September morning and I'm thinking about my car. I'm not usually the sort of person who pays attention to what I drive, so I'm surprised that I've become so obsessed with my vehicle. Traveling solo through British Columbia's Kootenay Rockies region on my first electric-car road trip, I'm worrying about where I'm going to recharge.

Despite a few anxious moments, I will eventually relax into this more sustainable – and recharging – way to road trip, as I explore four national parks, wander the back alleys of small towns filled with quirky outdoor art and seek out local, plant-based meals. The mountainous Kootenay Rockies is just one of several Canadian regions investing heavily in electric vehicle infrastructure.

I start my trip in Vancouver with a full battery and a smartphone full of route-planning apps. When I pull off the Trans-Canada Highway in Hope, two hours to the east, I don't really need to charge my car again. But I do need coffee and a triple-berry scone from the Blue Moose Coffee House, and Hope, I find, has more EV

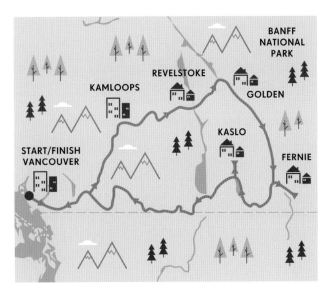

chargers than communities many times its size. At the junction of several routes that lead into BC's interior, Hope has long been a road-trip refueling stop. Perhaps it's not surprising that the town is investing in this newer power option.

Several hours later, in Revelstoke, I head for the back alleys. I browse paintings, sculpture and stained glass hanging in several alleyways behind local businesses – a street art project dubbed "Art Alleries." At nearby Terra Firma Café, I enjoy a hummus toastie, a thick sandwich spread with split pea hummus and roasted vegetables grown on the owners' organic farm.

Driving up the steep 16 mile (26km) Meadows in the Sky Parkway in Mount Revelstoke National Park brings my first glimpse of early-season snow amid the fall colors on the trails. Climbing the switchbacking road also sucks up a huge amount of battery charge. But I regain much of that on the drive

downhill, my battery recharging with the energy regenerated as I coast toward town.

Between Revelstoke and Golden, Hwy 1 bisects Glacier National Park, where the high peaks are topped with snow. In Golden, I gather my courage to explore the town's newest attraction: the Golden Skybridge. Taking a deep breath, I step cautiously onto Canada's highest suspension bridges, two swaying spans far above a deep canyon. Soon, I'm relaxed enough to enjoy the panoramas across the mountains.

It's raining as I continue east into Yoho National Park, so the crowds often surrounding the park's main attraction are absent. I zip up my jacket and scarcely notice the showers as I walk along the shore of deep-green Emerald Lake.

Back in Golden, at Reposados Tacos, I order vegetarian tacos to go. The broccolini with beet purée and the crisply battered avocado with pickled red onion are so vibrantly hued – and delicious – that I don't mind eating them in a motel parking lot while recharging the car.

In Radium Hot Springs, a blip of a town outside Kootenay National Park, I decide to top up my battery before heading into the park. I've just plugged into the charging station in front of the community center when another car pulls alongside. "Are you in a hurry to charge?" I ask the woman who gets out of her vehicle. "Not at all," she replies, then asks where I'm headed. Soon we're swapping notes about favorite hiking trails.

On her recommendation, I opt to hike the national park's Dog Lake Trail. I cross two short suspension bridges and trek into an old-growth forest, emerging onto another peaceful lakeshore.

When I arrive in Fernie, I'm excited to check into my own tiny house – a cute cabin at Snow Valley Lodging, with a petite kitchen, sofa and cozy sleeping loft. Although it's only a short walk to the town center, I don't go on foot. Fernie's city hall has a public charging station, where I plug in my car and go exploring.

I find another unexpected art project in Fernie's alleyways, where painters have converted public rubbish bins into colorful street installations. Poking around the laneway dumpsters, I spot serene landscapes, vivid abstract patterns and fanciful forest creatures. Fernie also has a kombucha brewery, Fernie Alpine Springs, where owner Simon Lefrancois leads me through a sampling of his fresh, crisp-tasting brews.

In Cranbrook, while charging the car outside the Ktunaxa Nation Tribal Council offices, I meet a colleague for an overflowing vegetable bowl at the Heid Out, which doubles as a craft brewery. She is a competitive cyclist, so before riding with her on NorthStar Rails to Trails, a 17-mile (28km) pathway, I rent an e-bike. For my benefit we pedal leisurely, stopping at several lookouts where I snap photos over the river and surrounding peaks.

I spend the night in the former St Eugene Mission, a hotel operated by local First Nations, where I learn about the building's dark history. From 1912 through 1970, the mission was one of the residential schools that Canada's government required Native children to attend, in a racist attempt to eliminate Indigenous cultures. I scan historic photos depicting generations of children who were forcibly removed from their families, and walk through this sobering heritage in the mission's small cultural center.

Continuing west, near Kaslo, I hike into the woods along the Kootenay River Trail. Suddenly, I spot a stone man leaning on a walking stick. Then I spy a child, also made of stone, crouching behind a boulder, and another who's peering out above a rock. I've found the *Hide and Seek* sculptures, playful artworks that Yvonne Boyd, Spring Shine and Christopher Petersen installed along this forest path.

I'm still smiling as I leave the woods and return to my car. I've got more charging stops to make before I'm back in the city, but I'm no longer worried. On this EV trip into British Columbia's mountains, I'm feeling recharged by my adventures. Soon my car will be, too.

ELECTRIFYING THE KOOTENAYS

Unless you're a long-distance cyclist or intrepid hiker, traveling car-free between the towns and mountain parks of the Kootenay Rockies is nearly impossible. But the Accelerate Kootenays program is making car travel greener, by providing funding for EV chargers. In the program's first phase, completed back in 2018, 40 Level 2 and 13 fast chargers were installed, and future phases are accelerating the pace at which new chargers are added.

"Despite a few anxious moments, I eventually relax into this more sustainable – and recharging – way to road trip"

Opposite, clockwise from top left: the Out of the Box dumpster art project in Fernie; bicycles for hire in Revelstoke; veggie treats at Golden's Reposados Tacos; braving a crossing of the Golden Skybridge. Previous page: the Kootenay Rockies in all their glory

DIRECTIONS

Start/Finish // Vancouver
Distance // 1304 miles (2100km)
Getting there // Fly into Vancouver International Airport. Find EV rentals in Vancouver through Zerocar (zerocar.ca) and Turo's car-share app (turo.com).
When to drive // June through early October. From October to April, winter tires are required on many BC highways.
What to pack // Mountain weather is changeable, so pack layers, rain gear and hiking boots.
Where to stay // Moberly Lodge, Golden (moberlylodge. com); Snow Valley Lodging, Fernie (snowvalleylodging.com); St Eugene Mission, Cranbrook (www.steugene.ca)
Things to know // Helpful apps include A Better Routeplanner and Plugshare for EV route planning; and Flo, ChargePoint and BC Hydro EV for unlocking charging stations.

MORE LIKE THIS
CANADIAN EV ADVENTURES

SEA-TO-SKY HIGHWAY, BRITISH COLUMBIA

It's only two hours from Vancouver to Whistler, but this drive between the mountains and the Pacific Ocean is one of Canada's most beautiful. Along Hwy 99, dubbed the Sea-to-Sky Highway, several kiosks provide information about the region's Indigenous peoples, along with stellar water and mountain views. Stop in the town of Squamish for a ride up the Sea-to-Sky Gondola, a hike among the peaks or a stand-up paddleboard excursion on Howe Sound. More adventures await in Whistler, from hiking, mountain biking, zip-lining and whitewater rafting during summer, to skiing, snowboarding and bobsledding in winter. Whistler delivers cultural adventures, too, at the excellent Audain Art Museum and multimedia Squamish-Lil'wat Cultural Centre, which explores two of the region's First Nations. You'll find plenty of EV charging stations at both ends of this scenic highway.
Start // Vancouver
Finish // Whistler
Distance // 80 miles (125 km)

GEORGIAN BAY CIRCLE ROUTE, ONTARIO

An EV road trip around Ontario's Georgian Bay – from Toronto to Manitoulin Island to several secluded waterfront provincial parks – takes some planning; the EV network is still developing in northern Ontario. But it's worth it for the hiking and paddling routes, and for the opportunities to learn more about Indigenous culture. From Toronto, travel northwest to Tobermory, exploring Bruce Peninsula National Park and charging your car, before catching the car ferry to Manitoulin Island. On the island, home to several First Nations, take a nature tour or medicine walk with a Native guide, and visit the exhibits at the Ojibwe Cultural Foundation. Cross the Little Current Swing Bridge to return to the mainland, then detour to Killarney Provincial Park to hike among pink granite or canoe the lakes.
Start/Finish // Toronto
Distance // 660 miles (1060 km)

SAGUENAY FJORD, QUÉBEC

Pilot your EV around one of the southernmost fjords in North America, when you travel through the Saguenay-Lac Saint-Jean region north of Québec City. Charge your car in the city, before driving north to Charlevoix, where you can sample your way along La Route des Saveurs, the self-guided Flavor Trail that takes you to local cheesemakers, craft brewers, cideries, bakeries and other food purveyors. Go whale-watching in Tadoussac, at the mouth of the St Lawrence River. Then turn west, taking in the mountain scenery as you follow the inlets along the Saguenay River and circle Lac Saint-Jean. You can take a cruise around the fjords or rent a bike and pedal its shores, before heading back to Québec City.
Start/Finish // Québec City
Distance // 545 miles (875 km)

Clockwise, from top left: the rocky Georgian Bay shore at Bruce Peninsula National Park, Ontario; whale watching in Tadoussac, Québec; a church overlooking Tadoussac Bay, Québec; the Sea-to-Sky Highway, British Columbia

LAND OF GIANTS: THE PACIFIC NORTHWEST

Tim Moore follows America's coastal route from Seattle to San Francisco to find free-spirited cities, Pacific vistas and forests of epic proportions.

Opened in 1926, Hwy 101 is laid along the United States' westernmost edge: 1540 miles (2479km) of ancient wood and wild water, linking the Pacific coast from Washington state to California. It's a route and a region that has always attracted adventurers and rebels, and somehow, for all the RVs and visitor centers, the 101 still retains that sense of wilderness and opportunity.

Seattle seems a fitting point of departure: the Northwest's dominant metropolis is also one of America's youngest, fastest-growing cities. A city of geeks and freaks that gave us Jimi Hendrix, Kurt Cobain, Microsoft and Amazon, Seattle is switched-on, radical and proud of it (and a great place to sample a microbrewed beer or three).

Leaving Seattle means a car ferry and a drive across the world's longest floating bridge, together sufficient to blow away any early morning cobwebs. At once the traffic thins and the trees close in, and after an hour or so at the rigorously enforced speed limit, you're into deepest, darkest Washington state: the Olympic Peninsula, a virgin enormity of forests and mountains that wasn't fully mapped until last century.

With a couple of hundred miles under your wheels, you will have grasped why license plates hail Washington as the Evergreen State. After the *Twilight*-heavy small town of Forks, and an optional side trip to the Hoh Rainforest's Hall of Mosses – where every bough is eerily draped in cobwebby beards of hanging vegetation – Hwy 101 swings southwest and soon hits the super-sized coastal scenery that will grace it for the bulk of its progress: a thousand-mile parade of lighthouse-topped bluffs and surf-sculpted sea stacks.

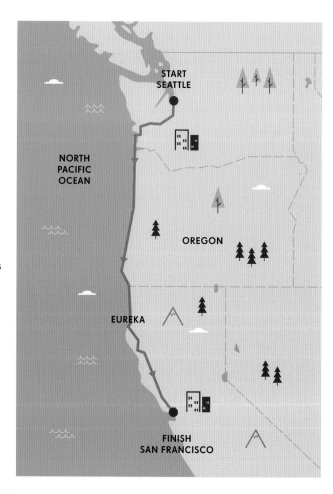

The mighty weather that carved this coast makes its presence thrillingly felt at Waikiki Beach, just outside Ilwaco. Heave the car door open against the roaring wind, clamber atop the bleached heaps of driftwood logs and behold an ocean that is Pacific in name only. Waikiki Beach is named in honor of a Hawai'ian sailor whose body was beached on its sands after an 1811 shipwreck – one of the countless victims of what still ranks among the world's most perilous maritime passages.

Drive onward into Oregon and the road is no longer yours alone, with RVs and long-distance cyclists joining the shiny lumber trucks whose payload leaves the roadside lined with drifts of red bark. Fish-canning ports give way to beach resorts, and the wildlife becomes ever-less retiring. A lively pod of gray whales may snort puffs of water into the clearing sky, and down in the surf below a viewpoint car park, some plump, sleek sea lions bark and loll recklessly in a spume-churned cove. Their well-fed presence pays tribute to a fecund ocean. Fish and chips is a regional institution, with even high-end salmon and halibut given the low-brow treatment.

Perched on a grassy headland and wedged between two magnificent state parks, Port Orford is a small working fishing port and the most westerly town in the lower 48 states. Boasting an artistic community, the ageless main street is home to glass-blowers and art galleries, and there's a restaurant where braised kale and butter lettuce have elbowed the coast's normally ubiquitous chowder clean off the menu.

> *"The 101 comes into its own as it approaches California – majestically engineered, a sinuous two-lane blacktop almost casually thrown along the coast"*

The miles come easy now, and the 101 comes into its own as it approaches California – broad, smooth and majestically engineered, a sinuous two-lane blacktop almost casually thrown along the jagged, rearing coast. Under a big blue sky, the open road has never seemed so open – until it's quite abruptly closed, hemmed in by colossal ochre trunks.

This is the redwood empire, the Prairie Creek Redwoods State Park, which was established in 1923 when the first stirrings of environmental panic kicked in. Fewer than 5 percent of old-growth redwoods survived the logging onslaught, most of them felled in the age before chainsaws, when cutting one down might take a team of loggers a month.

The world's tallest tree – a 379-footer (115m) – and the oldest redwood, predating the Roman empire by half a millennium, both stand in this forest, their locations kept secret for their own good. There is no such thing as a small old-growth redwood, of course, and strolling among them feels like a tour of some overbearing art installation. A sepulchral quiet reigns. Most of

THE TWILIGHT ZONE

Until 2005, the town of Forks was little more than a speck on the Washington state map – then along came Stephenie Meyer's *Twilight* saga and suddenly several thousand pilgrims were pitching up here every year. From a festival timed around *Twilight* character Bella's birthday to *Twilight* tours, themed accommodation and the local pizza parlor's Love at First Bite menu, Forks draws *Twilight* fans like, well... like vampires to blood.

From opposite, top left: Hwy 101 rounds Oregon's Cape Sebastian; surfers and wildlife abound en route; the beach at Mendocino; San Francisco's Golden Gate signals journey's end. Previous page: dwarfed by giant redwoods in Prairie Creek Redwoods State Park

the animal life is way up in the distant canopy. At ground level, nothing survives without the redwoods' blessing: the odd spindly hemlock clinging gratefully to one for support, sword ferns suckling on the mulch of a fallen "nest log" that will take several centuries to rot away.

The road flails about like a dying snake as it heads southwest back to the sea, twisting up through a farewell army of redwoods and the tourist trappings of a less-enlightened age: drive-through trees, chainsaw-carved representations of Bigfoot and $5 take-away redwood seedlings.

Then the trees part and a very different California emerges, one that is drier, browner and balder, where the thin coastal vegetation is decorated with garish tufts of pampas grass.

Seaside settlements soon begin to multiply, their names a reminder that this was Spanish-Mexican territory until the middle of the 19th century. The small town of Mendocino, however, is home to one of the state's oldest Protestant churches, looking down a handsome main street that actually recalls New England, complete with grand wooden houses and fancy old water towers.

A couple of hours south, the traffic builds and quickens; the 101 morphs from homely traveling companion to faceless freeway. The Golden Gate Bridge makes a grand finale to an epic drive, the giant leap for humankind that ushered in America's automobile age. And perhaps, after 1000 glorious miles, it's time for another local brew or two.

DIRECTIONS

Start // Seattle
Finish // San Francisco
Distance // 1050 miles (1690km)
Getting there // Seattle and San Francisco are well served by domestic and international flights.
When to drive // Winter can be dreary, but may appeal to storm watchers; gray whales migrate north from March to June or south from November to February. July to September is dry and sunny, but be prepared for a busier drive.
Where to stay // Wildspring Guest Habitat (www.wildspring.com) in Port Orford for wooded serenity.
Where to eat // Bowpicker (www.bowpicker.com), a trawler turned-chippie serves fish and chips at its battered best.
Hot tip // For a neon-and-jukebox roadhouse experience, stop by San Fran's It's Tops (www.itstopscoffeeshop.com).

MORE LIKE THIS
CLOSE TO THE SHORE

OKANAGAN VALLEY TOUR, BRITISH COLUMBIA

Filling up on sun-ripened fruit at roadside stalls has long been a highlight of traveling through the Okanagan on a hot summer day. Since the 1980s, the region has widened its embrace of the culinary world by striping its hillsides with grapes. More than 100 vineyards take advantage of the cool winters and long summers. Icewine, made from grapes frozen on the vine, is a unique take-home tipple. And when you're done soaking up the wine, you can soak up the scenery at the countless beaches along the way. This leisurely taste-tripping trawl keeps you within easy distance of Okanagan Lake, heading out north on Hwy 97 from Mission Hill, crossing the lake over the William R Bennett Bridge and then turning south along Lakeshore Road via a slight detour to Okanagan Lavender Farm. End your tour by treating your driver to something they can sample at Carmelis Goat Cheese Artisan.

Start // Mission Hill
Finish // Carmelis
Distance // 22 miles (35km)

O'AHU'S WINDWARD COAST

Amble down O'ahu's lushest, most verdant coast on this drive where turquoise waters and light-sand beaches share the dramatic backdrop of misty cliffs in the Ko'olau Range. Begin the drive in Honolulu, on the opposite coast, and slice your way through the range on the equally scenic Pali Hwy to Kailua. If it's been raining heavily, every fold and crevice in the jagged cliffs will have a fairytale waterfall streaming down it. Then take it slow on a serpentine cruise up the coast past untamed beaches, small farms, jungly hiking trails and lava-rock fishponds. Pull over at Kualoa Ranch for a tour of famous TV and movie locations, as seen in *Lost* and *Jurassic Park*. At the end of the drive you'll be rewarded with the shrimp trucks of Kahuku, where you can chow down on a plate of fresh crustaceans stir-fried with garlic and butter.

Start // Honolulu
Finish // Kahuku
Distance // 38 miles (61km)

CAPE ANN, MASSACHUSETTS

Somebody (a New Englander, no doubt) once said that "the humble clam... reaches its quintessence when coated and fried." The big-bellied bivalve – battered and fried – supposedly originated in Essex, Massachusetts, so Cape Ann is an ideal place to sample it. This North Shore route takes you from clam shack to clam shack, with breaks for beachcombing, bird-watching, gallery-hopping and picture taking. Before you head south down the 1A from Newburyport, take a detour to Plum Island to visit the Parker River Wildlife Refuge and its 800-plus species of birds, plants and animals. Further down the coast, break at Crane Beach, one of the longest and sandiest in the region, and, of course, Essex, for its maritime history, antique shops and succulent clams. With plenty of picnic tables overlooking the estuary, there's no better lunch stop.

Start // Newburyport
Finish // Gloucester
Distance // 54 miles (86km)

Clockwise, from top: heading for the surf on Waikīkī Beach, Hawai'i; an Okanagan Valley vineyard, winery and organic farm overlooking Okanagan Lake, British Columbia; Burnham Boat Building shipyard on the Essex River, Massachusetts

THE CIVIL WAR TOUR

Adam Karlin drives from Maryland to Virginia – and from the 21st century to the 19th and back again – on this itinerary into the heart of the United States' most formative conflict.

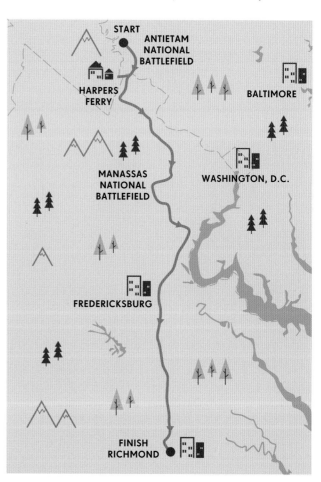

The sunrise is cresting over the hills of western Maryland. Grasshoppers are jumping through the tall grass, shaking dew off the blades, while the sparrows that hunt them whistle in the tree branches. Then the dawn truly hits, sunlight pouring pink and warm over the hills, onto the fields where the single bloodiest day in American military history unfolded.

I have spent much of my life traveling between two destinations, but when those destinations are tied to sites of historical significance, another journey occurs, and I slip somewhen else. Or at least I'd like to think I do, except the rustic peace of a national park is nothing like the smoke, fear and bloodshed that ruled here in 1862.

That's the contradiction of Civil War battlefields, some of the oldest intentionally preserved spaces in the United States – sites of mass violence that now showcase the bucolic serenity of the 19th-century countryside. You will find no greater concentration of Civil War battlefields than the DC Capitol Region, where the Union capital (Washington, DC) sat 100 miles (161km), as the crow flies, from the Confederate one (Richmond, Virginia). In the small space that separates and surrounds these two cities are battlefields where 100,000 Americans fell.

I am at Antietam National Battlefield, which represents the near northern edge of this battlefield bubble. Head about 50 miles (80km) northeast and you'll reach Gettysburg, Pennsylvania, where the most serious invasion of the Union, and the military ambitions of Confederate general Robert E Lee, were definitively checked and reversed. A little less than a year before Gettysburg, Lee squared off against the Union army here in Maryland, near the town of Sharpsburg, in a battle centered on Antietam Creek.

In the fields where soldiers once died in rows, only stalks of corn remain, bending in the breeze instead of in cannon smoke. The Sunken Road that was both a defensive position and an eventual abattoir is now a pleasant grass-and-dirt path. Union military cemeteries are inscribed with Irish and German surnames, marking the graves of immigrants who died for a country they barely even knew.

I found out about all of this via the National Park Service (NPS), which operates all of the sites listed in this tour unless otherwise noted. What the NPS couldn't help me do was process how these historical sites, and the related events, shaped the contemporary destinations and communities that have grown up around them. The NPS interpretive displays at Civil War sites are, in some ways, exhaustively informative, but they also hew to the "brother against brother" narrative that concludes with said brothers reuniting at the end of the war in national comity.

It's questionable if that comity ever existed before or after the war. From Antietam I drive 60 miles (96km) southwest to Harpers Ferry, West Virginia, a handsome, preserved town of slate-roofed houses and brick buildings that's perched on a rocky bend of the Potomac River. Tourists come here to bike the C&O Canal towpath or hike the surrounding hills. I am in search of stories about the abolitionist John Brown, who led a short-lived rebellion of enslaved people here – arguably the spark that stoked the bonfire of the Civil War. Brown himself believed peaceable debate would not create racial justice,

"In the fields where soldiers once died in rows, only stalks of corn remain, bending in the breeze instead of in cannon smoke"

and as I drive through a country riven by clashes over race relations, I wonder which century his words were meant to apply to.

When Brown's rebellion evolved into full-on war, one of the first pitched battles was fought at Bull Run River, near present-day Manassas, Virginia, 50 miles (80km) south of Harpers Ferry. Manassas National Battlefield Park has long been one of my favorite battlefields to visit, a little over 5000 acres (2023 hectares) of rolling green hills, thick woods and swift creeks divided by split-rail fences. This serene beauty is somewhat startling, given the battlefield is 30 miles (48km) west of Washington, DC, and located in an area otherwise overrun with suburban and exurban sprawl.

This was less the situation when I drove south to Fredericksburg, Virginia, where the downtown area extends out to the edges of nearby battlefields, of which there are four. These battles – Chancellorsville, Fredericksburg, the Wilderness, and Spotsylvania – are all interpreted at Fredericksburg and Spotsylvania National Military Park, one of the larger preserved battlefield parks in the region. In that park I find myself more concerned with military minutiae – who charged who and when – largely because the area

APPOMATTOX COURT HOUSE

About 95 miles (153km) west of Richmond is Appomattox Court House, the site of Robert E Lee's surrender. The moment was not the end of the war – skirmishes went on for months – but it nonetheless foretold the Confederacy's eventual defeat. To reach Appomattox, you can drive through "South Side" Virginia on Hwy 360 or Hwy 460; the road cuts through fields and farms that feel unchanged from the 19th century.

From opposite left: historic homes and stores on High Street in Harpers Ferry, West Virginia; silent canons at Manassas National Battlefield Park, Virginia. Previous page: a monument at Antietam National Battlefield, Maryland

is heavily wooded, and I find it difficult to slip into the abstract, time-bridging headspace that long sweeping views lend themselves to.

From here it's 60 more miles (96km) to Richmond, once the capital of the Confederacy, now a place to see how the 150-year-old Civil War shapes modern American politics. Richmond is the relatively liberal capital of the last state to desegregate its school system, a place where an enormous immigrant population and white identity politics are potent political forces.

I drive down Monument Ave, a gorgeous, tree-lined boulevard once filled with statuary deifying the leaders of the Confederacy. Those sculptures have since been removed; Richmond finally did away with a statue of Robert E Lee, the first monument placed on the avenue, in September of 2021. To wrap my head around both this history and its contemporary ripples, I head to the American Civil War Museum, where the war and its legacy are exhaustively examined by dedicated scholars and curators.

It's a captivating museum that manages to be both informative and interesting without feeling polemical. After I leave, I go in search of a drink to toast the end of my trip. But on the streets of Richmond, I soon come face to face with a public art exhibit on the white supremacist Unite the Right rally, which occurred not far from here, in Charlottesville. That event was stoked by a proposal to take down another Robert E Lee statue, and further marked by processions of Confederate flags – a reminder that even if my trip into the conflict was over, our nation's reckoning with it isn't.

DIRECTIONS

Start // Antietam, Maryland
Finish // Richmond, Virginia
Distance // 180 miles (290km)
Getting there // Three airports serve the region: Dulles and Reagan National in Washington, DC, and Baltimore-Washington International (BWI) in Baltimore. All offer car rental. It's about 75 miles (120km) to Antietam from Reagan National or BWI, and 55 miles (89km) from Dulles. Given DC traffic, BWI may be your easiest jumping-off point.
When to drive // Late April, May, October and November are ideal.
What to read // *Confederates in the Attic*, by Tony Horwitz, is a humorous yet incisive travelogue that partly focuses on Civil War sites, while *Team of Rivals*, by Doris Kearns Goodwin, is a biography of Abraham Lincoln during the war years.

Opposite, from top: the National Civil
Rights Museum at the former Lorraine
Motel, Tennessee; cypress trees in
Atchafalaya Basin, Louisiana

MORE LIKE THIS
TIME TRAVEL ITINERARIES

CIVIL RIGHTS IN THE SOUTH

The Civil Rights movement can be traced across the highways, city streets, and the cane and cotton fields of the South. Start in Little Rock, Arkansas, where the segregation barrier was (ostensibly) broken at Little Rock Central High School. From here drive east to Memphis and the National Civil Rights Museum, a series of sites centered on the Lorraine Motel, where Martin Luther King Jr was assassinated. Head south into the Mississippi Delta, a region still riven by startling poverty, and follow the Emmett Till Trail, a reminder of the brutality of 20th-century racial violence. Lynching itself is more broadly examined in Montgomery, Alabama, where the National Memorial for Peace and Justice and the Legacy Museum examine the struggle for equal rights as an ongoing conflict over the soul of the nation.

Start // Little Rock, Arkansas
Finish // Montgomery, Alabama
Distance // 550 miles (885km)

MARYLAND AND THE COLONIAL MARINES

The War of 1812 is one of the least-known American wars, partly because it lacks easy "good guy/bad guy" characterizations. Much of the course of the war was determined by former enslaved people, who joined the British as Colonial Marines with the understanding that freedom was the reward for enlistment. You can explore this little-known history starting in St Mary's City, where a living history museum recreates a 17th-century colonial capital. Colonial Marines flocked to the British Navy almost two centuries later, and helped defeat the American army outside of Washington, DC, at the Battle of Bladensburg, after which the freedmen went on to torch the White House. Finally, head to Fort McHenry in Baltimore, where the British advance was checked, after which many surviving Marines emigrated to Canada and the Caribbean.

Start // St Mary's City
Finish // Baltimore
Distance // 120 miles (195km)

CAJUN COUNTRY

When French-speaking Acadians fled Canada, many eventually ended up in Louisiana, where their name was anglicized to "Cajun" and their cultural influence grew. Start in New Orleans, which for the record is not a Cajun city, but is a convenient gateway to the rest of Louisiana. Drive southeast to Thibodeaux and the Wetlands Acadian Cultural Center, where you'll get a taste of the bayou, passing the oil and gas refineries that are the economic engine of Cajun country. From here head west through the haunting beauty of the Atchafalaya Basin to Lafayette, the unofficial capital of "Acadiana" (Cajun country), a city with fantastic food and better live music. Northeast of Lafayette are prairie towns like Mamou and Eunice, where Cajun dance halls playing centuries-old songs (and contemporary country) are the loudest thing going.

Start // New Orleans
Finish // Eunice
Distance // 230 miles (370km)

A DRIVE INTO DEATH VALLEY

Rainbow canyons, singing sand dunes and searing salt flats: Oliver Berry takes a Californian road trip through Death Valley National Park – and prays he comes out the other side alive.

It's just after 8:30am, and the temperature on the dash reads 95°F. By noon, it'll be closer to 105°, maybe even 110° if the sun really gets its mojo on. But in Furnace Creek, those kinds of temperatures barely register. Over a century ago, on July 10, 1913, the thermometer here topped out at 134.1°F (56.7°C), the highest temperature ever recorded, which means this is officially the hottest place on planet Earth – and for some reason, I've decided it's a brilliant place for a road trip. In summer.

Stifled and sweat-drenched, I decide I need air. I swig from my water bottle (temperature check: tepid to toasty), rub sunblock on my extremities and step out of the Jeep. Big mistake.

Outside, the heat hits me like a hairdryer. It feels like I've stuck my face into an oven. It's not just hot out here, it's way beyond that. Blistering, scorching, sizzling: none of these adjectives suffice. This is elemental heat, the kind only Mother Nature at her most ornery can conjure. I've camped in the Sahara, safaried in the South African savanna and gone walkabout in the Australian bush, but I've never felt heat like this. I last twenty seconds before I dive back into the 4WD, crank the air-con to max and stick my face up to the vent. Like many Death Valley road-trippers before me, I've learned a salutary lesson. Unless you really need to get out of the car, don't.

Sprawling east of the Sierra Nevada, Death Valley has struck fear and loathing into the minds of travelers since the 19th century. The valley got its English name from a group of hapless settlers called the Lost '49ers, who took an ill advised short cut en route to the Californian Gold Rush and barely escaped with their lives. For the region's Native Shoshone inhabitants, however, the valley is not a place of death, but prized red ochre, from whence came the original name: Timbisha (or Tümpisa), meaning "rock paint."

At 5347 sq miles (13,848 sq km), Death Valley is the largest national park in the Lower 48: it's roughly the same size as one Connecticut or two Delawares, although it can be crossed in a long day's drive. I've allowed myself two to explore some of the less-frequented corners. Hoping to avoid an unexpected breakdown, I've checked my water (twice), changed the oil, and stowed a can of gas and emergency supplies in the trunk just in case. That's overkill, maybe – but in Death Valley, it never pays to be unprepared.

The classic route runs from east to west along Hwy 190. I set out early from Death Valley Junction and reach my first landmark

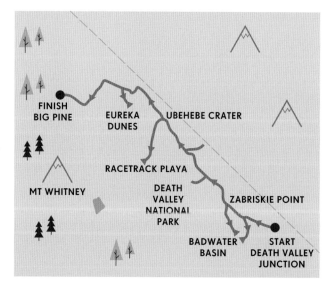

before dawn: Zabriskie Point, a rippled mass of ridges and rocks made famous by Michelangelo Antonioni's classic 1970 movie. It's famously beautiful at sunrise, and I'm not disappointed: the dawn reveals a chemical rainbow of colors – crimsons, scarlets, tangerines and sulfur yellows, a reminder of the rich veins of minerals buried in the valley's rocks. From Zabriskie Point, I tour the sights. I zoom up to Dante's View, where Luke and Ben looked down on Mos Eisley in the original *Star Wars* (Death Valley doubled as the desert planet of Tatooine). I stop at Badwater Basin, the lowest point in North America at 282ft (86m) below sea level: once an inland lake, it's now a shimmering salt flat encrusted with a layer of sodium chloride. I detour through the Technicolor canyon known as the Artist's Palette, and dally at the rubble-strewn Devil's Golf Course. I wander round the old Harmony Borax Works, one of many abandoned mines littering Death Valley, and visit the eerie ghost town of Leadfield, once a flourishing mining settlement, now an Ozymandian landscape of skeletal buildings and timber shacks. And I watch an unforgettable sunset over the blasted landscape of red rock and crimson plains at Titus Canyon.

Day two is for delving into Death Valley's secret corners. I meet an old friend, an LA based photographer who spends his winters touring the desert country. Together, we roll up to the rim of the Ubehebe Crater, a vast hollow half a mile wide that looks like the site of a great asteroid impact, but was actually caused by a massive exploding volcano.

From here, we head off-road, rattling past deserted gulches, wild ridges and barren flats, baked concrete-hard by the desert sun. We stop at the Racetrack Playa, a desolate plain where rocks seem to slide around of their own volition (the movement is actually a result of a combination of wind and ice). We judder along rocky backroads, picnic in shadowy canyons and, just for fun, try to fry an egg on the blacktop (verdict: it's possible, but inadvisable unless you like your eggs extra gritty). And like kids on vacation, we daydream away the drive, imagining ourselves as extraterrestrial explorers, steering a lunar rover across the surface of an uncharted planet, a million light years from home.

The sun is sinking over the mountains by the time we reach the sight I've most wanted to see: the mighty Eureka Dunes. Roughly 680ft (207m) high, these are the tallest sand dunes in North America: a sea of shifting sands straight out of *Star Wars: A New Hope*. Racing to beat the sunset, we scramble up the dunes, and sitting still, strain our ears to hear one of the desert's strangest phenomena: singing sand. At first, there's nothing, and then we catch it: a bassy, boomy drone, like the buzz of a faraway airplane, or a low note on a distant pipe organ. It swells and fades, echoes and reverberates – and we listen, mesmerized, until the moon rises over the mountains.

Driving into the darkness toward the mountain town of Big Pine, I aim to reflect on what a wild, weird place Death Valley is, and how lucky I feel to have seen it. But for now, all I can think about is a cold shower, cold air-con and best of all, a glacially cold beer.

VALLEY OF LIFE

Despite its name, Death Valley is actually full of life. Some 400 animal and 1000 plant species eke out a tough existence here, from kangaroo rats and desert tortoises to jackrabbits, roadrunners and rattlesnakes. But you'll have to be fortunate to see Death Valley's rarest spectacle: a super-bloom, when spring wildflowers carpet the desert floor. The phenomenon occurs around once a decade, when heavy winter rains bring extra moisture to the desert.

"This is elemental heat, the kind only Mother Nature at her most ornery can conjure"

Clockwise, from opposite: "sailing stones" and their paths on the Racetrack Playa; a curious coyote; the "singing sands" of the Eureka Dunes. Previous page: the desolate road toward the Devil's Golf Course

DIRECTIONS

Start // Death Valley Junction
Finish // Big Pine
Distance // 160 to 280 miles (357 to 451km), depending on the route.
Best time to drive // Winter and spring are ideal for exploring Death Valley: avoid the heat of midsummer if you can.
Where to stay // The gateway towns of Furnace Creek or Stovepipe Wells have a range of accommodation.
Hot tips // The main roads in Death Valley are paved, but to explore backcountry areas you'll require a 4WD with high clearance. Pack extra gas, check your spare tire and carry supplies just in case. The National Park Service advises that you drink at least 1 gallon (4 liters) of water per person per day in summer.
More info // www.nps.gov/deva

MORE LIKE THIS
DESERT DRIVES

THE CHIHUAHUAN DESERT

Sprawling across northern Mexico, west Texas and parts of southeastern Arizona, this huge desert is the real-deal Wild West – and the largest desert in North America at more than 193,050 sq miles (500,000 sq km). A century and a half ago, this was cowboy country, contested by Native Americans struggling to hold on to their ancestral lands and the ranchers and settlers who saw the commercial potential here for cattle-raising. The Chihuahuan Desert was often used as a backdrop in classic Westerns (John Wayne, Clint Eastwood and John Ford all made movies here) and it's not hard to see why, with its cinematic topography of craggy mesas, lonely canyons and cactus-studded plains. The desert's big ticket sight is Big Bend National Park, named after an oversized curve in the Rio Grande.
Start // El Paso, Texas
Finish // Big Bend National Park, Texas
Distance // 330 miles (531km)

JOSHUA TREE NATIONAL PARK

About 250 miles south of Death Valley, this surreal park encompasses 1235 sq miles (3199 sq km) and two distinct desert habitats, the Mojave and the Colorado, each with their own unique flora and fauna – including the eponymous Joshua tree, *Yucca brevifolia*, which can survive severe droughts and is superbly adapted to cope with the arid desert environment. It's a strange landscape, with strange plants and even stranger people (residents are famous for their alternative lifestyles). Go rock climbing in Echo Cove, hike the Arch Rock Trail and experience the old-timey vibes of Pioneertown – and don't miss the knockout vistas from Keys View. There are many backcountry roads to explore, either on foot, on horseback or in a 4WD – but stick to the trails, as the desert ecosystem is fragile, and tracks left here can last for decades.
Start/Finish // Palm Springs, California
Distance // 150 miles (241km)

THE PATAGONIAN DESERT

It might surprise you to learn that Patagonia is home to the world's eighth-largest desert: the sandy, stony expanse of the Patagonian Steppe, covering some 260,000 sq miles (673,000 sq km) of Argentina and Chile. This is big sky country, the land of the gaucho, who still herd cattle like the cowboys of old. You might spy them at work as you tour the desert – along with herds of guanaco, the wild cousin of the llama, which roam the steppe in prodigious numbers. The desert is roughly bordered by the Andes in the west and the Atlantic Ocean in the east, and stretches pretty much all the way to South America's southernmost tip. The classic road trip through here is along Ruta 40, a wild, unforgettable road that runs from mountain peaks to desert plains.
Start // Bariloche, Argentina
Finish // Torres del Paine, Chile
Distance // 1490 miles (2400km)

Clockwise, from top: near Big bend
National Park, Texas; the surreal
landscape of Joshua Tree National
Park, California; gauchos canter across
the Patagonian Steppe, with the cone
of Volcán Lanín in the background

ACROSS THE WORLD IN A SINGLE DAY

Adam Karlin loops around the lower half of Hawai'i, the Big Island, which packs a superlative amount of ecological diversity into a landmass that can be covered in under four hours.

If you're looking for an activity to take part in on a Big Island beach, I do not recommend a snowball fight.

Not because it's impossible. It is, in fact, quite possible, but only if you have a 4WD vehicle and a cooler – or, possibly, a pickup truck and a disregard for road safety.

I once met a chef at a local resort who decided to welcome some visiting friends from Minnesota with a taste of their frozen home. So, he climbed into his pickup, left the jungle of South Kona, drove to the top of Mauna Kea – where snow squalls, blizzards and ice are not uncommon in winter months – then filled the bed of the truck with snow, barreled down the mountain, pulled up to the beach where his friends were probably snapping some kind of #tropical selfies, and started the southernmost snowball battle in the United States.

Which is all to say: on Hawai'i, the Big Island, it is entirely feasible to drive from a beach to a desert to a rainforest to a snowfield all in the space of about 90 minutes or less, just depending on the traffic.

At just over 4000 sq miles (10,360 sq km), the Big Island is large in the sense that every other Hawai'ian island could fit within it, and small in the sense that it packs so much ecological and climatic diversity into such a compact package. How much diversity? Four of the world's five major climate zones can be found here. And those four climate zones overlap at the edges, yielding an ecological continent stuffed into the confines of an island.

A road trip along the southern half of the Hawai'i Belt Road, also known as the Māmalahoa Hwy, takes about four hours without stops – which, of course, I am making. I start this drive in Kailua-Kona, on the leeward (western) side of the island, blocked from Pacific winds and rain by the volcanic massifs of Mauna Kea and Mauna Loa, themselves the size of respectable Swiss summits.

Kailua-Kona is the most blatantly "mainland" town on the island. There are a ton of timeshares here, though the older mainlanders are balanced out with a good mix of locals and younger mainlanders. I doubt anyone working on the catamaran that takes me out for a night snorkeling tour with manta rays is over 30. If you're wondering what a manta ray night snorkel is like, imagine the most magical thing that's ever happened to you, then place it underwater and throw in dark sea angels with 18ft (5.5m) wingspans, and you're almost there.

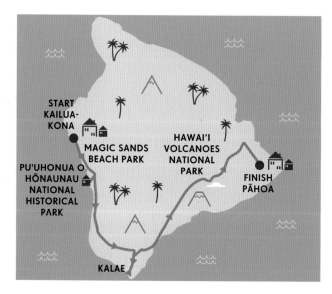

Before I leave Kailua-Kona, I take a quick detour north to the South Kohala deserts – and they are true, blistering, sun-beaten lava deserts. These may be dry zones, but they are blessed with white sand beaches that front pure turquoise water, which is why most of the island's resorts are here. Then I embark for my real journey south, making a first stop at Magic Sands Beach, also known as White Sands or La'aloa Bay. I prefer the name "Magic Sands" because it accurately captures the nature of this beach – it's there, and then it's not, thanks to an intense local tide system and wave cycles.

These conditions also make for some fine bodysurfing, and I spend a good deal of time letting the ocean swallow me up and spit me out, until it spits me out at the wrong angle, and I feel my back almost crack against the sandy sea bottom. The waters that surround the Big Island are great natural playgrounds, but they do not mess around.

From here I drive further south, into the green dream of South Kona, past jungle plots where generations of Japanese American families have harvested the Kona coffee that grows out of the volcanic soil. I pop in for a bite at Teshima's, a diner that balances

> "Here you will find jungle groves as thick and green as the day of creation, growing next to solidified lava flows where the engines of that creation have wrought immense destruction"

HILO

This trip doesn't even take in the entirety of the Belt Road. The northeast coast of the Big Island is anchored by its largest city: Hilo. Here you'll find a blend of cultures from across the Pacific rim, with some fine parks, excellent food and fascinating museums, including the 'Imiloa Astronomy Center, where traditional Hawai'ian exploration meets modern astronomy, and the Lyman Museum, focused on the history and culture of the island.

Clockwise, from above: spinner dolphins; Gemini North telescope, Mauna Kea; shaved ice in Hilo. Previous page: Kilauea's crater

Americana diner ambiance with Japanese country cuisine, then head for Pu'uhonua O Hōnaunau.

The "Place of Refuge" was once a temple complex where native Hawai'ians could claim sanctuary after violating the traditional legal code known as *kapu* (from which we derive the English "taboo"). The National Park Service maintains the *heiau* (temple), and I spend a pleasant half hour wandering the breezy grounds, but I'm also here to snorkel at next-door Two Step. Here, a reef pulses with a carnival of sea life that would require an extended David Attenborough reel to describe. In one 90-minute snorkeling session, I spot, among other species, yellow tang, green sea turtles, trumpetfish, and clouds of *humuhumunukunukuapua'a*, better known as the *humuhumu*, or reef triggerfish.

Now I drive still further south, through the rocky scrubland of Ka'ū district, the most remote on the island. Here, the winds of the Pacific roar onto Hawai'i free of obstruction, fishtailing my car as I spot the road spur that leads to Ka Lae – "South Point" – the southernmost tip of the United States.

I have reached the bottom of the Hawai'ian circle. Now my road turns north again, past the looming mountains of Hawai'i Volcanoes National Park, home of two active volcanoes, Kīlauea and Mauna Loa. It is one thing to say the Big Island is home to a fantastic array of ecosystems; it is another thing to see Kīlauea's steaming caldera and the elemental interplay that is at the heart of the nature this island so brilliantly showcases.

The lava-laced soil of the national park incubates an incredible fecundity of life, which is further helped along by the rains that lash the windward (eastern) side of the island. In Puna district, on the eastern edge, the Big Island's capacity for creation and destruction is most obviously realized: here you will find jungle groves as thick and green as the day of creation, growing next to solidified lava flows where the engines of that creation have wrought immense destruction. These paradoxes and balances are always present on this island, from its snow-topped peaks to the coral reefs that cling to its lava beaches, and every type of environment in between.

DIRECTIONS

Start // Kailua-Kona
Finish // Pahoa, Puna
Distance // 150 miles (240km)
Getting there // There are two major airports on the Big Island: Kailua-Kona International and Hilo International. You can rent cars at both.

When to drive // For all the Big Island's ecological diversity, its weather is pretty consistent. Locals notice the difference between winter and summer, but for most visitors it will feel warm and pleasant year-round. For the smallest crowds and the best deals, fall (September to November) is best. One of the busiest tourism weeks is Golden Week, which runs from April 29 to early May. Thousands of Japanese visitors come to the Hawai'ian islands during this time.

More info // www.gohawaii.com

MORE LIKE THIS
CONTRASTING LANDSCAPES

MARYLAND

Maryland calls itself "America in Miniature," and that's not marketing hyperbole. The ninth-smallest state in the country somehow manages to pack in mountains, hills, plains, forests, estuaries and oceanfront. You'll start in Cumberland, in the western panhandle, a region nestled within the Appalachian Mountains. From here drive east through green valleys, down into the hill country that surrounds the historically preserved downtown of Frederick. Then it's on past the suburbs that house a diverse mix of families, into the waterside town of Annapolis, home of the Naval Academy and a screensaver of a waterfront dotted with hundreds of sailboats. Cross the 4.3-mile (6.9km) Bay Bridge to the Eastern Shore, a region of tide-lapped wetlands and estuarine coastline, and push through to Ocean City, a Mid-Atlantic resort town brimming with beachside kitsch.
Start // Cumberland
Finish // Ocean City
Distance // 275 miles (470km)

NEWFOUNDLAND, CANADA

For a dramatic drive across a fantastic tableau of scenery, all confined to one island, head out to the salt-lashed island of Newfoundland. Start in the provincial capital of St John's, a collection of candy-colored homes clinging to stark, rocky cliffs. Now drive northwest, through hills studded with fir forests, stopping in the slate-and-stone town of Brigus, where Newfoundland's wild landscape is tamed. At least, it feels that way until you reach the Bonavista peninsula. Here, the misty green woods conceal quaint towns like Trinity, which is itself close to the coastal cliffs of the Skerwink Trail. Now head northwest through scrubby heath and boggy valleys to Twillingate, a place seemingly carved out of boulders and icebergs. Take a walk over the hills, which plunge down to the ocean, while a horror-movie fog descends over the craggy coast.
Start // St John's
Finish // Twillingate
Distance // 400 miles (645km)

ALASKA

From Anchorage you'll head east along the Glenn Highway past *Game of Thrones*-esque views of the icy wall of the Matanuska Glacier. Thread the winding mountain hairpins to come to the borders of Wrangell-St Elias National Park, the largest protected space in the US, a park so vast you could lose Switzerland inside it (and to be fair, the Swiss would feel at home amid all these rugged peaks). Turn north at the town of Glennallen and drive the Richardson Hwy. Now you've left the thick pine forests of southern Alaska for flinty, rocky valleys and icy bogs, yet while the ecosystems are different, they are no less dramatic. At Delta Junction, you can turn northwest to Fairbanks, where you can relax, and if it's late August to late April, maybe you'll even catch the northern lights.
Start // Anchorage
Finish // Fairbanks
Distance // 430 miles (690km)

Clockwise. from top: the northern lights on show at Mt Aurora near Fairbanks, Alaska; Cape Spear Lighthouse National Historic Site, Newfoundland; bicycles parked on the boardwalk next to Ocean City beach, Maryland

LOBSTAH AND LIGHTHOUSES ON MAINE'S ROUTE 1

This fabled highway follows craggy Atlantic coastline dotted with lobster shacks and historic lighthouses. Emily Matchar takes a salt-swept drive through Maine's coastal culture.

How to make your friends hate you in 60 seconds or less: tell them you're "sick of eating lobster."

Yes, I know it makes me sound like some kind of monocle-wearing robber baron. But it's simply how I feel after a week on Maine's Rte 1. I've had lobster salad and lobster rolls. I've had lobster bisque and lobster mac and cheese with a Ritz cracker topping. I've had numerous cartoonish red steamed lobsters, their juices squirting on my shirt as I attack their claws with a nutcracker (should have worn the bib). I've even had lobster ice cream (better than it sounds). And now, I am officially sick of lobster.

It's a good problem to have.

My journey to sick-of-lobster-ness starts in the southernmost Maine town of Kittery. My goal is simple: drive the "coastal route" portion of Maine's Rte 1 all the way to Mount Desert Island, taking in the views and eating as much Maine seafood as I can handle.

I cross the Piscataqua River from New Hampshire and find myself among outlet malls and motels and roadside diners. I make

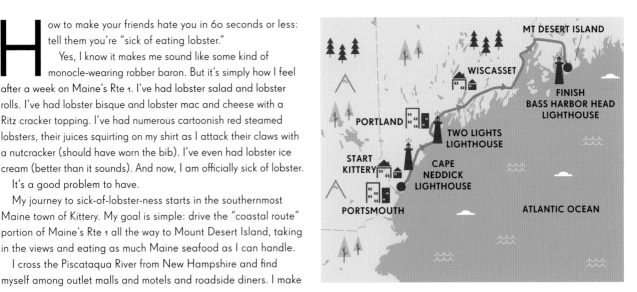

it less than three miles up Rte 1 before, stomach rumbling, I pull up to my first stop: Bob's Clam Hut.

Bob's has been selling fresh Maine seafood from a blue-shingled hut with a takeout window since 1956. As the name suggests, the specialty is plastic baskets heaped with small haystacks of golden-fried clam strips. I sit at a picnic table and plow through my pile of hot, chewy clam strips, their fried crusts salty and shattery, grease dripping down my fingers.

Groaningly full, I drive over to Fort Foster Park, where I stroll the pier above the rippling waters of the Piscataqua River estuary. Standing forlornly on a rocky ledge is the Whaleback Lighthouse, a granite beacon built in the late 1800s and in constant danger of being swept into the sea. Though it's early summer, the afternoon has grown chilly, and the wind whips my hair across my face as I make my way back to my car.

The brisk walk has brought back my appetite just in time for the short drive north to York, home to Fox's Lobster House. This gray-shingled seafood shack is a summerlong party, with regulars packing in for the lobsters that arrive at the back door by the boxful, still dripping with seawater. You can choose any size from 1.25lb "quarters" (0.57kg) to 2lb "deuces" (0.91kg), boiled and served with little plastic cups of melted butter.

But the thing that sets Fox's apart is its view. You could throw a lobster claw from the window and hit the Cape Neddick Light, aka "the Nubble," possibly Maine's most iconic lighthouse. This is the

Platonic ideal of the lighthouse, a stout white tower connected to an impossibly charming little red-roofed keeper's house, all atop a grassy promontory at the edge of the Atlantic. The day ends watching the sky darken over the lighthouse.

My next day involves ambling through the towns of the southern Maine coast: Ogunquit, Wells, Kennebunkport, Old Orchard Beach. This is pure vacationland, all antiques stores, B&Bs and vintage candy shops that make the entire downtown smell like fudge. I hit Cape Elizabeth in time for a late lunch at the Lobster Shack at Two Lights, another classic summer spot perched on the rocks beneath the Cape Elizabeth Light. This is the most powerful lighthouse in New England, its beam clearly visible for 27 miles.

After a mayo-dolloped, pickle-topped lobster roll, I head north along the edge of Cape Elizabeth to yet another legendary lighthouse. This is the Portland Head Light, Maine's oldest, built in 1791 overlooking the gray waters of Casco Bay. Construction began at the order of George Washington, and the light was originally lit with whale oil.

After a night in Portland, I drive through a light fog and onto the rocky, serrated shoreline of Midcoast Maine. The towns here are a little more austere than their southern neighbors, infused with the stoic auras of the shipbuilders and whalers who built them. I keep driving until I spot the apple-red shack of Red's Eats, a walk-up lobster roll shack on a riverbank in Wiscasset. I eat my roll in the car, butter dripping down my wrists, cooled by the briny breeze off the Sheepscot River.

I arrive in the tony village of Bar Harbor just after sunset, and stand next to my car for a few minutes, watching the lights sparkle on Frenchman Bay. Bar Harbor is on Mt Desert Island, which, despite its spelling, is pronounced "dessert." This turns out to be appropriate, as I find myself making an evening pitstop at Ben and Bill's Chocolate Emporium, home to the aforementioned lobster ice cream. It tastes like frozen lobster bisque – salty and buttery, with chunks of chewy frozen meat. I'll stick with rocky road.

Mt Desert Island is home to Acadia National Park, which is where I spend the last full day of my road trip. I slowly round the park's Scenic Loop, stopping to gawp at sea-pounded boulders, sheer granite cliffs and shockingly white beaches. The ocean is wilder here than anywhere else I've seen in Maine, exploding on the rocks in fireworks of foam.

By this point I am – I must admit – a little bit tired of lobster. But I've got one last dinner, and I want to make it count. Perched on a wooden dock above Bass Harbor, Thurston's Lobster Pound fits the bill. After gobbling down a "shedder" – a lobster that's recently shed its shell, whose meat is sweeter – I drive a bit south to see my last lighthouse. The Bass Harbor Head Lighthouse is not the most impressive – in fact, you might even call it stubby, if you were being mean. And yet. I may be sick of lobster, but I'm not sick of these views: sea and sky, salt and breeze, the beam of the lighthouse flashing on the surface of the darkening ocean.

LIVES OF LIGHTHOUSE KEEPERS

Between the years 1791 and 1910, 67 lighthouses were built along Maine's ragged coast. The lighthouse keepers battled the elements, rescued shipwreck victims and dealt with loneliness and boredom. Some tried to grow gardens, importing dirt from the mainland for potted plants. In 1866, the Lighthouse Board began sending books to lighthouse keepers to combat the monotony. By 1885, there were 420 such libraries.

"I eat my roll in the car, butter dripping down my wrists, cooled by the briny breeze off the Sheepscot River"

Opposite, from top: the ever-popular Red's Eats in Wiscasset; a fisherman and his catch in St George; the Bass Harbor Head Lighthouse in Acadia National Park. Previous pages: the Nubble Lighthouse and keeper's cottage on Cape Neddick in York

DIRECTIONS

Start // Kittery
Finish // Bass Harbor Head Lighthouse
Distance // 225 miles (362km)
Getting there // There are major airports in Boston and Portland, about an hour south and north of Kittery, respectively.
When to drive // Peak season in Maine runs from July 4 through Labor Day in early September. Prices are highest and hotels hardest to book. The shoulder season of late spring and early fall is lovely, though some establishments will be closed.
Where to stay // Coastal Maine has a wealth of accommodations, from quaint B&Bs to roadside motels to enormous summer resorts.
More info // The Maine Office of Tourism (visitmaine. com); the American Lighthouse Foundation (www. lighthousefoundation.org).

Opposite, from top: Seattle's Pike
Place Market, Washington; an oyster
roast underway at Bowen's Island
Restaurant along the Folly River,
South Carolina

MORE LIKE THIS
COASTAL DRIVES
FOR SEAFOOD-LOVERS

SAN FRANCISCO TO VANCOUVER

Start at Fisherman's Wharf in San
Francisco, where old-school Scoma's
serves an excellent *cioppino*, a seafood
stew invented by Italian immigrants in the
1800s. Sail across the Golden Gate Bridge
and tackle the golden hills of the northern
coast, the crashing Pacific on your left. As
you get into Oregon, the coast becomes
grayer and rockier – look for breaching
whales and small-town fried-seafood
stands. Slurp oysters in Willapa Bay,
Washington – the muddy estuary produces
20 percent of the nation's oysters – then
swing inland toward Seattle, where Pike
Place Market is famed for its salmon-
tossing fishmongers and steamed shellfish
stalls. Follow the foggy highway north,
then cross the border to Vancouver. Try
Indigenous-owned Salmon n' Bannock for
sage-smoked sockeye salmon, then hop the
car ferry for the 90-minute cruise through
the Gulf Islands to Victoria.
Start // San Francisco
Finish // Vancouver
Distance // 1000 miles (1610km)

CHARLESTON TO FOLLY ISLAND, SOUTH CAROLINA

Charleston's got enough sights – and
restaurants – to keep you occupied and
full for weeks. But if you fancy a drive to
a place with an entirely different flavor,
consider the jaunt from the Historic District
to Folly Beach, with a seafood stop in
the middle. As you leave the city, the key
landscape feature appears to be the
strip mall. But once you turn onto Bowens
Island Road, you feel the Sea Island spirit.
Palmetto trees sway, frogs ribbit from
tall grasses and marsh water gleams on
the horizon. Then it arises like a mirage:
a stilted wooden shack, the eaves of its
tin roof hung with twinkle lights. This is
Bowens Island Restaurant, a Charleston
institution for trays of oysters and cold
beers eaten marsh-side. Come at sunset
for unimpeachable views.
Start // Charleston
Finish // Folly Island
Distance // 10.2 miles (16.4km)

CHESAPEAKE BAY LOOP, MARYLAND

The United States' largest estuary, this
Mid-Atlantic bay is famed for its beauty
and its bounty: blue crabs, oysters,
rockfish and more. The loop of roads
and bridges around the Bay make for a
tranquil multiday road trip. From Baltimore,
head south to the Maryland capital of
Annapolis to admire the 18th-century
brick architecture and watch the bobbing
sailboats. On the water, Cantler's Riverside
Inn will serve you a mess of blue crabs,
Maryland-style: seasoned and dumped
on a butcher-paper-covered table. Take
the Chesapeake Bay Bridge, once one
of the world's longest, across the shining
waters to Maryland's rural Eastern Shore.
Hop from village to village, watching
herons soar, dolphins breach, and eating
all the seafood you can stand. Don't miss
Waterman's Crab House in Rock Hall.
Start/Finish // Baltimore
Distance // 170 miles (274km)

HIGHWAY 61 RE-REVISITED

Hwy 61 inspired Bob Dylan and countless other American legends. Garth Cartwright experiences the region that shaped rock and roll.

Hwy 61 runs from Wyoming, Minnesota, to New Orleans, Louisiana. Beyond traveling from America's chilly northern plains to its steamy southern swamps, Hwy 61 is, at least for me, the world's most famous road. This is due to the name of Bob Dylan's celebrated 1965 album: *Highway 61 Revisited*. But decades before Dylan returned to the birthplace of American music, many a blues musician was already following it in search of house-rent parties, Saturday-night fish fries and maybe even a record deal.

Hwy 61 spans 1407 miles (2264km) and while driving its entirety would be fascinating, I've never attempted to undertake such an immense trip. Instead, I stick with the southern end – nicknamed "the Blues Highway" – focused on what a pleasure it will surely be to drive.

Beginning in Memphis, Tennessee, I need a couple of days just to explore the city's rich music heritage – Sun Studios, where BB King, Howlin' Wolf, Elvis Presley and Roy Orbison started out; "Soulsville USA," the neighborhood that's home to the pioneering soul label Stax Records, which launched the careers of Otis Redding and Isaac Hayes; and then, of course, there's Graceland. There's also the National Civil Rights Museum, which puts into context the lives and struggles of Black Americans throughout this era. Evening finds me eating BBQ ribs – a Memphis specialty – then hitting the bars and clubs of downtown, and soaking up the sound of the city that helped create blues, soul, and rock and roll.

Leaving Memphis on the 61 is easy and, once outside the city limits, I find myself crossing the border into Mississippi. During the 1960s and the Civil Rights Movement, Mississippi gained a reputation for murderous racism, somewhere people fled from rather than traveled to. Today, the state remains one of the most racially divided in the United States, but from the outside, at least, it is peaceful. And the music that crystallized here a century ago now draws people like me, the blues tourists.

Cotton, which was once the dominant local industry, is still grown on vast plantations, but it's the sprouting casino signs that suggest the state's new growth industry. I pass Tunica, a mini Las Vegas situated right on the muddy Mississippi. I'm looking for

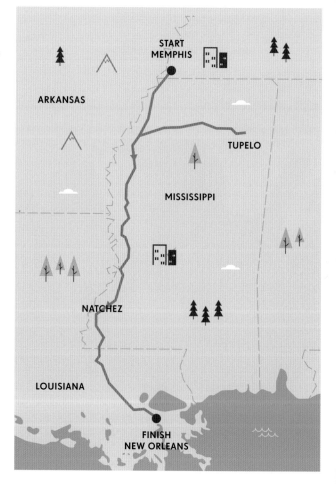

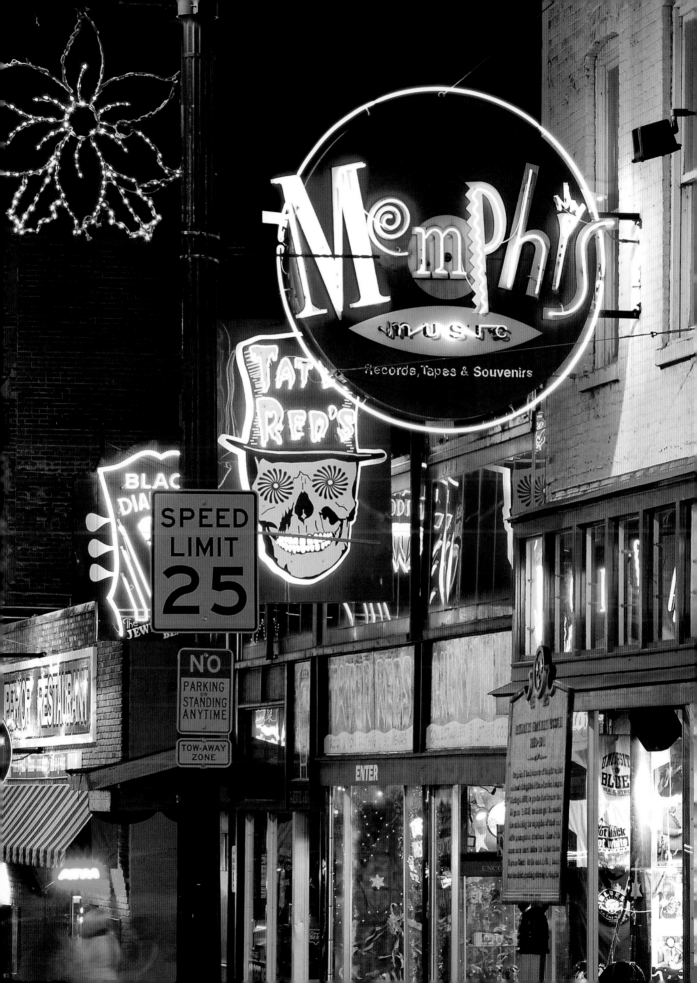

something more than gambling, however, and soon I start to see them: the roadside Blues Trail markers. They acknowledge the places where so many legendary blues men and women once lived, worked, recorded and died.

Around 90 minutes south of Memphis I'm approaching Clarksdale, a run-down cotton town turned draw for blues pilgrims. My first point of call is the excellent Delta Blues Museum, which tells the story of how the sound that was to become rock and soul took shape here. I then pay homage to the city's blues sites – here Bessie Smith died (after a car crash on Hwy 61), Ike Turner and Sam Cooke were born, and you can even drive over the actual crossroads where Robert Johnson sold his soul in *Cross Road Blues*. That certainly provides plenty of food for thought and, so inspired, I go and eat some tamales (a local favorite) in a diner.

Clarksdale's epicenter is Cat Head, a blues and folk art store, and a hive of local information. Armed with tips from its amiable proprietor, Roger Stolle, I head into town for the evening.

I start out at Ground Zero Blues Club, a sumptuous live music bar owned by actor and Mississippi resident Morgan Freeman, before I wander down to Red's, a juke joint that looks as if it was due for demolition sometime during the last century. Juke joints – the African American drinking and dancing clubs that were once prominent across much of the rural South – were how the blues became known. A few still stand and those that do often play host to local talent. At Red's, on a warm Friday night, Big-T is playing, the locals are dancing and the place is really rocking. Clarksdale also hosts the Juke Joint Festival every April: three days of beer, BBQ and blues.

MISSISSIPPI BLUES TRAIL

Since 2006, more than 200 Blues Trail markers have been placed across Mississippi. The plaques stand outside everything from cemeteries where musicians rest to juke joints, studios, record labels, homes, streets and even Parchman Farm, where many an unlucky musician did time. Maps are available and it's a fascinating drive as you explore the humble settings where one of the most atmospheric musical genres took shape.

Clockwise, from above: jazz musicians in New Orleans; riding New Orleans' streetcars; Creole architecture in New Orleans' French Quarter; Clarksdale, Mississippi, draws blues fans worldwide. Previous page: Beale Street in Memphis is another bluesy essential

The next morning, in need of some fresh air, I sign on for a guided canoe trip down the Mississippi, and feel as happy as Huckleberry Finn floating down the mighty river. Back in Clarksdale I head east to Oxford, home of the University of Mississippi – aka Ole Miss – and Rowan Oak, William Faulkner's house from 1930 until he died in 1962. A little further east is Tupelo, where a certain Elvis Aaron Presley was born in a two-room shack in 1935.

Back on Hwy 61, my next stop is Indianola, now home to a museum honoring its most famous son, BB King. Close by is Greenville, a small impoverished city that hosts the longest running blues festival in the US every year, at the very height of summer. The year I attended it was so hot I felt I was melting into the earth while the blues men casually strutted their stuff on stage. Where Clarksdale's juke joints are accommodating to visitors, Greenville's are rough: only seek one out with a local guide.

Continuing south I drop into two more towns – Vicksburg, a small city that played a leading role in the American Civil War, and just east of here, Jackson, the state's sleepy capital.

For me, however, it's the swampy and near-empty, rural Mississippi landscape where the 61 really gets evocative. The cotton plantations where musical legends were born and worked still stand, and the small towns that have been immortalized for me in blues songs – Natchez, Yazoo City, Sunflower, Merigold, Shelby – are still working towns, even if some of them seem to be on the verge of becoming ghost towns.

In *On the Road*, Jack Kerouac and Neal Cassady drove Hwy 61 to visit William Burroughs. When this task was complete, they then carried on to New Orleans. Having soaked up Mississippi's small-town lassitude and blues bars I follow their lead and drive on to the Big Easy.

"The cotton plantations where musical legends were born and worked still stand, often seemingly unchanged"

DIRECTIONS

Start // Memphis, Tennessee
Finish // New Orleans, Louisiana
Distance // 428 miles (689km)
Getting there // Memphis and New Orleans are well served by air and rail connections, as well as car rental outlets.
When to drive // Spring to autumn finds the Blues Highway at its most lively, but June to August can be extremely hot and humid. Live music generally happens on weekends, except in New Orleans where the good times roll every day.
Where to stay // Mississippi is the land of cheap motels. Both Memphis and New Orleans can be expensive; book accommodations in advance.
What to take // In summer, bring lots of loose clothing – you'll sweat like never before.
Detours // When entering Louisiana drive west to Lafayette; the capital of Cajun Country is home to great Cajun and zydeco music.

MORE LIKE THIS
MUSIC PILGRIMAGES

JAMAICAN REGGAE ROAD TRIP

Nobody did more to put Jamaica on the musical map than Bob Marley. A reggae-inspired drive could begin at the Rastafari Indigenous Village on the outskirts of Montego Bay, for an insight into the creed that played such a big role in Marley's life. Next, follow the main road past north coast beaches as far as Discovery Bay, before turning inland through labyrinthine hill country to reach the village of Nine Mile, where Marley lived the first 12 years of his life. Return to the coast between Ocho Rios and Buff Bay to approach the capital Kingston in the most spectacular way, by the zigzagging road through the forests of Blue River Mountains National Park. Kingston gives pride of place to the Bob Marley Museum, and is where to take the pulse of Jamaican music today.

Start // Montego Bay
Finish // Kingston
Distance // 175 miles (282km)

GRACELAND TO DOLLYWOOD, TENNESSEE

Put on your blue suede shoes before you step into your car on this star turn across Tennessee. Begin by the banks of the Mississippi in the state's southwest corner, where the city of Memphis helped launch the careers of Elvis Presley, BB King and countless others. Once you're done admiring the green shagpile of the Jungle Room in Graceland, take a neat diagonal across the state by way of Nashville, to discover upcoming talent in country music's capital. The scenery as you head further east is marked by parallel ridges as regular as a fretboard, until you reach Pigeon Forge, home region of Dolly Parton. You could end the trip on the rollercoasters of Dollywood, but another hundred miles will take you to Bristol on the Virginia state line, the officially acknowledged birthplace of country music.

Start // Memphis
Finish // Bristol
Distance // 534 miles (859km)

MOTOWN TO THE TWIN CITIES

There's something resonant about starting a road trip in Detroit, with its ever-present reminders of automotive history. But apart from a car engine coming to life, the signature sound of Michigan's largest city is Motown. The former Hitsville USA recording studio, now the Motown Museum, should be the first stop. After heading west past Gary, Indiana, home of the Jackson family, swing into Chicago, the northern pole of the blues. From jazz clubs to the Jay Pritzker Pavilion, there's no shortage of venues at the trip's halfway point. For a rural interlude, follow Hwy 14 to the banks of the Mississippi, then trace them upstream as far as Minneapolis-St Paul. As well as kicking off Bob Dylan's career, the Twin Cities were most famously home to Prince – his legacy lives on at the First Avenue club.

Start // Detroit, Michigan
Finish // Minneapolis, Minnesota
Distance // 703 miles (1131km)

*Clockwise, from top: the bright lights of Lower Broadway in Nashville,
Tennessee; a trombone player performs with a swing band at The Green
Mill in Detroit, Michigan; a tribute band entertains visitors to Bob
Marley's house and grave in Nine Mile, Jamaica*

TOURING NEW MEXICO'S GHOST TOWNS

Hugh McNaughtan drives between New Mexico's evocative ghost towns, vestiges of long-vanished mining booms that delve into the enchanting heart of this Southwestern state.

Taos' thriving community seems a strange place to begin a hunt for ghost towns, but spirits aplenty await here. The stacked adobe buildings of the Taos Pueblo, built a thousand years ago by the Northern Tiwa, is among the oldest continually inhabited places in the United States. Exploring the maze of multi-story red-walled structures, now a Unesco World Heritage Site, I sense the spirits of those who came before: the Ancestral Puebloans; the Spanish missionaries and colonialists who founded the nearby town; and the modern artists whom Taos enchanted. The romanticized reflections of Taos created by Georgia O'Keeffe, Alfred Stieglitz, Ansel Adams and others can be viewed in the town's three museums, as can the work of 20th-century Puebloan artists such as Albert Looking Elk, Juan Mirabal and Albert Lujan.

From Taos, the air turns crisper as I climb above 8000ft (2440m). The road passes 13,161ft (4011m) Wheeler Peak – New Mexico's highest point – en route to Colfax, Dawson and Folsom. Not much of Colfax survives, but the grass-swaddled brick-and-adobe remains of its hotel and other buildings show the scale of a town that boomed between the 1890s and 1920s as a stop on the Atchison, Topeka and Santa Fe Railway. The Great Depression and the unaffordability of gas eventually sealed the fate of this community that, surrounded by pasture and mineral wealth, had promised so much.

Despite peaking at over 9000 souls in the early 20th century, nearby Dawson offers more ghosts than town. Following two mine explosions that killed nearly 400, the town struggled on until the pits finally fell silent in the 1950s. The Phelps Dodge Company sold most of Dawson's buildings, leaving a cemetery of iron crosses as testament to a community that had its own newspaper, baseball team, golf course and ten coal mines.

Still inhabited by a few determined souls, Folsom is richly evocative. Dating to the 1880s, when the Colorado and Southern Railway brought prosperity, it's now studded with atmospheric buildings like the Folsom Hotel, the Folsom Supply Store and the remains of ranchers' homesteads. Walking tumbledown streets smeared with melting snow, it's easy to imagine the days when the outlaw Tom "Black Jack" Ketchum made a habit of holding up trains here. His third attempt (in 1899) was his last – he was captured and hanged in Clayton.

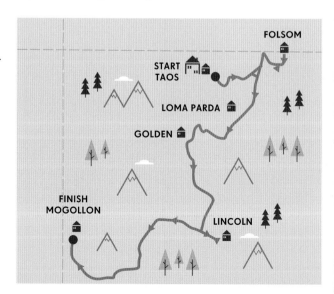

"It's possible to imagine the ghosts of those who lost their lives during a violent, dissolute heyday"

BANDELIER

The rugged landscape of the Bandelier National Monument is spread over 19 sq miles (50 sq km) of volcanic rock, cut with canyons and mesas. It's been inhabited for more than 10,000 years, and the dwellings cut into implausibly high rock faces, the haunting petroglyphs and the stone ruins evoke civilization across countless generations – from prehistory, to Ancestral Puebloans, to their descendants today. It can be explored via 70 miles (113km) of trails.

As I swing south, I'm drawn to the infamous ghost town of Loma Parda, or Brown Hill. The fortunes of this quiet farming town flipped in 1854, when Fort Union was established just six miles away. With the fleshpots of Santa Fe impractically distant, Loma Parda became the natural choice of the bored soldiery, quickly earning the nickname "Sodom on the Mora" (the Mora being the river that waters the town). As I now creep my way through derelict stone buildings, it's possible to imagine the ghosts of those who lost their lives during a violent, dissolute heyday that lasted until 1891. Now a national monument, the remains of Fort Union, active during the Apache Wars of the 1870s, are no less evocative.

The luster of gold, which brought so many West, lives on in a cluster of ghost towns between Santa Fe and Albuquerque – Cerillos, Hagan, Madrid, and, especially, Golden, which exploded into modern history with the first gold strike west of the Mississippi in 1825. It bloomed with saloons, miners' cottages, a school, post office and everything you'd associate with a Wild West town. Golden's character endures through its extensive remains, especially the beautifully restored church of San Francisco (featured in the 2021 movie *The Harder They Fall*), and the Golden General Merchandise Store, built in 1918 and now restored as Henderson's Store.

Gold was not the only precious payload sought in these hills – to the north of Cerillos, turquoise has been mined for more than 1000 years, while coal is the raison d'être of Hagan and Madrid. Cerillos is more complete than Hagan: with more than 19 historically recognized buildings, dirt streetscapes and timber-fronted stores, its official Historic District offers a delightful ramble. Madrid is something else again. It's a ghost town in name only, with more than 40 restored shops, galleries and taverns.

Wild West names don't come much more famous than Billy the Kid, who draws me onward to Lincoln. Founded by Hispanic settlers as Las Placitas del Rio Bonito in 1850, Lincoln was renamed in honor of the assassinated president in 1869, and is now a state monument. Its main street, Billy the Kid Trail, recalls the outlaw gunman who took part in the 1878 shootout known as the Battle of Lincoln. I find the town's storied past still remarkably tangible – whether kicking back at the Wortley Hotel, owned by Sheriff Pat Garrett, who brought the Kid to justice; wandering the two-story 1870s courthouse in which William H. Bonney (the Kid's original moniker) was confined; or handling the rough stone of the Torreon, the circular tower that shielded early Hispanic inhabitants from Apache raids.

Heading west to Truth or Consequences brings me within striking distance of some of New Mexico's remotest ghost towns, fringing the vast Gila National Forest. Just southwest of town is Hillsboro, a living ghost town that houses artists, storekeepers and ranchers

in its well-preserved buildings. Further on, the road hits Kingston – which flared brilliantly and brightly from the 1880s until the silver bust of 1893 – and Pinos Altos, where an 1860 gold strike brought droves of prospectors, clashes with Chiricahua Apache and a legacy of handsome, tumbledown buildings such as the Pinos Altos Opera House.

Last stop, deep in the Gila wilderness, is the isolated, *truly* Wild West town of Mogollon, listed on the National Register of Historic Places. Its historic district, scattered with the edifices of saloons, stores and municipal buildings, attests to its once-fabulous gold and silver wealth, if not the violence that came with its transient mining population and remoteness. Nowhere brings this history more alive than Graveyard Gulch, a half-mile walk through abandoned diggings to the cemetery where so many delved, dreamed and died in the town's glory days.

Opposite, from top: Dawson Cemetery, legacy of coal mining disasters; original buildings still standing in Cerillos. Previous page: the ruins of the transportation corral, Fort Union National Monument

DIRECTIONS

Start // Taos
Finish // Mogollon
Distance // 881 miles (1418km)
Getting there // The closest international airport is in Albuquerque, the state capital, where you can rent a car to drive the 135 miles (217km) north to Taos – stopping at Bandelier National Monument if time allows.
When to drive // With large sections of the drive passing through elevations above 6000 feet (1830m), winter snow can present problems. Spring (March to May) and fall (September and October) are best.
Where to stay // Mabel Dodge Luhan House (www.mabeldodgeluhan.com) was the one-time home of Taos' famous art patron; the Hurd La Rinconada Ranch (www.hurdgallery.com) doubles as an art gallery outside Lincoln; the Cosmic Campground (www.fs.usda.gov), near Mogollon, is dedicated to stargazing.

MORE LIKE THIS
PIONEER TRAILS

IOWA'S MORMON TRAIL

The bare prairies of southern Iowa evoke one of the lesser-known westward treks of American history – the Mormon exodus from Illinois to Utah. In 1846, religious intolerance forced a vanguard of Mormon leaders to leave their home of Nauvoo, cross the frozen Mississippi into Iowa, and begin a torturous 300-mile winter odyssey to Council Bluffs on the Missouri River, where they planned to join the Oregon Trail. Sites of interest along the way include: the Nauvoo Historical Landmark and Joseph Smith Historical site in Illinois; the Linger Longer Park and Sugar Creek staging point, where the emigrants grouped before their freezing ordeal; the Van Buren Courthouse, where the Nauvoo Militia Band performed for money to support the trekkers; and the Mount Pigsah Historic Site, where reconstructed huts and a cemetery attest to the travails of Latter-Day Saints.
Start // Nauvoo
Finish // Council Bluffs
Distance // 300 miles (483km)

SOUTH DAKOTA'S BLACK HILLS

Few places in the Midwest carry the historical weight of the Black Hills of South Dakota. Sacred to the Lakota Sioux, these granite-strewn mountains, carpeted in dark forests of spruce, ponderosa pine and juniper, were promised to their Native owners in perpetuity in the Fort Laramie Treaty of 1868. However, Lieutenant Colonel George Custer's expedition of 1874 led to the discovery of gold, which was followed by an inevitable surge of fortune-seekers, and the Battle of Little Bighorn and the Great Sioux War. Start amongst the pink sandstone of the spa town Hot Springs, then drive north through Wind Cave National Park, one of the largest caves in the world. Beyond lies Custer, where gold was first discovered, the Crazy Horse Memorial, Black Elk Peak, Mount Rushmore and ultimately Deadwood, the quintessential gold-rush town.
Start // Hot Springs
Finish // Deadwood
Distance // 100 miles (160km)

MAKING MISSOURI

Missouri's complicated pioneer past offers plenty of historic sights to road-trippers. French-Canadian Ste Geneviève, generally acknowledged as the first permanent European settlement in the state, dates to 1750 and is the ideal place to begin a historical treasure hunt. An hour's drive north, St Louis embodies the state's unstable past – founded in 1764 and named for the 13th-century King Louis IX of France, it was almost immediately ceded to Spain, returned to the French in 1800, then incorporated into the United States as part of the Louisiana Purchase of 1803. To the north is Hannibal, Mark Twain's boyhood home; to the west Independence, President Harry S Truman's hometown and the beginning of the California, Oregon and Santa Fe Trails; while north again, St Joseph was the eastern terminus of the fabled Pony Express.
Start // Ste Geneviève
Finish // St Joseph
Distance // 442 miles (711km)

Clockwise, from top: bison roam in Custer State Park, South Dakota; the Crazy Horse Memorial in South Dakota's Black Hills; Main Street in Hannibal, Missouri

TOP OF THE WORLD HIGHWAY

Adam Weymouth explores the history of the Yukon gold rush as he winds from Alaska to Canada through dramatic peaks, on one of the most northerly highways in the world.

I am driving east after three months in Alaska, on my way to Canada. By midmorning I am drinking thin coffee from a gas station in the nondescript town of Tok, just an hour or two shy of the border. I could easily make it there for lunch, but there's a left turn just up the road at Tetlin Junction, offering another way into Canada. It follows the Taylor Hwy, and then the Top of the World Hwy – named both for its altitude and latitude. It is very much the scenic route, and to do it justice will add several days on to my journey. I cannot resist.

Immediately the road begins to climb. The spruce forest appears to have no end. Occasional stretches of trees are blackened, ravaged by the fires of previous summers – they will not rot quickly in the dry air, but stand like this until they fall. It is a beautiful day, clear as a bell, and there are expansive views across the rounded hills of the Yukon–Tanana Uplands to the jagged ridge of the Alaska Range beyond, its peaks still snowbound in midsummer. The Fortymile caribou herd, about 40,000 strong, pass this way on their annual migration. Their prints are in the dust of the roadside, like a series of quotation marks leading off to the distant hills.

The settlement of Chicken – summer population 23, winter population seven – lies 40 miles (64km) before the Canadian border. The story has it that Chicken is so named because the original residents, a ragtag of gold prospectors, were unable to spell ptarmigan, the local bird and delicacy, and ptarmigan tastes a little like chicken, so what the hell? The town of Eagle is 90 miles (145km) to the north, with a name that cannot help but seem like one-upmanship. Between mid-October and mid-March there is no road into or out of Chicken. "We're not snowed in," one of the year-round residents tells me, in what feels like a well-rehearsed line,

"the rest of them are snowed out." I park up in the campground and pitch my tent. I order a beer and a burger in the local bar, and when I fall into bed around midnight, the sky is still pink, a protracted sunset that will merge into a sunrise at around three in the morning.

The next day I go exploring. Up Chicken Creek there are small-scale dredging operations, many of them family-run outfits. Gold mining is not confined to the past, as I had first thought before coming to Alaska, but for some is still a viable way to make a living, especially with the price as it has been. Yet while the fabled nuggets, big as a fist, do exist, mostly it is hard graft for scant

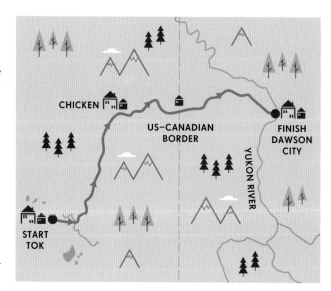

reward. I ask one old-timer what the attraction must be. His eyes gleam. "The attraction?" he says. "It's just...*gold*. It's like liquid sun, or something."

I drive on. Above the treeline now, the road winds through the peaks, with distant views of the Tombstone Mountains and huge, unpeopled spaces. I stop the car and climb a summit to try and take it all in. The border crossing is a small cluster of huts that I can see from miles off, a pocket of human life in all this wilderness. On the Canadian side the road is mostly unpaved, and I drive it slowly, gawping. Eventually a series of switchbacks descend to meet the Yukon River. There is an exquisite campsite here, on the Yukon's western bank, and I park up and pitch my tent. Later that evening I walk down to the water and catch the free ferry across into town.

Chicken had close to 100 residents at the peak of its 1891 gold rush, but Dawson City has an altogether grander story. The Klondike's first big strike came in 1896. In 1897, the population of Dawson hit 5000. By 1898 it was 40,000. By 1902, the city had government buildings, a power plant, four newspapers, several churches, a library, a court of law, a water-works department, several schools, a swimming pool, a bowling alley and a curling club. But gold extraction had already peaked. Today the population of Dawson City is 1375.

Dawson has kept its wonky boardwalks and left its streets unpaved. Diamond Tooth Gertie's Gambling Hall has three cancan shows a night. The poet Robert Service's cabin is here, as is one-half of author Jack London's. Men and women dressed in petticoats and buckskin lead tours around the town, telling stories of strange things that happen under the midnight sun. Every night in the Downtown Hotel, its original front wood-paneled, a man with a beard and wearing a captain's hat serves up Sourtoe Cocktails, a shot of liquor with an apparently human toe afloat in it, like a wizened monkey nut with a nail. "You can drink it fast, you can drink it slow," state the rules on the wall, "but your lips must touch the toe." The implication is that in a frontier town, we are only a few laws away from drinking body parts.

The get-rich-quick spirit remains here. The wildly successful reality TV show *Gold Rush*, credited for bringing a new generation to gold mining, is filmed in the hills around town. The next day, I head out on one of the tours to try my hand at panning, and after an hour spent ankle-deep in a creek sloshing water around a pan, I have a couple of specks of gold in a vial to show for my time. These gains represent quite a lot less than minimum wage, but I do feel proud of myself.

That evening I climb Midnight Dome behind the town. The sun is still up, that rich dusk light. The mighty Yukon, 1000 miles from the sea but already a huge river, unwinds into the distance. The highway goes the other way, hugging the Yukon upriver toward Whitehorse, in the direction I will be driving. Canada stretches out before me, at this moment seeming boundless.

FIRST NATIONS HISTORY

It must not be forgotten that the Yukon gold rush was a disaster for the Native population. In the space of a single year the Tr'ondëk Hwëch'in were evicted from the lands and fishing grounds their people had always known, and decimated by the diseases, abuse and religion that the prospectors brought with them. The Dänojà Zho Cultural Centre in Dawson City gives an excellent introduction to Native culture and history.

Clockwise, from above: caribou migrating at the Alaska-Canada border; panning for gold in Dawson City; from Chicken to anywhere; at Diamond Tooth Gertie's, Dawson City. Previous page: Fortymile River region

"Above the treeline now, the road winds through the peaks, with distant views of the Tombstone Mountains and huge, unpeopled spaces"

DIRECTIONS

Start // Tok, Alaska
Finish // Dawson City, Yukon Territory
Distance // 187 miles (301km)
How to get there // Tok is a three-hour drive from the small, lively city of Fairbanks.
When to drive // The highway is open from May until the first snowfall, but the border crossing closes mid-September. You'll need to pass through customs between 9am and 9pm.
What to take // A full tank of gas. There is one filling station in Chicken, and from then on there's nothing until Dawson.
Where to stay // For a true wilderness experience, book a log cabin at Clinton Creek (www.clintoncreekhideaway. com). Or travel by RV and park up at Chicken Gold Camp and Outpost (www.chickengold.com).

*Opposite, from top: the Igreja Santa
Rita dos Pardos Libertos (Church of
Santa Rita) in Paraty, Brazil; the
Sutter Creek Ice Cream Emporium,
off Hwy 49, California*

MORE LIKE THIS
GOING FOR GOLD

GOLD COUNTY, CALIFORNIA

Hwy 49 hugs the contours of the Sierras,
and is named for the 49ers, the prospectors
who descended on the state in the years
following 1849, chasing rumors of untold
wealth. Many of the once raucous frontier
towns are now cleaned up, much better for
finding an excellent steak or a local wine
than a brothel, but spots like Auburn and
Nevada City retain many of their charming
mid-19th-century buildings. Drive south and
stop in Placerville, where nearby Apple
Hill is a patchwork of orchards offering
everything from pie to hot cider. History is
around every corner: Dutch Flat has the
Golden Drift Museum, you can pan for
gold at South Yuba River State Park, while
Columbia is a living museum, a recreation
of a 19th-century gold rush town, albeit
without the violence and the dysentery.
Start // Vinton
Finish // Oakhurst
Distance // 295 miles (475km)

GOLD RUSH TRAIL, FRASER CANYON, CANADA

This trail, tracing the shape of the Fraser
River, was once a network of fur-trading
routes used by the First Nations in their
dealings with the Hudson Bay Company.
Then, between 1858 and 1862, as a series
of gold strikes lured prospectors in, it
rapidly expanded. Today it cuts a broad
and diverse swathe through some of British
Columbia's finest landscapes, many of
the towns along its length birthed into
existence by the 19th-century quest for
gold. Stampeders would have stocked up
in New Westminster before making the
long journey north, and some of the historic
roadhouses that sustained them en route
still exist. Barkerville, formerly a ghost town
left behind once the rush subsided, now
has over 120 buildings that have been
brought back to life, with trading and
partying like it's 1862.
Start // New Westminster
Finish // Barkerville
Distance // 454 miles (730km)

CAMINHO VELHO, ESTRADA REAL, BRAZIL

In 1697, the Portuguese in Brazil began
constructing roads using the labor
of enslaved Africans, with the aim of
extracting gold and diamonds from the
interior and sending them on to Lisbon. The
Estrada Real Institute has since revitalized
this network of trails, with the Caminho
Velho (Old Path) following the first of these
routes. Once taking 60 days to cover on
horseback, it's now a comfortable week's
drive, passing through verdant landscapes
and some of the country's most beautiful
colonial-era cities. Ouro Preto is a Unesco
World Heritage Site, with precipitous
cobblestone streets, baroque buildings
and the Nossa Senhora do Pilar church,
decorated with 957lb (434kg) of gold. The
road reaches the ocean at Paraty, in the
18th century one of Brazil's most important
ports, surrounded by rainforest and with
handsome beaches to explore.
Start // Ouro Preto
Finish // Paraty
Distance // 441 miles (710km)

SOUTHERN UTAH NATIONAL PARK CIRCUIT

Greg Bloom cuts a swath through southern Utah's canyonlands, taking in five national parks, three scenic byways and close to a dozen protected areas.

"This is the most beautiful place on Earth."

So begins *Desert Solitaire* (1968), Edward Abbey's account of a summer spent in the canyonlands of southern Utah, and I couldn't agree with him more. It is a land where the scorched red earth does impossible things, and each bend in the road produces a jaw-dropping moment. Yet writing about road trips in the context of Abbey is conflicting. The pugnacious environmentalist rued the very existence of roads in his spiritual home and muse. To truly experience the canyonlands, he wrote, get out of the car and "walk, better yet crawl, on hands and knees, over the sandstone and through the thornbush and cactus."

I sympathize with Abbey's point of view. But exploring deserts on hands and knees involves more time than most of us have. So I drive. Often. I am always sure to set aside plenty of time for hikes in the area's magnificent wilderness. Abbey would approve.

On a recent trip I set my sights on the three heavy hitters of Utah's national parks: Arches, Bryce and Zion. I had visited each individually, but never together in one glorious swoop. The drive was the icing on the cake: 475 mouthwatering miles (764km) along the scenic byways of southern Utah. The route has no name, but is rather an agglomeration of several famous drives, many with names that will be familiar to US road-trip aficionados – Trail of the Ancients,

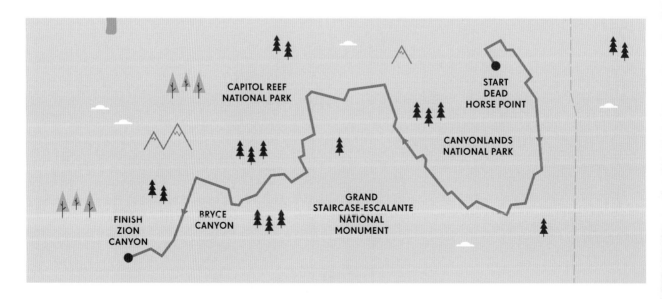

> *"Wind, frost, rain and rivers have been slicing and dicing the ruddy sandstone into fantastic shapes for eons"*

Bicentennial Scenic Byway and the mind-blowing Hwy 12 (dubbed, rather awkwardly, "A Journey Through Time Scenic Byway").

The building block of the American Southwest's stupendous canyons, arches, mesas and grottoes is sandstone, a malleable substance formed by the hardening of sediment over time. Wind, frost, rain and rivers – most notably the Colorado – have been slicing and dicing the ruddy sandstone into fantastic shapes for eons, and will continue to do so for eons more.

The most famous product of this is the Grand Canyon, just south of the Utah border in Arizona. A couple of hundred miles (about 300km) up the Colorado River from the Grand Canyon's north rim is Dead Horse Point, which overlooks Canyonlands National Park at the confluence of the Colorado and Green Rivers. After a morning spent hiking in nearby Arches National Park, where Abbey was a ranger in the 1950s, my road trip begins. The massive abyss beneath Dead Horse Point plays tricks with one's sense of space. To the east, the snow-draped La Sal Mountains lord over the canyon's burgundy-toned eastern rim. This is southern Utah: serene, brutal, inspiring.

From Dead Horse Point, I follow the Trail of the Ancients due south and then west toward my next hiking stops, Natural Bridges National Monument and Capitol Reef National Park. Abbey loved the summer here, but it's not the best time to visit. For one thing, the national parks are overrun with RVs, as Abbey predicted would happen. Summer is also unbearably hot. March is about perfect: cool and crisp for those day hikes, and not too crowded.

I leave the Trail of the Ancients behind at Natural Bridges and follow the Bicentennial Scenic Byway through Capitol Reef, then pick up Hwy 12 in Torrey and drive south to Bryce Canyon. This entire stretch is mesmerizing, the road snaking into snowy pine forest and down into dusty red desert, skirting huge mesas. There are myriad potential side trips, many bearing cheeky names like Cheesebox Canyon, Kodachrome Basin, Moss Back Butte and Dirty Devil River.

By the time I reach Bryce Canyon National Park I think I've lost the ability to be impressed. I haven't. Erosion has sculpted the crumbly earth into fields of colorful totem-pole-like formations called hoodoos that change color by the hour. My hike is under sunny skies but there's a nip in the air – at over 8000ft (2440m), Bryce is the highest of these national parks. On my way back to the car, a snow squall moves in. I watch as the hoodoos, their tops dusted white, transmogrify into the distinguished old men of the high Utah desert.

Leaving the snow behind me, I descend toward Zion National Park, 80 miles (128km) west and a couple of thousand feet lower. I opt for a half-day hike to Observation Point, 2100ft (640m) above the Zion Canyon floor. There are several slot canyons – narrow alleyways cut into the sandstone – to negotiate along the way, and from the top we can look straight down to the valley, where the Virgin River dances among Zion's imposing cliffs.

From Zion I have ample opportunities to extend the road trip. It's only two hours to the Grand Canyon or five to Death Valley. Alas, this time I head home, leaving Abbey's Country to continue its intricate pas de deux with time.

HOLE-IN-THE-ROCK

Predecessor to the scenic byways of southwestern Utah, the Hole-in-the-Rock route was a wagon road, from Escalante (along present-day Hwy 12) to Bluff, built by Mormon settlers in the late 1800s. The route, in use for a year, crossed the Colorado River via an actual hole in the rock, a steep notch in a cliff. Ropes and oxen lowered wagons down the notch, which can be visited by road from Escalante or boat from Lake Powell.

Opposite, clockwise from left: Native American cave art in Capitol Reef National Park; extraordinary sandstone formations in Arches National Park; snowy slopes in Bryce Canyon National Park. Previous page: the Watchman peak in Zion National Park

DIRECTIONS

Start // Dead Horse Point State Park
Finish // Zion National Park
Distance // 475 miles (764km)
Getting there // Dead Horse Point is near Moab, accessible by air or by road from Salt Lake City, 230 miles (370km) northeast. Zion is 160 miles (257km) from Las Vegas.
When to drive // Low season rules: go October to March.
Where to stay // Zion Lodge in Zion Canyon (www.zionlodge.com; reserve months in advance); Gonzo Inn (www.gonzoinn.com) on the main drag in Moab; Capitol Reef Inn & Cafe (www.capitolreefinn.com) in Torrey.
Climate // It's seriously cold at night in the desert from October to April. Days are mild outside of summer's heat.
Hot tip // Some of the best side trips are accessible via unpaved roads, so hiring a 4WD makes sense.

Opposite, clockwise from top: the lure of the Florida Keys, at the beach; and at the bar; the towering trees of Kings Canyon National Park, California

MORE LIKE THIS
AUTHORS' ITINERARIES

JOHN MUIR'S COUNTRY, SIERRA NEVADA

What the canyonlands were to Edward Abbey, the Sierras were to John Muir a couple of generations earlier. The legendary conservationist and Sierra Club founder was also one of the early American travel writers, producing volumes on his excursions into this wild mountain range near the California–Nevada border. This trip takes in a trio of Californian national parks from north to south: Yosemite, Kings Canyon and Sequoia. You'll see the expected big trees, big cliffs and big waterfalls, along with lesser-known gems like the Kings Canyon Scenic Byway (Hwy 180) – 50 miles (80km) of alpine eye candy, culminating in the dramatic descent into Kings Canyon. This is high-altitude driving: in the cold months many roads close and chains are mandatory. It goes without saying that there are amazing hiking opportunities along this route, including the John Muir Trail.

Start // Yosemite National Park
Finish // Sequoia National Park
Distance // 260 miles (418km)

STEPHEN KING'S COUNTRY, MAINE

Stephen King has two homes in Maine, and many of his gritty horror stories are set in the state. From Portland, take maritime Rte 1 "downeast" to Ellsworth, then detour south and loop around the Acadia Scenic Byway, one of 31 All-American Roads. The coastal route brings you past icons (the LL Bean store, the Bath Iron Works), natural wonders (the entire coastline), architectural marvels (the 1827 Pemaquid lighthouse, Bucksport's Penobscot Narrows Bridge), picturesque harbors (Camden, Bar Harbor) and unexpected artist havens (Portland, Belfast, Rockland). Get out of the car and hike in the Camden Hills or Acadia National Park. Or take a car ferry to explore the Fox Islands or Deer Isle. End up in pleasant Bangor, King's part-time residence and gateway to Maine's wild north. Crowds thin and the foliage is spectacular in the autumn; be ready for inclement weather at any time of year.

Start // Portland
Finish // Bangor
Distance // Approx 300 miles (482km)

JIMMY BUFFETT'S COUNTRY, THE FLORIDA KEYS

It's tempting to call the Florida Keys Hemingway's country, but the author only lived in Key West for eight years and the area didn't inspire his books. Tennessee Williams lived in Key West for decades, and Thomas McGuane caroused there with other authors in the 1970s and set his classic novel, *Ninety-Two in the Shade*, in Key West. Ultimately, however, the Keys are Jimmy Buffett territory. The "Margaritaville" crooner got his start in Key West and has written countless songs and several bestselling short-story collections about the Keys. Perhaps it's the drive to Key West that inspires so many artists and writers. The Florida Keys Scenic Highway, a prestigious All-American Road, traverses a magnificent seascape as it hops, one bridge at a time, among the Keys' myriad islands. Hurricanes are a threat from July to November, so check the radar to ensure you aren't driving into one. (For wildlife spotting, see p182.)

Start // Key Largo
Finish // Key West
Distance // 110 miles (177km)

JUST FOR KICKS: ROUTE 66

The Mother Road knows America best: Andrea Sachs covers more than 2400 miles (3860km), eight states and nearly a century of red, white and blue moments on Route 66.

I finish the 2448-mile (3940km) drive before I've even begun. "End" reads the Route 66 sign on Jackson Blvd, Chicago. I circle the block, searching for a plain brown square, an arrow pointing west. "Begin" urges a sign on Adams St. I bounce in my car seat and do as I am told.

Route 66, the legendary highway connecting Chicago to Los Angeles, dates from 1926, but only 80 percent of the original road still exists – hence the navigational confusion. It has also been realigned several times, before being decommissioned in 1985 and replaced with five different interstates. Because of its patchwork condition, I find myself flitting between old and new segments,

smooth and bumpy. With so many attractions – monumental and kitschy, natural and plastic – along the route, I fall woefully behind schedule. "Route 66 time is different," Jerry McClanahan, a cartographer and artist, tells me at his gallery in Chandler, Oklahoma. "If it's quick, you're not doing Route 66."

Over the decades, the road has attracted American dreamers. In the early 20th century, they piled into jalopies to escape the Dust Bowl and find work during the Great Depression. In WWII, soldiers followed the road in the name of duty. In the mid-century, liberated motorists embraced car culture, and later counterculture. Now, nostalgia-seekers like myself take Route 66 to travel back in time.

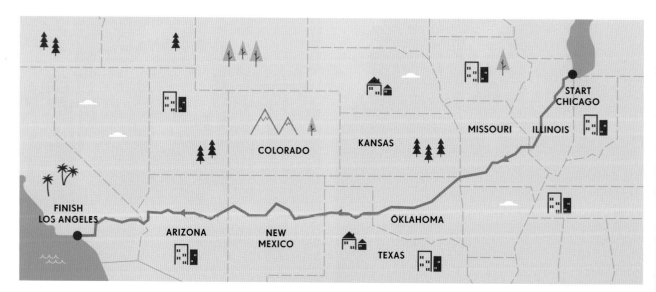

I meet Jim Jones, a living remnant of the road. At the Route 66 Association Hall of Fame & Museum in Pontiac, Illinois, he reminisces about the highway that defined his youth.

"I was seven years old and pumping gas," he says of a 1940 photo of himself and his brother in his hometown. "Odell had 13 gas stations and 951 people. Dad made a good living."

In 1947, the Jones clan drove the entire route, camping along the way. Sixty-six years later, Jim repeated the trip, staying in hotels. I ask him how the road had changed over the years.

"It's more of a history-oriented highway today," he says. "People drive it for the nostalgia."

In Adrian, Texas, the midway point of Route 66, I nearly kiss the sign informing travelers that Chicago and LA are an equidistant 1139 miles (1833km) away. I cross the empty street to the Midpoint Café and ask the owner's daughter if the restaurant honors the halfway achievement. "Eat a piece of ugly pie," she says.

Her father joins me at the counter. He plucks some old postcards from a rack to illustrate Adrian's former self as a robust railroad town. The community once supported five cafes open 24/7; today, the sole surviving restaurant closes at 4pm.

"Route 66 was the lifeblood of the town, because of all the traffic," says another customer, Finis Brown, the town mayor. "It still is."

One of the most exhilarating sections is the 159 miles (256km) of uninterrupted road in western Arizona. I brake only for wild ferrets and Angel Delgadillo. Angel's reputation precedes him by more than 1700 miles (2736km). When your nickname is "the Godfather of Route 66," you amass a vast fan base. The barber, who was born

REBRANDING WILLIAMS

Williams was the final town to be bypassed by the interstate, but the Arizona outpost didn't die. Instead, it rebounded as the Gateway to the Grand Canyon. The Grand Canyon Railway runs train services to the South Rim of the national park. The town also plays up its Wild West character with shootout performances. For a traffic-free ride, the Route 66 Zipline transports passengers in a flying car that reaches speeds of up to 30mph (48km/h).

Clockwise, from above: riding the Route into California; the lifeguard post at Santa Monica Pier where the journey ends; you know you're on the right road in Winslow, Arizona. Previous page: roadside in the Route 66 town of Seligman, Arizona

in 1927, grew up with his Mexican parents and eight siblings in a modest home on Route 66 in Seligman, Arizona.

"The people in the cars looked so down and out," he said of the Dust Bowl migrants. "We'd say, 'Here comes a poor Okie. He's only got one mattress. And here come rich Okies. They have two mattresses.'"

The date that makes Angel shudder is September 22, 1978, when the interstate south of town opened, killing the town's livelihood.

"They turned off the lights on Main Street," he lamented.

In February 1987, Angel organized a meeting seeking historic designation for the 89 miles (143km) of road from Seligman to Kingman. The group urged lawmakers to post historic signs, which would help preserve the road. Angel's perseverance paid off, and his victory inspired other communities to embrace the cause as well.

"Seligman has the distinction of being the town where Route 66 got its rebirth," he says. "We helped save a little bit of America."

Route 66 originally terminated on Broadway and Seventh St in downtown LA. Two weeks after leaving Chicago, I roll up to the intersection, park and excitedly jump up and down on the pavement outside Clifton's Cafeteria. I ask a bystander if there was a historical marker I could high-five. The restaurant's owner points to a small blue sign: "Original terminus of Route 66 (1926–1939)."

On Santa Monica Pier, the last of the three finales, I approach Ian Bowen, who is tucked inside a Route 66 kiosk. He shakes my hand, "Congratulations." Several minutes later, a couple from North Dakota receive the same reception.

While standing in line to snap a picture of the "End of the Trail" sign, I compare notes with the Dakotans. Much to our delight, we had both taken a wrong turn in Chicago. In our photos, we flash knowing smiles that we had done Route 66 right.

"'Route 66 time is different,' Jerry McClanahan tells me. 'If it's quick, you're not doing Route 66'"

DIRECTIONS

Start // Chicago
Finish // Los Angeles
Distance // 2448 miles (3940km) and eight states
Getting there // Pick up your rental car from Chicago's O'Hare or Midway airports or, if you are driving west to east, Los Angeles International Airport.
When to drive // Late spring, summer and early autumn are best. In summer, book lodgings in advance as many of the vintage motels sell out. Also be aware that some attractions and shops keep small-town hours, even during peak months.
Maps // Most GPS units and mapping apps ignore Route 66 and kick drivers on to the interstates or major highways. Jerry McClanahan's *EZ66 Guide for Travelers* is invaluable. The author plots every turn along the route with sightseeing and dining suggestions, historical snippets and more.
Hot tip // Don't let your fuel gauge drop below halfway, especially in the Southwest, where gas stations are sparse.

Opposite, clockwise from top:
sunrise over Florida's Key West;
the former home of artist and
bat enthusiast Edward Gorey
in Cape Cod, Massachusetts;
refreshment options off the
Overseas Hwy, Florida

MORE LIKE THIS
CLASSIC US DRIVES

OVERSEAS HIGHWAY, FLORIDA

The 113-mile (182km) Overseas Hwy ribbons through the Florida Keys, from Key Largo to Key West, the country's southernmost city. The All-American Road features 42 spans, including the famous Seven Mile Bridge (cue *True Lies*). In many spots along the route, you'll feel like a bug gliding on the water. Look left for the Atlantic, right for the Gulf of Mexico and up for pelicans, osprey and great white herons. Follow the mile-markers to such Keysian attractions as John Pennekamp Coral Reef and Bahia Honda state parks, which offer stellar diving. For drier wildlife, the National Key Deer Refuge is home to the smallest North American deer, while at the Turtle Hospital, patients await their return to sea. When you're out of road, exit the car and enter a bar. Order a Key West classic, the Key lime margarita. If you're traveling during hurricane season, remember that there's only one way in, and out, of Key West.

Start // Key Largo
Finish // Key West
Distance // 113 miles (182km)

KANCAMAGUS HIGHWAY, NEW HAMPSHIRE

The Kancamagus Hwy – "the Kanc" for short – delves into nature and doesn't return to civilization for a glorious 34 miles (56km). Opened in 1959, the American Scenic Byway starts at the junction of Route 16 in Conway and meanders through the White Mountains before finishing in Lincoln. You'll trade restaurants, hotels, gas stations and cell phone coverage for views of the Swift River, hiking trails of varying endurance levels and possibly a moose sighting. The Russell-Colbath House, the only original structure remaining from the town of Passaconaway, peeks at New England life in the 1800s. In the warmer months, cool off in the spray of Sabbaday Falls; in autumn, soak up the colors from the Kancamagus Pass (870m). Some spots require a parking pass, which you can purchase on-site at a kiosk (US$5 for the day), ranger station or visitor center.

Start // Conway
Finish // Lincoln
Distance // 34 miles (56km)

ROUTE 6, MASSACHUSETTS

Rte 6 started modestly, as a jaunt from eastern Massachusetts to Brewster, New York State. By 1937, the highway stretched to Long Beach, California, and, for a spell, held the honor of the longest transcontinental highway in the country – total mileage: 3652 (5877km). Realignments and renumberings removed the road from its podium. However, in the Bay State, you can still drive the Grand Army of the Republic Highway (its more reverential name) from its original departure point in Provincetown, along Cape Cod, over the Sagamore Bridge and to the border with Rhode Island. The road passes through historic beach towns, such as Yarmouth Port (one spine-tingling attraction: the Edward Gorey House) and Sandwich, the oldest on the Cape. Rte 6 also partly parallels the nearly 40-mile (64km) Cape Cod National Seashore. In the summer, beachgoers jam the road.

Start // Provincetown, Massachusetts
Finish // Providence, Rhode Island
Distance // 119 miles (192km)

TWO SIDES OF THE SOUTH

Southern charm meets Southern Gothic, with some hard-hitting truths along the way, on Clifton Wilkinson's drive between two of the United States' most characterful cities, Charleston and Savannah.

I begin my road trip not on four wheels but on four legs, sitting on a horse-drawn carriage that trundles around South Carolina's largest city, Charleston, with a gentle clip-clop. History is what's drawn me here, American friends having recommended Charleston and its equally elegant sister, Savannah, as the ideal vacation for this history-loving Brit.

Two southern belles await, and the carriage is the perfect way to see the first. Charles Town, as it was originally called, was founded in 1670 and named after British monarch King Charles II. The canopy over the carriage is welcome, providing shade against a sun that, even in May, glares down on one colonnaded balcony, pretty porch and perfect lawn after another.

My friends were right. The private homes and public buildings here are beautiful, displaying centuries of wealth that have made the city the hugely popular destination it is today. I'm busy admiring these paragons of architectural design when we arrive at the Old Slave Mart, where I'm confronted with the stark evidence of where Charleston's wealth came from: slavery. Running concurrently with a past full of money and mansions is one full of human misery. Charleston, by some estimates, was where around half of all enslaved Africans arrived in the British Colonies and subsequently the United States. The Old Slave Mart, now a museum, was a place of horror that only stopped functioning in 1863.

Given Charleston's dominant role in the slave trade, it seems apt that one of its star attractions is Fort Sumter. This island fortification in the city's harbor is where the Civil War started. Here, in April 1861, South Carolinian militia fired on Union troops holding the fort and four years of bloodshed began, during which Lincoln issued the Emancipation Proclamation, which officially ended slavery.

I jump in my rental car and head south, conflicted in my opinion of Charleston and wondering what the rest of the trip will produce. The road that runs to Savannah, Hwy 17, is a quiet two-laner that feels almost rural, lined with trees and grassy shoulders. Even though it's just two hours between the cities, I've decided to break the journey with a visit to the coast, so at Gardens Corner I turn south onto Hwy 21 to begin my detour.

Water soon becomes as prevalent as land, the bridges connecting South Carolina's Sea Islands hovering just above the marshy landscape's waterline. I pause in handsome, wealthy Beaufort for a wander along its streets filled with antebellum houses and tempting

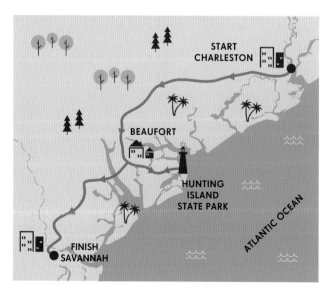

"I'm confronted with the stark evidence of where Charleston's wealth came from: slavery"

restaurants, but the coast is calling. Back in the car, it's a short drive that I take slowly to get to the Atlantic's edge, in the form of Hunting Island State Park.

The thick maritime forest abruptly stops when it reaches the park's five miles of white sands, and the ocean rolls in. The Atlantic is quiet the day I visit, waves breaking gently on the beach, but the elegant, eerie remains of dead trees that punctuate the shore are evidence of the erosive power of the salt water here, rushing in during storms and killing the forest by degrees. The bare stumps create an unsettling but engrossing atmosphere and I head to the lighthouse, the only publicly accessible one in South Carolina, to climb its 167 steps for a better view. Back at ground level a sign tells me that loggerhead turtles nest here. I'm too early to witness any action, but I leave happy that this place is still a refuge for these endangered creatures.

As I reluctantly leave the ocean, the next hour's drive is a pleasant blur of countryside and few cars, until I cross the South Carolina–Georgia border and the single-lane road starts rising toward the impressive Talmadge Memorial Bridge. The low sides provide wonderful views of the Savannah River and city – and also reinforce just how high this bridge is (185ft/56m). Suddenly, as I'm approaching the bridge's highest point, in my rearview mirror I spot a motorcycle closing in fast. And then another. And another. Within a few seconds there are at least two dozen bikers surrounding my car, whooping at each other and the views – they are oblivious to the large drop just a few feet away and, apparently, to the intimidated driver in their midst. I'm escorted by this cavalcade until the bridge ends, where the road curves toward the city and the bikers peel off.

I park in one of Savannah's 22 celebrated squares, where my genteel B&B overlooks a manicured garden with dappled sunlight emerging through the trees. Like Charleston, Savannah is a place to explore on foot and I'm eager to do so. The compact layout, dotted with squares and parks, is reminiscent of a British city, which is unsurprising as Savannah, like Charleston, was founded by the British in 1733. I marvel at the houses that compete with one another in grandeur and join a walking tour to discover more of the history.

As with its South Carolina sibling, the beauty here has an ugly side in the form of a history intertwined with the trade in enslaved people. But Savannah also has a ghoulish aspect as well: the city has established itself as the home of Southern Gothic, with several reputedly haunted houses. The most famous is the 150-year-old redbrick Mercer House, scene of a shooting in 1981 by the homeowner, which killed a young man. The story was told in the book and film *Midnight in the Garden of Good and Evil*. I decide to indulge my interest in the macabre with a drive to one of Savannah's most celebrated sights, Bonaventure Cemetery. Even with a blinding midday sun there's an unnerving atmosphere here, created by the creeping, creepy Spanish moss hanging from the oak trees and the many statues, including of young children, that rise among the headstones. Like much on this trip there's a juxtaposition of the beautiful with the disturbing in the cemetery, and as such it's a fitting end to my tale of two cities.

HARRIET TUBMAN BRIDGE

On Hwy 17, before the turnoff for Beaufort, stands a bridge honoring one of antislavery's greatest advocates, Harriet Tubman. Crossing the Combahee River, the bridge recalls a Civil War raid in 1863 led by Tubman herself. Union troops, including 150 African Americans, fought Confederates to liberate a group of former enslaved people. Over 700 traveled north, many joining the Union Army, and Tubman received recognition in the shape of an eponymous bridge.

Opposite, clockwise from top: atmospheric Bonaventure Cemetery in Savannah; the Old Slave Mart Museum in Charleston; high tide on Hunting Island. Previous page: Charleston's St Philip's Church

DIRECTIONS

Start // Charleston, South Carolina
Finish // Savannah, Georgia
Distance // 153 miles (246km)
Getting there // Both cities have small airports. Both are also on the Amtrak Silver Meteor train line, linking them with New York and Washington to the north and Miami to the south.
When to drive // Summers round these parts are anything but charming, so aim for a visit in spring or fall.
Where to stay // Charleston and Savannah have some amazing places to stay, generally with plenty of historical character, but prices are high and options get booked well in advance, so reserve early.
More info // Visit charlestoncvb.com and visitsavannah.com for details on accommodations, restaurants and sights.

MORE LIKE THIS
DRIVING THROUGH HISTORY

ST AUGUSTINE TO CAPE CANAVERAL

Road trip through 400 years of history on an easy drive along Florida's Atlantic Coast. Begin in St Augustine, the oldest European city in North America, founded in 1565. Beneath a touristy veneer are some seriously wonderful museums and Spanish Colonial architecture, with a highlight being the Castillo de San Marcos fortress. A short drive south through oceanside towns, including Daytona Beach (famous for its NASCAR race), brings you forward four centuries to the heady days of the 1960s Space Race at Cape Canaveral, located on the appropriately named Space Coast. Numerous rockets have launched from here, including the Apollo missions that went to the Moon, and you can continue to catch blastoffs even today. Find out all about the history of space exploration at the Kennedy Space Center.

Start // St Augustine, Florida
Finish // Cape Canaveral, Florida
Distance // 127 miles (204km)

BOSTON TO PROVINCETOWN

Boston is one of the most important historical cities in the United States. The events connected to the American War of Independence that took place here are formative (from the Boston Tea Party to the Boston Massacre) making the 2.5-mile (4km) Freedom Trail, a walking route through the city that joins the historical dots, an obligatory attraction. Driving south, the route along Cape Cod delves further into the past with the famous Plymouth Rock, the spot where the Pilgrim Fathers supposedly disembarked in 1620. Hwy 6 then loops round the cape and ends up in charming Provincetown (P-town to its friends). Today a focus of LGBTIQ+ tourism and cute waterfront architecture, it was also where the *Mayflower* originally anchored and the male passengers agreed to the rules of self-governance laid out in the Mayflower Compact.

Start // Boston, Massachusetts
Finish // Provincetown, Massachusetts
Distance // 116 miles (187km)

A TRIO OF NEVADA TOWNS

Pioneering endeavors and mining mayhem combine in three attractive Nevada towns. Furthest north is Virginia City where a huge silver streak, the Comstock Lode, was discovered in 1859, making the place a boomtown for the next 20 years. The main street today looks like a film set and the saloons and museums recall the town's glory days. A quick drive south brings you to Carson City, state capital and home to museums exploring the town's past, from pioneer stopover to an intriguing railroad history. Continuing south and up into the eastern slopes of the Sierra Nevada mountains, the road leads to picturesque Genoa. The oldest settlement in Nevada, founded as a trading post by Mormons in 1851, its most popular attraction today is, ironically, the Genoa Bar and Saloon.

Start // Virginia City
Finish // Genoa
Distance // 28 miles (45km)

Clockwise, from top: the Boston
skyline framed by the USS
Constitution, Massachusetts; inside
Kennedy Space Center, Florida;
Nevada's oldest saloon in Genoa

COOL RUNNINGS:
CANADA'S ICEFIELDS PARKWAY

Snowcapped peaks, glinting glaciers, azure lakes and more wildlife than your average safari –
Oliver Berry finds the road from Lake Louise to Jasper is hard to top for scenic splendor.

'm only half an hour into my road trip into the Canadian Rockies, and I've already come to a screeching halt. A moose has parked himself on the asphalt. Antlers speckled with dew, breath clouding in the autumn air, he's rooted in the middle of the highway, chewing on some grass while he checks the view. I've been waiting 10 minutes. He hasn't budged an inch.

I honk my horn. The moose doesn't seem bothered. I try revving the engine. The moose just keeps on chewing. I lean my head out and holler for him to shift his hide, haul ass, vamoose. Nothing. I ponder the wisdom of manhandling him out of the way, but since the moose outweighs me by 700lb (320kg) and his antlers look capable of turning me into a plate of short ribs, I decide against it. If Mr Moose feels like standing in the road a while – well, I'll just have to wait.

Happily, the Icefields Parkway is possibly the best place on the planet to find yourself in a traffic jam, moose-based or otherwise. Not that there's much traffic. Stretching for 143 epic miles (230km) between Lake Louise and Jasper, this wild, mountain-framed road

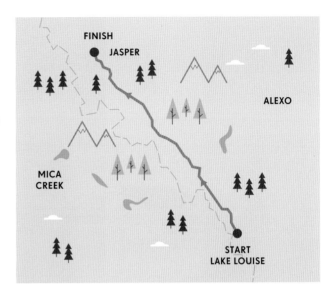

"At times, the highway feels more like a safari park. Only here, the wildlife is just that — wild"

is one of the most beautiful drives on Earth. From vast ice fields to plunging valleys, glacial lakes to serrated peaks, it packs more scenery into the drive than any road I've ever driven.

"Having some trouble, sir?" drawls a mustachioed park ranger, as his 4WD slows to a halt alongside my car. "Let's see if we can't get things moving." The ranger nudges his vehicle forward, flanking the moose. The animal reluctantly trudges off into the grass, leaving the highway clear. "Sometimes all it takes is a little persuasion. Safe driving!" The ranger smiles as he rolls off into the distance.

It's the first of many memorable wildlife encounters on the Icefields Parkway. Near Bow Lake, sipping coffee at the old hostelry of Num-Ti-Jah Lodge, I watch a pair of eagles soaring overhead as they search for prey. Further north, from the trail over Parker Ridge, I spy a family of mountain goats picking their way along the canyon walls, like a troupe of acrobats dressed in fur coats. When I stop for lunch at the Saskatchewan River Crossing, I listen to the peeps of pikas and the whistles of marmots. And once, near the Athabasca Falls, about 25 miles (32km) south of Jasper, I spy a mother black bear and two cubs foraging for berries in the wildflower meadows.

Sometimes, the Icefields Parkway feels more like a safari park than a public highway, only here, the wildlife is just that – wild. But while the animals are fascinating, it's the scenery that makes the Parkway special. Based along the route of an old packhorse trail established by First Nations people and fur traders, the road was completed in 1940 to join Banff and Jasper national parks. It's a thread of civilization fringed by sprawling wilderness. Craggy peaks spike the skyline to east and west, and beyond lies wild backcountry barely changed since the days when Stoney, Kootenay and Blackfeet Nations called this land home. Waterfalls thunder down rock walls. Lakes sparkle electric blue. Then there are the glaciers that gave the road its name: more than 100, glinting like gems in the mountainside.

Sadly, climate change now threatens these icy wonders. Even the mightiest have shrunk dramatically in size over recent decades. At the Athabasca Glacier, about halfway along the Parkway, I stop at the Icefield Centre, and take a 90-minute trip onto the glacier itself in an all-terrain snowcat. It's a thrilling detour as the vehicle bumps and jolts over the ice, grinding its way onto the vast Columbia Icefield – at 125 sq miles (325 sq km), the largest expanse of ice in the Rockies. At the top, passengers snap selfies surrounded by a boundless sea of ice: frozen in waves, cracked by crevasses, glinting like glass and tinted with a rainbow of icy colors. It's sobering to think that one day even this great glacier might melt into memory.

But for now, there are more natural wonders to explore ahead: a hike along the craggy ravine of Sunwapta Canyon, a detour to see the thunderous crash of the Athabasca Falls, an afternoon picnic with a view of the pyramid-shaped Mt Fryatt. It's well after dark when I finally pull into Jasper, and I've only traveled 143 miles (230km), but I head to bcd happy in the knowledge that I've driven some of North America's most spectacular scenery.

Tomorrow, I think I might just hop back in the car, pull a U-turn and do it all over again.

SEEKING YOGI

Bears are top of the must-see list, but they're hard to spot. The best time is between August and September, when they forage in preparation for hibernation. Look out for them in bushy meadows, avalanche corridors and near railway tracks. Grizzlies are larger, and distinguishable by their dish-shaped face and neck hump. Black bears, despite their name, can also be brown, red or cinnamon. Keep a respectful distance and stay inside your car if you spot a bear.

Opposite, clockwise from top left: all-terrain snow coaches take visitors onto the icefields; caution – black bear crossing; the Canadian Rockies provide stunning scenery. Previous pages: the slowly receding Athabasca Glacier

DIRECTIONS

Start // Lake Louise
Finish // Jasper Town
Distance // 143 miles (230km)
Getting there // Calgary International Airport is a two-hour drive from Lake Louise. The nearest international airport to Jasper is in Edmonton, a four-hour drive.
When to drive // Late autumn to avoid summer traffic.
What to take // Binoculars for wildlife spotting, hiking boots for trails, food and drink for roadside picnics.
Where to stay // Simpson's Num-Ti-Jah Lodge; The Crossing Resort (www.thecrossingresort.com).
Car rental // Major rental firms can be found in both Banff and Jasper.
More info // www.icefieldsparkway.com; www.travelalberta.com

*Opposite, from top: the Alaskan
Hwy crossing the Yukon; the rugged
peaks of Grand Teton National
Park, Wyoming*

MORE LIKE THIS
WILDERNESS DRIVES

ALASKAN HIGHWAY

If it's true wilderness you want, head north – way north. At nearly 1400 miles (2232km) long, the Alaskan Hwy is one of the longest roads in North America, running all the way from Dawson Creek in British Columbia to Delta Junction in Alaska. It was built during WWII to connect the rest of the US with Alaska, and for years still had long stretches of gravel road, although it's now paved along its entire length. It's a very different prospect from most American road trips – you won't find any motels or malls, and gas stations are few and far between, but what you get in exchange is wilderness and wildlife in abundance. This is one road trip that really does deserve to be called epic, in every sense of the word.

Start // Dawson Creek, British Columbia
Finish // Delta Junction, Alaska
Distance // 1387 miles (2232km)

DEMPSTER HIGHWAY, CANADA

If you're looking for another drive of magnitude and challenge, Canada's Dempster Hwy fits the bill. This hard-packed, gravel road branches off the North Klondike Hwy near Dawson City, Yukon, and swings north through pristine wilderness for 457 miles (740km) before ending in Inuvik, the northernmost town of any size in Canada's Northwest Territories, way beyond the Arctic Circle. And if that's not enough, you can now drive all the way to Tuktoyaktuk, a tiny settlement on the shores of the Arctic Ocean, 90 miles (147km) north of Inuvik. It's a gorgeous, lonely drive that takes in dense forest (you may spot grizzly bears), snow-tipped mountains and vast expanses of flat tundra. There are two tiny settlements near Inuvik – Fort McPherson and Tsiigehtchic, where you have to take a car ferry. For this whole trip, be sure to rent a 4WD, take two spare tires, and fill up on gas. Bring emergency supplies in case you break down; there is practically no phone reception here.

Start // Dawson City
Finish // Inuvik
Distance // 457 miles (740km)

GRAND TETON TO YELLOWSTONE, WYOMING

Yellowstone is nature's tour de force. Its unique supervolcano features half the world's geysers, the country's largest high-altitude lake and a mass of blue-ribbon rivers and waterfalls. To the south, Grand Teton National Park complements with craggy peaks, peaceful waterways and sublime alpine terrain. Wildlife spotting can start at Jackson, where elk, bison and bighorn sheep congregate in winter at the National Elk Refuge, and grizzly sightings are not uncommon as soon as you head out onto the Moose-Wilson Rd. The wet lowlands at Oxbow Bend provide a scenic spot to view moose, elk, bald eagles and other birds, while bear (or bison) jams are sometimes an issue from Yellowstone Lake on. Beyond the Grand Canyon of the Yellowstone, head east toward Lamar Valley, dubbed the Serengeti of North America for its herds of bison, elk and the occasional grizzly or coyote. It's also the place to spot wolves, particularly in spring.

Start // Jackson
Finish // Mammoth
Distance // 250 miles (402km)

ON THE TRAIL OF THE LONESOME PINE

The 574-mile (924km) route through the Blue Ridge Mountains is one of America's legendary road trips – for Marcel Theroux, it's the scene for a drama of change and renewal.

The two roads that run down the spine of the southern Appalachians, Skyline Drive and the Blue Ridge Parkway, were built specifically for sightseers and tourists. They are winding, sedate – the speed limit never exceeds 45mph (72km/h) – and closed to commercial vehicles. There isn't a "Gas Food Lodging" sign anywhere in sight, nor a gleam of neon. To find fast food and even gas, you have to leave the route briefly and venture into the back roads of Virginia and North Carolina.

Getting your kicks is a possibility, getting lost in the sticks is a virtual certainty. But the rewards for forgoing roads with higher speeds and corporate amenities are immense. This is a route filled with tales of moonshine, disappearing customs and the Appalachians' own take on jazz: old-time music and bluegrass.

It's getting close to Halloween when I join the northern end of Skyline Drive after a leisurely breakfast in the town of Front Royal. I feel like the slow speed of the roads is the whole point. There's no one behind me beeping or impatient to overtake. The route

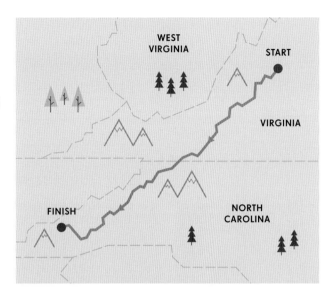

winds through mountain scenery with views that stretch for miles to distant vanishing points; the colors span a vast range: from the cheese-on-toast yellow of the tulip poplar to the vibrant red of sourwoods and maples.

Skyline Drive is the shorter of the two roads, sitting at their combined northern end. At 105 miles (169km) long, it can be covered easily in a day, though, at the higher elevations, the weather can be very fickle. Towards mid-afternoon, somewhere around milepost 78, mist swirls over the road and as I slow the car, a strange form appears on the pavement directly ahead of me. It's a large black bear, galumphing into the trees on the other side. It's only visible for a few seconds, but the whole atmosphere of the mountain seems instantly different: wilder and more threatening. At milepost 105, skyline drive comes to an end; from here the route continues on the longer Blue Ridge Parkway.

Half a day's drive along the parkway, close to milepost 213, sits the storied Blue Ridge Music Center. Overnight, high winds have felled a tree and taken down the power lines. Starved of electricity, the videos and recordings in the center don't work and, suddenly, we're a bit closer to the music's roots: two men in a shady corner, playing unamplified instruments, singing about the dark and the light of life in the mountains.

Every afternoon during the months that the center is open, local musicians play here for free. Today, 72-year-old Bobby Patterson is plucking a resonator banjo, accompanied by Willard Gayheart, 82. The music – gospel and secular – is still a vital part of life in

"The slow speed of the roads is the whole point. The route winds through mountain scenery with views that stretch for miles"

the region. Willard explains that, barely a generation ago, farmers hosted parties as a way of repaying neighbors for their help in bringing in a harvest. Hired musicians and tubs of moonshine would be the reward for a day of collective effort.

The ranger at the Blue Ridge Music Center rolls her eyes when I show her where I'm headed on the map. There's a weather warning: more heavy rain and high winds are expected toward evening. To stay off the top of the parkway, I leave the route and take the state roads, crossing the border from Virginia into North Carolina and passing small towns, Baptist churches, commercial Christmas tree plantations and huge patches of pumpkins, grown for Halloween.

But there's no avoiding the Blue Ridge Parkway. I'm booked to stay in a cabin close to milepost 256, so in the late afternoon, I bid small-town America farewell and head off back up the mountain.

The weather is worsening and the road has become astonishingly eerie: a riot of windblown leaves, heaving branches and fog gathering in the dips. By some miracle, I find the lodge just as night is falling. My cabin, overhung with waving branches

MEN AT WORK

The construction of Skyline Drive and the Blue Ridge Parkway began after the Great Depression in the 1930s, partly under Roosevelt's New Deal. Young, unskilled, unmarried men were enrolled in the Civilian Conservation Corps (CCC) and put to work on projects to protect the country's natural resources. The construction of the roads created jobs in the region, but also displaced residents along their lengths – some voluntarily, others forcibly.

From opposite left: scenic stops, local traffic and many bends make this a leisurely trip; the leaves and trees of Virginia ensure a vivid autumn drive. Previous pages: forest surrounds the Linn Cove Viaduct

and sitting in a hollow, clearly resembles the set of a horror film, but tucked up safely in bed, I hear no bears, or serial killers, just the death-throes of the storm.

By morning, the bad weather has finally passed. The rain and wind have denuded many trees, but the sun blazes through the ones that are left. At Linn Cove Viaduct I drive through some of the most uplifting scenery of the whole route. The viaduct itself is an architectural marvel. The last section of the route to be constructed, it was designed to have minimal impact on its surroundings. It seems to float above the slopes of Grandfather Mountain. From it, I look down on the huge belt of uplands that spread along the eastern seaboard of the United States all the way from New Jersey to Alabama.

I turn-off at milepost 385 to the town of Asheville, with barely half a day's drive to go until the southern end of the parkway. It's a good place to stop and celebrate the journey's conclusion – a lively, affluent place with a dynamic music and arts scene.

At the recommendation of two local musicians, I head to bluegrass night in Jack of the Wood, one of Asheville's live-music venues. The audience includes young hipsters who look like they've just finished a hard day logging or gathering ginseng. Flannel shirts, work boots, baseball caps and facial hair are the order of the day. The evening is a celebration of what's local, renewable, homemade. It seems that just as Appalachia's last mountain people are relinquishing their old ways, a new generation is looking to them for inspiration.

DIRECTIONS

Start // Skyline Drive's northern terminus lies at an intersection with Rte 340 near the town of Front Royal.
Finish // The Blue Ridge Parkway's southern end lies at the junction with Rte 441 on the boundary between the Great Smoky Mountains National Park and the Eastern Cherokee Reservation in North Carolina.
Distance // 574 miles (924km)
Getting there // Front Royal is about 1½ hours' drive west of Washington, DC.
Further away // From the end of the drive, head to Asheville, NC – a drive of a little over an hour.
When to drive // Fall. The broadleaved trees start their slow-motion firework display toward the end of September.
More info // www.visitskylinedrive.org; www. blueridgeparkway.org

Opposite: the Adirondacks in flaming color, New York

MORE LIKE THIS
LEAF PEEPING DRIVES

ADIRONDACK TRAIL, NEW YORK

Though it's New England that has the firmest hold on the imagination when it comes to fall color, it's actually upstate New York and the Adirondack Mountains that have some of the largest stands of old-growth forest in the Eastern US. There are a dozen scenic byways running through more than 9000 sq miles (23,000 sq km) of rippling mountains. While the 140-mile (225km) Central Adirondack Trail takes an east-west arc through the preserve, the 188-mile (303km) Adirondack Trail runs up the middle, largely following Rte 30. There are plenty of opportunities for hikes and waterside leaf peeping, from Great Sacandaga Lake to Indian, Tupper and Upper Saranac Lakes, as well as harvest festivals, apple picking and historic sites such as 1760s Johnson Hall and the 1876 Log Hotel that's now the Adirondack Experience museum.
Start // Fonda
Finish // Malone
Distance // 188 miles (303km)

PEI TIP TO TIP, CANADA

The smallest of Canada's provinces, Prince Edward Island takes on the same autumnal tints as its Atlantic neighbors, but its geology adds a subtle boost. The island is largely made of red sandstone, which gives the soil here its special hue. Deep among the woods and farmsteads, more than a dozen scenic heritage roads have been left unpaved to show the rich red clay, mirrored for a few precious weeks by the tree boughs arching above. Although some tourist businesses might have closed by the time the leaves are at their reddest, it's still a fantastic season to sample the island's seafood and farm produce, walk the dunes of Prince Edward Island National Park, and make a stop at Green Gables – the farmhouse home to the fictional red-haired heroine Anne.
Start // East Point
Finish // North Cape
Distance // 165 miles (266km)

AMONG THE GREAT LAKES, MICHIGAN

Surrounded on most sides by Lakes Huron, Michigan and Superior, Michigan's Upper Peninsula stretches more than 300 miles (480km) end to end, with comparatively few residents but plenty of forest. The 4-mile (6.4km) Mackinac Bridge, the UP's primary link to the "mainland," marks the official starting point for a tour. With some time set aside, given the distances involved here, you could crisscross between the shores of the Great Lakes, stopping at such prime spots for foliage as Tahquamenon Falls State Park, a Niagara in miniature, and the 19th-century lakeside ghost town of Fayette. At the end of the Keweenaw Peninsula, Copper Harbor is a tiny port on Lake Superior, whose 8.8-mile (14.2km) Brockway Mountain Drive offers some of the loftiest viewpoints between the Rockies and the Alleghenies – a truly grand finale.
Start // Mackinaw City
Finish // Copper Harbor
Distance // 438 miles (705km)

DRIVING AMERICA'S LONELIEST ROAD

Overlooked historic sites of the American West dot this drive, on which Ryan Ver Berkmoes is drawn by 1100 miles (1770km) of open road disappearing into the far horizon.

Bypassed by busy I-80 and largely forgotten, US 50 – a once vital cross-country link in the United States' web of highways – is a strip of gray asphalt and cracked concrete that meanders through no places in particular, across great swaths of the West. It's a route pioneers once endured – you can still see wagon wheel ruts here and there. These flinty folk would approve of boosters in Nevada in the 1980s, who took US 50 and its sparse traditional highlights, applied the very essence of the old bromide, "When life serves you lemons, make lemonade," and gave it the moniker: "America's loneliest road."

For anyone like me who gets itchy at the mere thought of a road stretching to the horizon and beyond, the promise of a lonely road is as alluring as California was to dreaming pioneers clumping West.

I've driven US 50 going east and going west, and I prefer the former, driving upstream against the tide of forgotten strivers and seeing what they left in their wake. And it's not just the odd failed frontier outpost, either. Across Nevada, Utah and Colorado, US 50 passes all manner of places America has tried to forget over the decades. From old outposts forgotten almost the day they were built to vast concentration camps where tens of thousands of American citizens were held against their will, and all framed by stark,

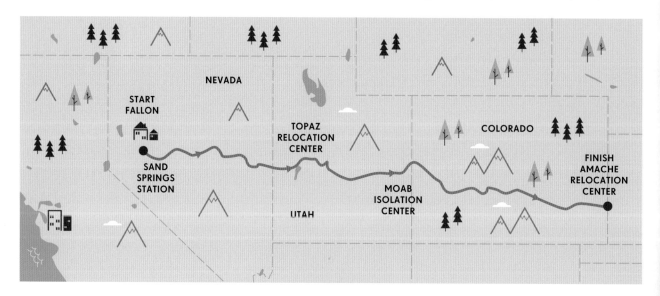

DRIVING MORE
OF US 50

This drive takes in 1,137 miles (1830km) of the 3,073 (4946km) miles that US 50 covers from Ocean City, Maryland to Sacramento, California. Heading west from Fallon, US 50 crosses the Nevada desert to the stark setting of Virginia City. From here the scenery's spectacular as the road crosses the Sierras, skirting the south edge of Lake Tahoe before the long descent to Sacramento. Going east from this drive's end point, the road cuts a swath through middle America, including Kansas City, and Cincinnati, where there's the unmissable National Underground Railroad museum. It finishes at Ocean City, right on the Atlantic.

"I pull over and just soak up the silent majesty, feeling like an astronaut who is no more than an infinitesimal speck in the emptiness of space"

windshield-filling expanses that embody the moonscapes of Buzz Aldrin's famous quote: "Magnificent desolation."

I start in Fallon, Nevada, where the last lights of the Reno exurbs fade out behind me. At the engaging Churchill County Museum, I meet the characters who've previously passed by as well as those who forsook the golden promise of California to make a life here, amid a surrounding color palette that runs from gray to brown. It's a well-curated primer for the road ahead.

Barely a half hour on, Sand Springs Station is an apt name for a forlorn stop on the route of the Pony Express, the failed Fedex precursor that has an outsize place in history, given it only lasted 17 months. Nothing but sand seems to spring from the arid earth, certainly not water. Among the ruins of stone buildings is a sign

with a visitor's description from 1860:

"The water near this vile hole was thick and stale with sulphury salts: it blistered even the hands. The station house was... roofless and chairless, filthy and squalid, with a smokey fire in one corner, and a table in the centre of an impure floor, the walls open to every wind, and the interior full of dust. Of the employees, all loitered and sauntered about... as cretins, except one, who lay on the ground crippled and apparently dying by the fall of a horse on his breast bone."

Continuing east through horizon-filling vistas of emptiness, I pull over and just soak up the silent majesty, feeling like an astronaut who is no more than an infinitesimal speck in the emptiness of space.

Up and over the aptly named Confusion Range, US 50 enters Utah. Near a wide spot in the road known as Hinckley, I careen along empty gravel roads through a rocky plain that on many maps simply reads 'Lava.' A few bleak miles and my first glimpse of green is a tiny sign, signaling I've arrived at a place of forgotten shame. The 'Topaz Relocation Site' was a concentration camp for over 11,000 men, women and children of Japanese descent during WWII. Almost all were American citizens who lost everything they had through forced relocation from their farms, businesses and homes in California to this desert in 1942.

There is little to remember these people, or the extraordinary violation of their rights as humans and citizens. I try to imagine counting the long winters here, peering into the far, featureless distance for any hint of a land beyond.

Midway through Utah, US 50 joins up with the fast-moving blur of I-70 for a spell. Secrets are never far. I take the turnoff for the geologic fantasyland of Arches National Park but stop in scrubland, a few miles short of the selfie-snapping crowds. A vandalized sign notes that this was the location of the 'Moab Isolation Center.' Today, no trace remains of this place internees of the Japanese concentration camps were moved to if they had the temerity to protest the violation of their rights. (Many were decorated veterans of the American Army in WWI.) Standing there in the relentless wind, I recall what the camp commandant told one of the inmates: "Anybody could die here, and they will never find his body."

US 50 manages to miss the literal rarified air of the resort end of the Rockies and the zoom-zoom of booming Denver, instead weaving through the tousled old steel city of Pueblo and onto the plains of eastern Colorado, which are as flat as stereotypical Kansas – except Kansas isn't this flat. Still, like so much of this drive, I am mesmerized by the stark colors. Here the endless blue sky is underpinned by ribbons of yellow grain and brown earth.

Bent's Old Fort National Historic Site is a faithful reconstruction of a tan adobe trading post complex where early pioneers and Native Americans traded goods in the 1830s, until floods of white settlers overwhelmed the tribes. Walking the trails around the fort, which weave between the clattering leaves of the cottonwood trees along the banks of the Arkansas River, I'm transported back 200 years.

My final US 50 stop is another Japanese-American concentration camp, this one with the euphemistic name 'Amache Relocation Center.' Remarkably – compared to Topaz – there is something to see here. Through the years, local students have restored sections of the camp, which held over 7,000. Among the exhibits, I pause to bear witness to slivers of the lives lived here: a few hardy ornamental shrubs planted by inmates who were clinging to their humanity.

US 50 continues into Kansas, where the metronomic rhythm of small towns along the route feels like civilization after the boundless solitude before.

From opposite: a cannon guards Bent's Old Fort National Historic Site; the crumbling walls of Sand Springs Pony Express Station. Previous page: US 50's magnificent desolation

DIRECTIONS

Start // Fallon, Nevada
End // Colorado-Kansas border
Distance // 1,137 miles (1,830km)
Getting there // Reno's airport is served by all major airlines and has car rental counters for all major firms. It's 65 miles (105km) west of Fallon.
When to go // As pioneers on wagon trains found out, summer is blazingly hot whereas blizzards can close the road in winter. Spring and fall are ideal times for this drive.
Where to stay // Overnight in larger towns and cities like Ely, Nevada; Salina, Utah; and Grand Junction, Gunnison and Pueblo in Colorado. Note that it can be 100 miles (161km) or more between gas stations in western Utah and Nevada.
What to listen to // Download the superb podcast *Order 9066*. Produced by the Smithsonian, it's an oral history of survivors of the Japanese-American concentration camps.

Opposite, from top: the eponymous cacti of Saguaro National Park; the historic suspension bridge over the Ohio River, just off the National Road in Wheeling, West Virginia

MORE LIKE THIS
AMERICA'S UNSTORIED ROADS

I-10 ACROSS ARIZONA AND NEW MEXICO

Cacti, colored deserts and fantastical eroded peaks keep the fast ride east on I-10 across Arizona and New Mexico visually interesting. But it's the stops where you discover history as dramatic as the landscapes that count. Casa Grande Ruins National Monument is the Gothic cathedral of the Hohokum people, who built this adobe tower – a veritable mixed-use high-rise – in the 12th century. Their petroglyphs enliven Saguaro National Park, which is named for its iconic cacti. The nearly indiscernible Butte Camp recalls the vast Japanese-American concentration camp that stood in this empty expanse. Just up the road from Las Cruces is the brilliant-white fantasyland of White Sands National Monument and – on the two days a year when it's open to the public – the Trinity Site, where the first atomic bomb was exploded.
Start // Phoenix, Arizona
Finish // Los Cruces, New Mexico
Distance // 388 miles (624km)

US 61 IN MISSISSIPPI AND TENNESSEE

US 61 in Mississippi is hyped as "the blues trail," but it's a challenge to find blues music along much of it today. Rather, on its Mississippi-River-hugging route through forgotten hamlets and horizon-filling cotton fields, the road plunges through the heart of America's enduring civil rights struggle. Vicksburg's National Military Park covers an epic Civil War battlefield where slaveholding Confederates held out for weeks against the Union Army. Excursions take in sites seared into the national conscience. Greenwood anchors the rural locales where Emmitt Till lived his final days before his murder. A house in Holly Springs documents the life of Ida B Wells, who fought against lynching and for voting rights, starting in the 1880s, an era when the notion of a black woman doing this was inconceivable. And Memphis has its superb museums devoted to racial justice and Martin Luther King.
Start // Vicksburg, Mississippi
Finish // Memphis, Tennessee
Distance // 221 miles (356km)

THE NATIONAL ROAD

The first federally built road in the US was the National Road, running from the Potomac River in western Maryland across the steep hills of Pennsylvania and the rolling farmlands of the Midwest, to the burg of Vandalia in the wilds of downstate Illinois, where funds ran out in the early 1830s. Today much of the route survives as US 36 across Pennsylvania, West Virginia, Ohio, Indiana and Illinois. It should be called the Heartland Road as it arrows through middle America. Often thought of as the Rust Belt for its dead industries, a trip here uncovers Amazon warehouses as vast as any old steel mill, farm towns trying to stay relevant, and booming cities like Columbus and Indianapolis. In the humble diners that often serve delicious food along the route, you'll hear first-hand the arguments and forces roiling today's American political landscape.
Start // Cumberland, Maryland
Finish // Vandalia, Illinois
Distance // 654 miles (1,053km)

SIERRA STARS: LAKE TAHOE TO YOSEMITE

While searching for hiking trails beneath glacier-carved peaks, Amy Balfour drives past brilliant blue lakes, High Sierra meadows, granite domes and the oldest "thirst parlor" in Nevada.

Soaring skyward on the eastern fringes of California, the Sierra Nevada range is a visual feast. Pine forests hug its slopes and valleys. Alpine lakes sparkle. Waterfalls plunge. Granite peaks and domes, carved by glaciers, add a rugged grandeur that has inspired the likes of photographer Ansel Adams and painter Albert Bierstadt. And with luminous day-long beauty, the mountains were fittingly dubbed the Range of Light by naturalist John Muir.

The Sierra Nevada stretches north-south for 430 miles (692km), linking the southern end of the Cascade Range near Lassen Peak to the Mojave Desert. More than 500 of its peaks rise above 10,000ft (3050m). It's also home to three national parks: Yosemite, Kings Canyon and Sequoia. My plan is to maximize the scenery – and minimize the traffic – while driving to bucket-list trails from Lake Tahoe south to Yosemite.

My adventure begins on the shores of Lake Tahoe. Known for its magnificent deep blue waters, the lake straddles the California–Nevada state line at a lofty 6245ft (1900m). A two-lane road encircles its 72-mile (116km) shoreline, carving a narrow path between the fortress-like mountains and the lake's pristine waters.

On the Nevada side, the ADA-accessible Tahoe East Shore Trail links the ski town of Incline Village with Sand Harbor State Park 3 miles (4.8km) south. Beside a lakeside boardwalk, I scrutinize the still waters. The lake is famed for its clarity, but algal growth has at times reduced visibility in recent years. The popular "Keep Tahoe Blue" bumper sticker underscores local concerns.

Across the lake, the Rubicon Trail in California rollercoasters up and down the shoreline for 4.5 miles (7.2km), unfurling between the lake and a forest thick with pines, firs and cedars. A historic

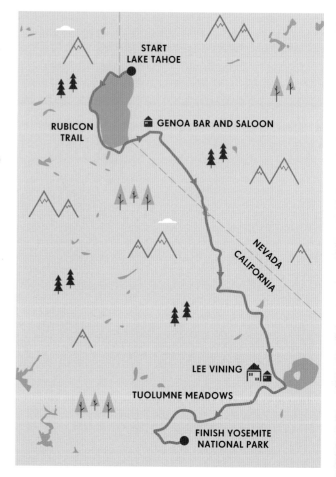

lighthouse, sandy coves, campgrounds festive with families and tranquil Emerald Bay are memorable diversions during my hike the next morning. I turn around near Vikingsholm, a Scandinavian-style mansion built in 1929.

Bursting at its dusty seams with knick-knackery and half-truths, the Genoa Bar and Saloon back in Nevada is a direct portal to the old West. According to the brochure the bartender hands me, this cozy watering hole on the eastern flanks of the Sierra-adjacent Carson Range dates from 1853, making it the oldest "thirst parlor" in Nevada. Looking around, I tend to believe this statement – but truth can be hard to pinpoint in and around the Sierra, a land of hidden mines, doomed pioneers and celebrated jumping frogs.

Behind me, somewhere, hangs Raquel Welch's leopard-print bra. She left it here, they say, during a movie shoot. To my left, an original wanted poster offers a reward for the capture of the murderer of Abraham Lincoln. I decide I like it here and order a beer.

East of the saloon, I follow the Eastern Sierra Scenic Byway (Hwy 395) south, encountering peaks that hunker dramatically over the flat Great Basin landscape. The highway rolls into tiny Lee Vining, a gateway town on the east side of Yosemite National Park. With its roadside ice-cream shack, homey mom-and-pop motels and plentiful souvenir shops, the town borders on kitschy.

At sunset, Mono Lake shimmers with a reflective blue sheen. From my shoreline perch north of town the lake exudes an eerie pull, with swaths of yellow-tinged sand and desert scrub illuminated against its still waters and dark volcanic cinder cones.

"The lake exudes an eerie pull, with swaths of yellow-tinged sand and desert scrub illuminated against its still waters and dark volcanic cinder cones"

More than one million years old and formed by the forces of fire and ice, the alkaline lake – which has no outlet – is among the oldest in the United States.

In the morning I rise early to beat the traffic into Yosemite. From Hwy 395 the narrow Lee Vining Scenic Byway (Hwy 120) shoots from the chalky-white Great Basin desertscape to the lush High Sierra in a mere 12 miles (19km) – while clinging to the flank of a steep mountain smothered in loose scree. The enormous granite mountains that surround my car glow a luminous pink in the morning light, but their grandeur feels vaguely ominous – likely due to the harrowing drop lurking beside the shoulder of the road.

The Tioga Pass entrance to Yosemite sits at 9945ft (3030m) – atop the loftiest highway pass in the Sierra Nevada. From here I drive west on Tioga Rd into a subalpine dream: a High Sierra landscape of jagged peaks, glacier-polished granite domes, soaring lodgepole pine forests and alpine lakes that shimmer a dazzling blue. The Lyell and Dana Forks of the Tuolumne River and several creeks drop from the surrounding Sierra Crest to feed

THE DONNER PARTY

The ill-fated Donner Party became trapped on Donner Pass as their wagon train rolled west during the brutal winter of 1846–47. Only 47 of the 89 pioneers survived. Their grisly tale of survival, which descended into cannibalism, is explored in the visitor center at Donner Memorial State Park, northwest of Lake Tahoe. The park is also home to Donner Lake, which has kayak and stand-up paddleboard rentals and a pleasant campground.

From opposite left: bikers on the road from Lee Vining into Yosemite National Park; Mono Lake, surrounded by calcareous tufa rock formations. Previous page: Tioga Pass, gateway to Yosemite National Park

the Tuolumne Meadows, which are dotted with wildflowers for a few glorious months in summer and early fall.

I hike through pines to the base of Lembert Dome. One of many granite domes scattered across the park, it was formed during the Tioga glacial period 20,000 years ago. My hiking boots maintain a reassuring grip on its barren southern slope as I scramble up to the summit. I'm not afraid of heights, but the exposed drop at the end of the slope is, well, scary.

A final push lands me on the 9450ft (2880m) summit, where 360-degree views are the payoff for the hair-raising scramble. To the east, the Sierra Crest stretches from Mt Conness to the Kuna Crest. The Cathedral Range punctuates the skyline to the south. Below me, to the west, lie the Tuolumne Meadows. John Muir, an early advocate for the park, called the meadows a "spacious and delightful high-pleasure ground."

My journey continues on Tioga Rd, where I picnic beside Tenaya Lake on smooth granite shores. Next up is Olmsted Point, which overlooks a stark landscape of glaciated rocks and glacier-carved monoliths. My adventure concludes in Yosemite Valley 50 miles (80km) south, where temperatures are warmer and the crowds noticeably thicker.

Before driving into Yosemite, I pull over for the panorama from Tunnel View, which overlooks the highlights ahead: El Capitan rising to the north, pine forests and meadows blanketing the valley floor, and Bridalveil Fall dropping to the south. A peek-a-boo glimpse of Half Dome ties together the entire scene.

DIRECTIONS

Start // Lake Tahoe
Finish // Yosemite National Park
Distance // 215 miles (346km)
Getting there // Lake Tahoe is 200 miles (322km) northeast of San Francisco via I-80. Alternatively, fly into Reno, Nevada, instead. It's a mere 35 miles (56km) to the northwest via scenic Hwy 431, the Mt Rose Scenic Byway.
When to drive // Tioga Road is open when it's clear of heavy snow, which is usually June through October. Lake Tahoe is packed with ski resorts, so highways are regularly plowed in winter, but tire chains may be required on snowy days.
Where to stay // Cedar House Sport Hotel in Truckee; Basecamp Tahoe City in Tahoe City; The Ahwahnee in Yosemite National Park
More info // visitinglaketahoe.com

Opposite: the towering giant sequoia
known as General Sherman in
Sequoia National Park, California

MORE LIKE THIS
SIERRA NEVADA DRIVES

KINGS CANYON & SEQUOIA NATIONAL PARKS

Superlatives abound in Kings Canyon and Sequoia, two adjacent national parks marked by their enormous sequoia trees, powerful waterfalls and glacial valleys. Kings Canyon Scenic Byway drops for 30 dramatic miles (48km) within its namesake canyon, twisting past chiseled rock faces laced with waterfalls. Hiking trails to Mist Falls and Zumwalt Meadow begin near Roads End, which overlooks the mighty Kings River. Enormous sequoia trees cluster at General Grant Grove, with more big trees visible along the Generals Hwy, which links Kings Canyon National Park with Sequoia National Park to the south. Here, the General Sherman Tree, the world's biggest tree by volume, rises 275ft (84m) in the Giant Forest. Drive Crescent Meadow Rd to the Tunnel Log, then tackle the dizzyingly scenic drive into Mineral King Valley.

Start // Kings Canyon National Park
Finish // Sequoia National Park
Distance // 160 miles (257km)

EASTERN SIERRA SCENIC BYWAY

Running north-south along the base of the Sierra Nevada, Hwy 395 is the no-nonsense sidekick to a colorful cast of geologic wonders, outdoor adventures and thought-provoking historic sites. The southern gateway is tiny Lone Pine, a convenient basecamp for exploring the rounded rock formations of the Alabama Hills, which glow photogenically at sunset. Just west, Mt Whitney soars to 14,505ft (4421m) – the tallest peak in the Lower 48. A permit is needed to hike to its summit. During WWII more than 10,000 people of Japanese ancestry were incarcerated at a concentration camp at the Manzanar Historic Site. The Methuselah tree, more than 4800 years old, hangs tight in the Ancient Bristlecone Pine Forest. Hike, mountain bike and ski Mammoth Lakes, a four-season playground. The surreal volcanic formation at the Devils Postpile National Monument is just west.

Start // Lone Pine
Finish // Mammoth Lakes
Distance // 155 miles (250km)

EBBETTS PASS SCENIC BYWAY

From the western Sierra, Hwy 4 jogs through a handful of mountain hamlets and forests before crossing Ebbetts Pass, which is only open in summer and fall. For outdoor fanatics, the drive is practically a road trip through paradise. Adventure options include hiking through sequoias, paddling tranquil lakes, climbing granite boulders and strapping on skis or snowshoes in winter. The trip kicks off in Murphys, a picturesque gold rush town where wine tasting rooms and great indie restaurants line the main drag. Enormous sequoias and hiking trails are plentiful in Calaveras Big Trees State Park, while sandy beaches border gorgeous Lake Alpine. Ebbetts Pass offers top-of-the world scenery at 8736ft (2662m) while Hope Valley is a verdant wonderland of wildflowers, grassy meadows and burbling streams all encircled by Sierra Nevada peaks.

Start // Murphys
Finish // Hope Valley
Distance // 95 miles (155km)

ON CAPE BRETON'S CABOT TRAIL

Joe Bindloss encounters Nova Scotia's windblown coastline, a rich blend of Gaelic, Acadian and Mi'kmaq cultures, vibrant fall foliage and a stunning national park on Canada's Cabot Trail.

L ife on the island of Cape Breton, in the far eastern corner of Canada, goes with the flow. Lobster boats chug into the horizon; whales rise and fall beyond the shore; bears lumber through the island's boreal forests; the Atlantic wind carries the rhythmic notes of Gaelic fiddles.

Surrounded by the Gulf of St Lawrence on one side and the Atlantic Ocean on the other, Cape Breton's northern half is home to the Cabot Trail, a beautiful 185-mile (297km) road that hugs cliffs, then winds and climbs over the Cape Breton highlands before dropping down to grass-covered sand dunes and tranquil hamlets.

Alexander Graham Bell, he of telephone-invention fame and a regular visitor to the island, declared that of all the natural places he'd seen around the world, "Cape Breton outrivals them all."

But the Cabot Trail is more than a drive with stunning geography, ocean vistas, wilderness and wildlife. It's also a cultural circuit enriched by charismatic inhabitants and centuries-old traditions. The Mi'kmaq people inhabited the island when the first Europeans, led by explorer John Cabot, arrived in 1497. In later centuries, many Scottish, Irish and English settled. So did Acadians, descendants of the French, all contributing to a colorful Gaelic melange.

Many fishing villages were not accessible by land until as late as the 1930s, when car travel over the Cape Breton highlands became possible. In 1936, the Cape Breton Highlands National Park was created in the northern section of the island, preserving 366 sq miles (949 sq km) of coastal wilderness, forests and mountains. The road – which encompasses much of the park – was gradually paved in sections between 1940 and 1961.

The route itself is circular so I can head in either direction (though the cliff-clinging, counterclockwise trip offers the best views). Driving

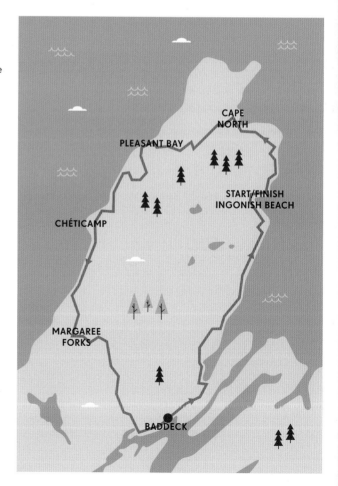

"The road winds through corridors of pine and spruce, before I emerge at a cliff edge and a view of the icy ocean"

here is a pleasant, leisurely experience. While the maximum speed is between 35mph and 50mph (60–80km/h), the trail has a pace of its own; locals regularly stop their vehicles in the middle of the highway – for a pedestrian, a moose or simply a friendly chat with a neighbor heading in the oncoming direction.

Officially, the Cabot Trail starts and ends in Baddeck, a pretty harbor town on Bras d'Or Lake. I take a quick predrive look in the Alexander Graham Bell National Historic Site, a museum that displays Bell's fascinating inventions, including his hydrofoil.

From Baddeck, I head north to St Ann's, home of the Colaisde na Gàidhlig, the only Gaelic college in North America, where you can learn to speak the language, step-dance or play the bagpipes.

The road then winds through corridors of pine and spruce, before I emerge at a cliff edge and a view of the icy ocean. In its northern section the road heads around the national park, whose hiking trails and campgrounds make it the perfect stop for adventurers.

You should get used to stopping. At North River, you can jump in a kayak and paddle up an inlet while keeping an eye out for whales and otters. At Ingonish Beach, enjoy a round of golf at Highlands Links, a gorgeous course designed by Stanley Thompson in 1939.

I have my sights set further north. Back on the trail, at Cape North on the northernmost tip, a detour takes me to the tiny fishing port of Bay St Lawrence. Here I jump aboard a whale-watching boat and cruise alongside the bay's rugged coastline, whose numerous waterfalls and sea caves are just as beautiful as the pilot whales and dolphins that swim around the boat.

Back on land and feeling peckish, I head from Cape North to the remote settlement of Meat Cove, so named because in the 1700s, European settlers slaughtered moose, deer and bear there (for antlers and hides). It's a must-visit for the cove's only chowder hut that whips up seafood chowder, lobster rolls and crab sandwiches.

The northwestern shore of Cape Breton – between Cape North and Pleasant Bay – has magnificent "look-offs," viewing points that frequently dot the route. These showcase the island's deciduous trees – birch and maple – that transform into an explosion of autumn colors. Bald eagles frequently soar overhead.

Heading south at Pleasant Bay, steep cliffs morph into lowlands comprising grass-covered dunes and sandy beaches. A shock of striped red, white and blue flags (and even buildings) signifies my arrival into Chéticamp, a village that proudly proclaims its French Acadian roots. A sign also states cheekily that the locals are "Proud to be Hookers," a nod to Chéticamp's expert hooked-rug makers. The best examples of their work are exhibited in the hooked-rug museum, Les Trois Pignons (www.lestroispignons.com).

Another cultural event is the annual Celtic Colours International Festival in October, when local and international artists fiddle, pipe and dance in churches and school halls.

But whatever the time of year, it's worth the drive just to kick up your heels at a *ceilidh* (pronounced cay-lee), a Gaelic gathering where all are welcome to eat, drink and be merry to a backdrop of local folk music, and Cape Breton's exceptional hospitality.

PARKLIFE

In summer, Parks Canada (www.pc.gc.ca) offers a range of fabulous activities in the Cape Breton Highlands National Park. You can hike at sunset along the scenic Skyline Trail with a park interpreter, enjoy the gourmet contents of a Parks Canada picnic basket, or learn to cook, crack and feast on a lobster. At night, rub shoulders with the region's ghosts on a lantern walk or wander through the park with a guide to view the star-filled sky.

Opposite, clockwise from top left: moose are a common sight on Cape Breton; an Acadian lighthouse in Chéticamp; winding through Cape Breton. Previous page: the Cabot Trail undulates around a cliffside

DIRECTIONS

Start/Finish // Baddeck
Distance // 185 miles (297km)
Getting there // Sydney, the capital of Cape Breton, is a one-hour flight from Halifax Stanfield International Airport on the Nova Scotia peninsula. By car, it's a 4½-hour drive from Halifax to Sydney via the Canso Causeway.
When to drive // June to the end of October is the prime season. During autumn the deciduous trees show their true colors and hundreds of performers kick up a musical Gaelic storm at the Celtic Colours International Festival.
Where to stay // Keltic Lodge (kelticlodge.ca) is a handsome lodge above the Highlands Links Golf Course, perched on a cliff overlooking the Ingonish Beach.
Where to eat // Don't miss the fishcakes at the Rusty Anchor Restaurant (therustyanchorrestaurant.com).

Opposite, from top: Trail Ridge Road makes its way through high alpine tundra in Rocky Mountain National Park, Colorado; Waimea River wends through the magnificent Waimea Canyon on Kaua'i, Hawai'i

MORE LIKE THIS
DRAMATIC LANDSCAPES

WAIMEA CANYON DRIVE, KAUA'I

These islands may be small but they present some immense scenery for road tripping. On Kaua'i, of all its unique wonders, none can touch Waimea Canyon for grandeur. A gargantuan chasm of ancient lava rock 10 miles (16km) long and more than 3500ft (1067m) deep in places, it's nicknamed the Grand Canyon of the Pacific for good reason. Drives here on a clear day are phenomenal. A paved road follows the entire length of the canyon, climbing from the coast 19 miles (31km) to Pu'u o Kila lookout point. Along the way, the Garden Isle gives a rollicking display of its tropical attributes: a rippling rust-red valley, lush moss-green foliage and streaming waterfalls. Waipo'o Falls drop Rapunzel-like over a height of 800ft (244m) and can be spied from numerous points along the drive.
Start // Waimea
Finish // Pu'u o Kila Lookout
Distance // 19 miles (31km)

WHITE RIM ROAD, UTAH

The otherworldly terrain of Canyonlands National Park is intimidating enough, but once you leave the asphalt for the gravel of the White Rim Road, it feels like driving on Mars. Sneaking along the edge of sheer cliff walls, and open only to 4WD vehicles and mountain bikers with special permits, this epic 100-mile (161km) loop was constructed by Cold War-era uranium miners, encircling the Island in the Sky mesa. You'll find campsites but no water in this arid, desert country; if you want creature comforts and roads with guardrails you've come to the wrong canyon. The payoff comes in the best desert views this side of Olympus Mons.
Start // Junction of Potash Rd and Schafer Trail
Finish // Mineral Bottom Rd
Distance // 100 miles (161km)

TRAIL RIDGE ROAD, COLORADO

In Colorado's Rocky Mountain National Park, the foreboding peaks look like an impassable barrier. But Trail Ridge Road does cross it, and in stunning fashion. Climbing up to 12,183ft (3713m), the western end of Hwy 34 is the highest paved through-road in the country. (The road up Colorado's Mt Evans reaches 14,240ft/4340m, but you have to go back the way you came.) About 11 miles of the route runs above the tree line, opening up vistas across the peaks and into the thickly wooded valleys below, perhaps with sightings of elk lower down or bighorn sheep higher up. The driving season is short, with snowplows usually opening the highway around Memorial Day in May (early road-trippers might still find snowbanks either side); most of the drive beyond the Many Parks Curve Overlook closes again in mid-October.
Start // Estes Park
Finish // Grand Lake
Distance // 47 miles (76km)

SOUTH AMERICA

A HIGHWAY RUNS THROUGH IT

Kevin Raub tackles Brazil's Transpantaneira Highway, crossing a slice of the world's largest wetlands while dodging caimans, capybaras, anteaters and mesmerizing birdlife en route.

Brazil's Transpantaneira "Highway" (MT-060) begins in the one-horse town of Poconé – although there are actually way more horses than that, and very few of anything else.

Before setting out, I'd advise fortifying yourself with a bite to eat in Mato Grosso's capital, Cuiabá, 65 miles (104km) northwest. Home to nearly a million people, it's a hectic city blessed with an abundance of excellent restaurants. These serve the hearty cowboy cuisine of the Pantanal – piranha soup, grilled catfish with deep-red annatto, cassava stew, succulent grilled meats, chicken with rice, and locally harvested *pequi* fruit.

Conversely, Poconé is only home to 33,300 people and has a distinct lack of interesting dining options. I know this because it's lunchtime and I'm hungry, having made the mistake of setting out from Cuiabá without eating. I tap a local bus driver for some restaurant intel. He's parked on the side of the road, feet propped up on the open windowsill, seemingly dozing in and out of consciousness. "You're looking for lunch?" he asks, smiling wryly. "In Poconé, even the restaurants close for lunch!" In other words, I should have eaten in Cuiabá.

The Transpantaneira Hwy was originally built in 1973, with the idea of crossing the entirety of the Pantanal. In theory, the road would have connected Cuiabá with the neighboring state of Mato Grosso do Sul and its capital, Corumba, on the border with Bolivia. As the toucan flies, it would have only been a 256-mile (412km) undertaking. But building a road across the world's largest tropical wetlands was a wholly unrealistic project (to say nothing of the environmental catastrophe that would have been wrought) – part of the road is completely flooded during the rainy season, rendering it useless for half the year.

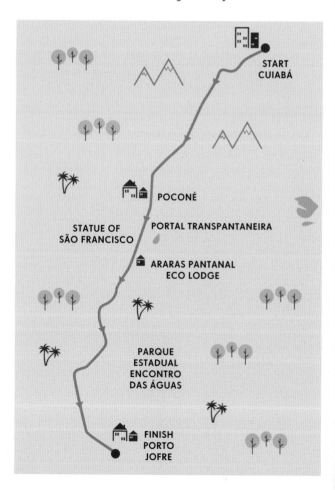

"*Every minute or two I apply the brakes in order to ogle something potentially deadly, shockingly docile or deliriously cute*"

As soon as the roadworks reached the Cuiabá River, in what today is referred to as Porto Jofre, it became clear that a large bridge would need to be built, so the project was wisely halted. Today, the Transpantaneira is a 91-mile (147km) dirt road that traverses around 120 bridges, most of which are of the rickety wooden variety.

A highway it is not. But to take on the small, drivable portion is to navigate one of the most dramatic and wildlife-rich panoramas on Earth. This gargantuan, Unesco-listed floodplain is slightly larger than Kyrgyzstan, marginally smaller than Belarus, and 10 times the size of the Florida Everglades. A road trip here reveals astonishing changes of scenery – grasslands, lakes, dry forests, rivers and gallery forests.

I have driven the Transpantaneira three times and if I *only* consider the birdlife I've seen, my mind is blown – hyacinth macaws, toucans, jabiru storks, herons, egrets, spoonbills, ibis, cuckoos and kingfishers. A total of 656 bird species have been recorded and they are everywhere, in astonishing sizes and colors. Yet there's so much more to the Pantanal.

Despite the lack of food, the town of Poconé does have gas – the last fill-up opportunity on this route. I had set off in a standard rental from Cuiabá, which is all you need in dry season... provided it hasn't recently rained. Heading southwest out of Poconé, the scenery is a far cry from the state's name – *mato grosso* means "thick forest" in Portuguese. Flat ranchland and wide-open spaces dominate the landscape in all directions.

Around Km 16 comes the first requisite stop, the Portal Transpantaneira. This Instagram-ready wooden gate declares in Portuguese: *Aqui começa o Pantanal do Mato Grosso* ("Here begins the Mato Grosso Pantanal"). A few kilometers later, the wonderful 30ft (7m) tall statue of São Francisco, the protector of ecology, provides another photo op.

From here on it becomes slow going. Dodging giant potholes and easing over suspect bridges is par for the course. I'm not timing it, but just about every minute or two I apply the brakes in order to ogle something potentially deadly, shockingly docile or deliriously cute. Remarkable fauna crowds each mile from this point onwards.

The road is teeming with *jacaré* (caimans), a cousin of the alligator. In between the gatherings of these crocodilian bandits, a pack of capybaras sit idling here and there, often with their backsides facing the road – a stance that gives them a distinct air of not giving a damn. A giant anteater (a rare spotting!) hobbles over the distant plain. And a couple of attached-at-the-hip macaws squawk across the horizon, their distinct soundtrack instantly recognizable to anyone who spends time in the Pantanal.

I stop at the pioneering Araras Pantanal Eco Lodge (Km 32), which delivers a winning trifecta – the road's most luxurious accommodations, its most sustainably focused ethos and its best food. All of those are the realized dreams of legendary conservationist André Thuronyi. I ramble up one of the lodge's three observation towers, the perfect perch for spotting the rare hyacinth macaws for which the lodge is named. This majestically blue bird is the largest parrot by length in the world. They fly in pairs (macaws tend to couple up for life) and seeing these outstretched marvels gliding side-by-side is a true testament to Mother Nature's magic.

In debatably foolish fashion, I go for a run as the sun sets. There is a lot in the Pantanal that could potentially kill someone, and I might present an alluring challenge – but I'm hyped up on survival-of-the-fittest adrenaline, along with the sounds of things that go bump at twilight.

The next day, the grid is left well behind at Km 65 – from here on out, everything runs on generator and solar power. Just off the road, massive jabiru storks (known colloquially as *tuiuiú*) bob across the landscape, doing their signature shuffle while searching for eels, fish and aquatic snakes.

At Km 105, still-denser vegetation emerges. This is wild, wild country. Ahead, Porto Jofre is set to mark the end of the road, but not before a toucan flies by, the bright orange of its signature beak streaking across my sightline through the windshield. And here I thought they only existed on boxes of Fruit Loops.

JAGUARS

The Pantanal is one of the few places on Earth that large numbers of jaguars call home, but habitat loss coupled with recent drought and wildfires are seriously threatening the largest cat in the Americas. However, with a population as high as 4000 by some estimates, the Holy Grail of Pantanal wildlife sightings remains possible. Porto Jofre is famous for sightings, especially on the Cuiabá River and its channels, from June to November.

Opposite, clockwise from top left: toucans, jaguars and giant anteaters can be spotted in the Pantanal. Previous page: the Transpantaneira Hwy crosses many channels; a pair of skimmers and a pair of jabiru storks

DIRECTIONS

Start // Cuiabá
Finish // Porto Jofre
Distance // 156 miles (251km)
Getting there // Marechal Rondon International Airport in Cuiabá is the nearest airport and the jumping-off point for all trips in the Northern Pantanal. From there, it's a 62-mile (100km) drive to Poconé. You can rent cars at the airport.
When to drive // May to October
What to take // A full tank of gas and insect repellent.
Pit stop // BarAra (Km 32.5) is popular for beer, *galinhada* (chicken and rice stew) and fried *pacu* (river fish) ribs.
Tour operators // Ailton Lara at Pantanal Nature (www.pantanalnature.com.br) is a jaguar specialist. He also owns Pantanal Jaguar Camp (www.pantanaljaguarcamp.br) in Porto Jofre.

*Opposite: the powerful Iguazú
Falls cover the border between
Argentina and Brazil*

MORE LIKE THIS
SOUTH AMERICAN NATURE

A PARANÁ RIVER RUN

The Paraná River, a 3030-mile (4880km) beast raveling through Brazil, Paraguay and Argentina, is part of the larger Paraguay-Paraná System, responsible for the annual flooding that makes the Pantanal one of the world's most magical bowls of biodiversity. This ride runs parallel to the river in Argentina's northeastern corner, ending at the mighty Iguazú Falls on the Brazilian border. Heading out from the Iberá Provincial Nature Reserve, across a mix of unpaved and paved roads, a landscape of burnt-red earth and tropical forest emerges. You can visit the beautiful tea plantation at Establecimiento Las Marías, one of Argentina's largest yerba mate producers; Saltos Del Moconá, a unique waterfall running parallel to the river for an astonishing 1.8 miles (3km); and the Jesuit ruins at San Ignacio Miní. Finally, Iguazú: the world's largest waterfall.
Start // Colonia Carlos Pellegrini
Finish // Puerto Iguazú
Distance // 337 miles (543km)

ECUADOR'S SPONDYLUS

Ecuador's epic coastal run, dubbed the Spondylus (or Ruta del Sol) by a government tourism initiative, crosses all the coastal provinces of Ecuador. This route has it all – nature reserves, jungle, beaches, wildlife and ruins. Highlights include Ecuador's only coastal national park (Parque Nacional Machalilla), the Indigenous community of Agua Blanca, sweeping sunset views at Mirador de Salango and numerous idyllic beaches. Los Frailes, for example, is a particularly pretty patch of sand between Machalilla and Puerto López. Don't miss trading your wheels for a boat to reach Isla de la Plata, touted as a "poor man's Galapagos." A spondylus, incidentally, is a sacred seashell used as a symbol of prosperity in pre-Columbian times.
Start // Atacames
Finish // Salinas
Distance // 352 miles (566km)

URUGUAY'S INLAND HIGHLIGHTS

When it comes to Uruguay, the capital Montevideo and the coast almost always command the attention of travelers. But the interior hides a boatload of off-the-beaten path natural wonders. Begin just south of the Brazilian border at Parque Natural Regional Valle del Lunarejo, which is flush with dense green foliage, freshwater-carved canyons, caves, vertical rock walls and waterfalls. Over 150 bird species have been recorded here, alongside intriguing wildlife such as small anteaters, margays (wild cats), coatis, prehensile-tailed porcupines and gray brocket deer. From here, Ruta 5 cuts through the heart of Uruguay. Small towns like San Gregorio de Polanco entice with beach opportunities on Rincón del Bonete lake; and Cerro de los Cuervos (Vulture Gorge) is home to many of the country's best hiking trails.
Start // Parque Natural Regional Valle del Lunarejo
Finish // Cerro de los Cuervos
Distance // 323 miles (520km)

ECUADOR'S AVENUE OF THE VOLCANOES

Regis St Louis breathes in crisp mountain air as he drives past highland villages, topaz lagoons and towering peaks on this journey across the Ecuadorian Andes.

The longest mountain range in the world snakes along the western reaches of South America, stretching some 5500 miles (8851km) from Venezuela to southern Patagonia. Ecuador has only a small section of the Andes, though its soaring peaks do not lack for drama. Dubbed the "Avenue of the Volcanoes" by 19th-century German naturalist Alexander von Humboldt, the Inter-Andean Valley courses along the spine of this relatively compact nation, and is flanked by more than 70 mountains and volcanoes – over two dozen of which are still active.

This landscape of fire and ice forms a magnificent backdrop to both tiny Indigenous villages and sprawling cities, as well as cloud forests, glacial lakes and misty grasslands. I aim to see some of its biggest peaks while getting a taste of Andean culture as I drive the roads between Ecuador's highland cities.

Wisps of morning fog cling to the rooftops as I stand in line for the TeleferiQo, an aerial tram that glides up the slopes of Volcán Pichincha above Quito. A young family joins me as we board the glass-walled gondola and soar across meadows and eucalypts, then high above the tree line to Cruz Loma, the terminus of the tramway. At the top a sign reads *Precaución: 4100m de altura. Despacio – No corra* (Warning: 4100m elevation. Go slowly – don't run). Far below me, Quito stretches along the valley floor, a vast agglomeration of homes, office towers and churches interrupted by dark patches of green – the city's parks, which are the only recognizable landmarks from this height. Verdant hills frame the city on either side, while rolling clouds engulf distant Volcán Cayambe and the peaks beyond.

"*Caballo?*" a man leading a horse calls to me as I contemplate the view. It turns out Cruz Loma is a bit shy of the mountain's high

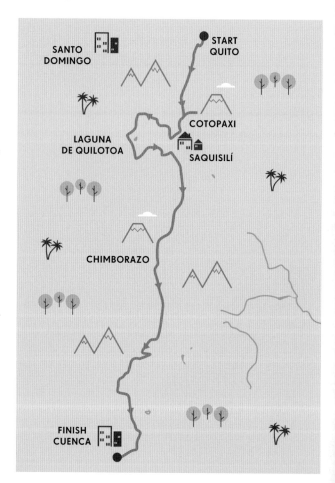

point. You can hire horses or rely on your own feet for the final four-hour slog to the 15,407ft (4696m) summit of Pichincha. Since I feel winded just tying my shoes, and the road is calling to me, I forgo the climb and return to the bottom.

The sun is in full force, casting a spectral glare through my windshield as I join the traffic heading south and make my way onto a well-paved stretch of the Carretera Panaméricana, a road that traverses Ecuador north and south (and is one chink of the 19,000-mile chain of roadways connecting Alaska with southern Chile). I spot lush mountains through my passenger window, the low brooding humps of Corazón (an inactive stratovolcano) as well as occasional glimpses of the twin snow-dusted peaks of the Illinizas further off. The best views, though, are to the west, and at one brief stretch in the road, the clouds finally dissipate, revealing a full and majestic profile of Cotopaxi, my next destination.

The clouds arrive, obscuring all but the lower slopes of the mountain, as I roll into my lodging for the night. The elegantly rustic Hacienda San Agustín de Callo was once a monastery and before that an Incan stronghold, and there are still a few mortarless walls standing that display the craftsmanship of Incan builders. By the 18th century, the hacienda was already hosting notable guests including Alexander von Humboldt and English mountain climber Edward Whymper. I feel as though I've slipped back a few centuries as I sip tea by the fireplace and listen to the wind howling outside the drawing room.

The next day I rise just after dawn for a vivid glimpse of Cotopaxi at first light. Its near-perfect conical shape looks almost like a child's rendering of the prototypical volcano, with its snow-encrusted summit shimmering in the early morning sun. Before departing, I take a stroll on the variety of alpine meadow known as the *páramo*. Off in the distance I see a few woolly quadrupeds (llamas? alpacas?) that cast a furtive glance my way before disappearing over the horizon.

Near the settlement of Guaytacama, I leave the Panaméricana behind and drive on toward the small village of Saquisilí. Pedestrians pack the streets as I near the Plaza Grande. Today is Thursday, Saquisili's big market day, which brings villagers from across the region to shop and sell their wares at hectic squares across town. Woven baskets, shiny saddles, piles of corn, slender stalks of sugarcane, buckets of bright red tomatoes, heavy tapestries and cooking pots of all shapes and sizes pack the stands. Tailors work antique-looking sewing machines, while the scent of grilled meat wafts over the plaza from a row of food stalls. On the outskirts of town, the animal market is also doing a lively trade as Kichwa-speaking farmers haggle over chickens, rabbits, sheep, goats and llamas, as well as *cuy* (guinea pig), which is a delicacy in these parts.

The sun is still shining as I head west along a narrow two-lane road past rolling farmlands and green hills, with peaks crowding the horizon. The going gets steeper and the views more striking as I zigzag up steep switchbacks above plunging valleys. I pass through Indigenous settlements with powerful sounding names like Chisulchi, Sigchos and Chugchilán, before finally arriving at a viewpoint overlooking one of Ecuador's most striking sights. Some 1300ft (400m) below me lies the volcanic crater lake of Laguna de Quilotoa. Peaks surround blue-green waters that reflect the clouds overhead.

My final leg of the journey takes me past Chimborazo, Ecuador's tallest peak at 20,549ft (6263m), and Sangay, the country's most active volcano – the glacier-topped mountain has been erupting since 2019. The following day I reach the outskirts of Cuenca. The shadows are lengthening as I stop at Mirador Turi. From here, the whole city spreads before me, and the street lamps around town glow faintly in the late afternoon. I follow the line of mountains framing the city off to the north, and try to imagine what lies beyond: the great line of volcanoes that march from here to the Ecuadorian capital. More than towering landmarks, they seem to embody the soul of this Andean nation.

TIGUA PAINTINGS

During the 1970s, a young Indigenous man from the community of Tigua near Laguna Quilotoa began painting colorful scenes from Kichwa legends. The artist, who spent his days growing potatoes and tending llamas, depicted these legends against the beautiful Andean scenery where he lived. Toaquiza's art has brought fame to Tigua, and today more than 300 painters are at work in the highlands, with about 20 studios in the community itself.

"Verdant hills frame the city on either side, while rolling clouds engulf distant Volcán Cayambe and the peaks beyond"

Opposite: vicuña and Volkswagen near Volcán Chimborazo. Previous Page: due to the Earth's bulge, Chimborazo is our closest point to the stars

DIRECTIONS

Start // Quito
Finish // Cuenca
Distance // 392 miles (631km)
Getting there // Quito has direct flights from Miami, Atlanta, Houston, Madrid and several cities in Latin America.
When to drive // June to September are the warmest, driest months in the highlands. January to April is cooler and wetter.
Where to stay // La Basílica Hotel (www.hotelbasilicaquito. com) in Quito's historic center has fine rooms and kind staff. Cuenca's Hotel Victoria occupies a grand 17th-century mansion overlooking the river.
Slow travel // Take things slowly, especially off the main highways. Be mindful of pedestrians, livestock and potholes.
Detours // Just west of Cuenca, you'll find the wildlife-rich Parque Nacional Caja, with trails across misty grasslands.

MORE LIKE THIS
ENCOUNTERING
MOUNTAIN CULTURES

PRE-COLUMBIAN CULTURES, CHILE

The vast region of Norte Grande stretches from coastal hills to Andean peaks across one of the driest deserts on Earth. Before heading into the highlands, visit the Museo de Sitio Colón 10 in the seaside city of Arica, where some 32 excavated Chinchorro mummies lie in situ. It's a short drive east into the Azapa Valley, where you can learn about the world's oldest known mummies (dating back to 7000 BCE) in the Museo Arqueológico San Miguel de Azapa, then follow the winding road skyward to Putre, an Aymara village perched at a dizzying elevation of 11,581ft (3530m). Leave the beaten path behind for a trip into Parque Nacional Lauca, a Unesco Biosphere Reserve that's home to remote highland villages set amid snow-sprinkled volcanoes, sparkling lakes and isolated hot springs.

Start // Arica
Finish // Parque Nacional Lauca
Distance // 979 miles (1575km)

THE CHIRIQUÍ HIGHLANDS, PANAMA

People from Chiriquí claim their province has it all: Panama's tallest mountains, longest rivers and most fertile valleys. Chiriquí is also a place of incomparable beauty. From the lowland village of David, you'll head north to Boquete, a small town with a spring-like climate year-round and misty cloud forests outside of town. Keep heading higher to reach the small settlement of El Salto. From here, you'll leave the car behind for an ascent up Volcán Baru, Panama's highest peak, with views of both the Atlantic and the Pacific Oceans on clear days. Zigzag your way to the other side of Baru to reach serene mountain villages like Volcán, Bambito and Cerro Punta. Near the road's end, take a hike in Parque Internacional La Amistad, harboring an impressive array of wildlife.

Start // David
Finish // Parque Internacional La Amistad
Distance // 122 miles (196km)

NEWFOUND GAP ROAD, NORTH CAROLINA

The only paved route that bisects the Great Smoky Mountains National Park also provides a taste of frontier life. Starting in Cherokee, North Carolina, you'll soon reach the Mountain Farm Museum, which evokes life on a typical farmstead of the late 19th century. In the summer the barnyard is full of livestock, and down-home music jams sometimes happen on the porch. Up the road, Mingus Mill is a turbine-powered mill that grinds wheat and corn much as it has since its opening in 1886. Further on, stop for a hike along the Kephart Prong Trail, where you can wander past the ruins of an old Civilian Conservation Corps (CCC) camp dating back to 1933. Don't miss the views from the Rockefeller Memorial, where President Franklin D Roosevelt formally dedicated the park in 1940.

Start // Cherokee, North Carolina
Finish // Gatlinburg, Tennessee
Distance // 33 miles (53km)

Clockwise, from top: the Great Smoky Mountains National Park, North Carolina; Parinacota church in Parque Nacional Lauca, Chile; the Caldera River in Boquete, Panama

THE SALAR DE UYUNI

A sea of salt, vibrantly colored lakes, weird rock formations, steaming fumaroles and floating islands await Etain O'Carroll in the hauntingly surreal landscape of southwest Bolivia.

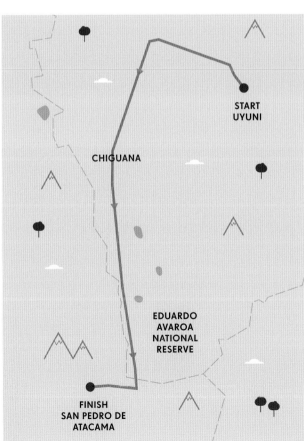

START
UYUNI

CHIGUANA

EDUARDO
AVAROA
NATIONAL
RESERVE

FINISH
SAN PEDRO DE
ATACAMA

Dazzlingly white and near featureless, the Salar de Uyuni is the world's largest salt pan. It covers an unfathomably large chunk of Bolivia's most remote highlands and is all that remains of ancient Lago Minchín. It has no roads, no services and no landmarks for navigation, making it a surreal and otherworldly place to travel. In the wrong conditions it's also dangerous. From December to April a pool of water covers the surface turning it into a vast mirror that magically reflects the sky, but also causes openings in the crust that can collapse under the weight of a vehicle.

Car rental companies refuse to let you take their vehicles here, so joining a tour or hiring a guide with a 4WD is practically the only option for exploration. That's not a bad thing, however: the scenery is so mesmerizing and the experience so immersive you'll be glad to leave the driving to someone else.

An expedition across the salar begins in the small town of Uyuni in southwestern Bolivia. It sits at an altitude of 11,985ft (3653m) and is surrounded by scorched desert and jagged mountains. Tour operators prowl the streets, each of them offering a special trip (the usual route), a reduced rate (the standard cost) and a promise of rain.

The tour takes from three to four days, crossing some of the 4633 sq miles (12,000 sq km) of the salar and continuing through the Atacama Desert to San Pedro de Atacama in Chile. Upon leaving Uyuni, a bumpy, rutted desert road leads out to the edge of the salt pan where a rough ramp extends across the thin veil of salt by the edge of the salar. Even experienced local drivers have

been known to become stuck at this point. It doesn't take us long before we're surrounded by an eerie glow, though. The immense blanket of white stretches as far as the eye can see in every direction, mountains float above the distant horizon and the glare is almost unbearable.

The salt is split into interlocking geometrical shapes and is so flat that NASA calibrates its satellite sensors here. A floating spot on the horizon turns out to be Isla del Pescado, a volcanic outcrop covered in towering, 400-year-old cacti. Vicuñas (the smallest member of the camel family) roam through the scrub, and from the top I get my first proper glimpse of the salar, endlessly white and enigmatic. The immense cacti are silhouetted against the sea of white, with jagged peaks and snow-capped volcanoes dwarfed in the distance. It's unlike anything I have ever seen and feels like a million miles from anywhere.

We set off again and head for the far side of the salar, crossing mile after mile of nothingness. An ominous silence descends as we drive though a patch of pooled water. My heart drops as I feel the wheels sinking into the slush. We are soon up to the axles in water, tense and fearful, but eventually lurch out onto the shore.

Herds of llamas and vicuñas startle and scatter as we pull up in a tiny village of adobe houses. This is the Atacama Desert, the driest in the world, and by morning every drop of moisture has been sucked from my skin. We drive on past spectacular mountain ranges and smoking volcanoes through a region that is completely uninhabited and untouched. We gain elevation steadily and at Laguna Chiguana see rare James's flamingos huddled together against a backdrop of turquoise water, sweeping dunes and brooding mountains.

Next up is the so-called Dalí Desert, where bizarre, free-standing rock columns litter the valley floor. The most magnificent, the Árbol de Piedra (Stone Tree), is a sculptural form scooped out into smooth curves and sharp edges by the sheer force of nature.

We haven't encountered another soul all day and by evening pull up at Laguna Colorada, a large pool of what looks like toxic tomato soup surrounded by white dunes of salt. Harmless minerals and algae color the water; the dunes are borax, set against a backdrop of black mountains and immense blue sky.

It is mesmerizing. The sun is just beginning to set and it is bitterly cold. We are now at an elevation of over 13,120ft (4000m)

LITHIUM LAKE

As ancient Lago Minchín receded and dried out, it left behind a shallow pool of water rich in precious minerals. The Salar de Uyuni is estimated to be the world's largest reserve of lithium, an ultra-light metal used in smartphone and electric car batteries. Until now, extraction has been on a relatively small scale, but there are plans to dramatically increase output, though the process poses environmental concerns for this fragile ecosystem.

"We pile out onto a steaming landscape that looks as if it could be the set of a 1970s science-fiction film"

From opposite: the Atacama Desert is the world's driest; a well-earned rest in San Pedro de Atacama, Chile, the final stop. Previous pages, from left: a 4WD atop the surreally beautiful salar; sunrise on the salt pans

and even the short walk to our rustic hostel leaves me breathless. I go to bed early but find it impossible to sleep.

We rise before dawn on the final day of the trip, tired and bleary eyed as we set off for the Sol de Mañana geothermal field. As the sun rises, we pile out onto a steaming landscape that looks as if it could be the set of a 1970s science-fiction film. Mud pots splutter and boil, billowing clouds of vapor rise out of the ground, fumaroles hiss, and a thick whiff of sulfur hangs in the air. We are at an elevation of 16,400ft (5000m), but it feels as if we are entering the very belly of the Earth.

We have one more stop before crossing the border, Laguna Verde, a vivid turquoise lake that changes color as the wind disturbs sediments in the water. Behind it, the perfect cone of Volcán Licancábur rises sharply into the sky, the last of our Bolivian landmarks. We cross the border, a ramshackle trailer and a post in the ground, and switch to a luxury minibus and immaculately paved roads. The scenery is no less spectacular, and San Pedro promises good food, hot showers and cozy beds but, unfortunately, none of the adventure. This is one trip I can't imagine I'll ever forget.

DIRECTIONS

Start // Uyuni, Bolivia
Finish // San Pedro de Atacama, Chile
Distance // 310 miles (500km)
Getting there // Fly into La Paz then head (by air/bus) to Oruro, then train.
When to drive // May to November for access to all areas. From December to April parts of the salar will be impassable, but pooling water creates a mirror effect.
Self-driving // Only possible in your own 4WD. Take local advice seriously. Follow other vehicles across the salar and bring food, fuel, water and plenty of spares.
Tour operators // Choose wisely and ask about guides' experience, training, vehicle condition and equipment.
Hot tip // Tours run in both directions but are significantly cheaper from Uyuni.

Opposite, from top: workers extracting
salt at Salinas de Maras, Peru;
Bonneville Salt Flats, Utah

MORE LIKE THIS
SALT PAN DRIVES

BONNEVILLE FLATS, UTAH, USA

Motorheads can get a slice of racing
history on the Bonneville Salt Flats on the
Utah–Nevada border. Numerous land
speed records have been set here and you
can get your own taste of the mesmerizing
surroundings by taking a drive across the
30,000 acres (12,140 hectares) of salt. The
flats are graded for racing so don't get
any ideas about setting your own records
– pressure ridges and standing water can
result in a very different end to your drive
– but the otherworldly surroundings and
shimmering mirages make a drive here a
surreal experience. In recent years, surface
conditions have been deteriorating, so stay
away from the edges, where you can easily
get stuck in the mud. If at all possible, try
to follow the tracks of other vehicles and
avoid pools of water. Don't forget to wash
your car thoroughly once you are back on
the road.
Start/Finish // Wendover
Distance // 25 miles (40km)

SALAR DE ATACAMA, CHILE

Polar regions aside, Chile's Atacama
Desert is Earth's highest and driest
desert, and a stunning region to drive.
Sandwiched between the ocean and the
Andes, parts of this place haven't felt
rain for over 400 years (possibly ever),
yet sometimes snowflakes fall. A place of
exquisite extremes, it is possible to drive
from the capital in a week via the Pacific
coast, stopping at Chile's hectic culture
capital Valparaíso, plus Viña del Mar, La
Serena and Copiapó. The desert drive
proper begins after turning away from the
coast at Antofagasta to reach the gateway
town of Calama. From here, head to San
Pedro de Atacama, once the epicenter of
a Paleolithic culture and now a brilliant
base for exploring the desert's jewels,
including the Salar de Atacama salt flat,
stunning Valle de la Luna (Moon Valley)
and the extraordinary El Tatio geyser
field. From here, continue into Argentina
through Reserva Nacional Los Flamencos,
or venture into Bolivia via Eduardo Avaroa
National Reserve.
Start // Santiago
Finish // San Pedro de Atacama
Distance // 1060 miles (1705km)

SALINERAS DE MARAS, PERU

Peru's Sacred Valley gets twisty as the Río
Urubamba flows toward Machu Picchu, but
in the area around Cuzco, the landscape
is broader and the roads more forgiving.
Among the most memorable sights here are
the Salineras de Maras: tiers of pinkish-
white salt pans tucked into a side valley.
You can get there on a gentle uphill walk of
a mile, across the bridge from Tarabamba,
or via the rougher but more view-filled
approach from above, near Maras. There's
plenty to see along the highway between
Cuzco and Urubamba, including the
archaeological site of Chinchero and the
lofty roadside viewpoint at Machuqolqa
– all amid rolling farmlands watched over
by snowcapped peaks. For more marvels
of Inca landscaping, take a detour to the
strange concentric circles of Moray, or finish
in Ollantaytambo where the valley rises up.
Start // Cuzco
Finish // Ollantaytambo
Distance // 48 miles (77km)

CULTURAL JOURNEYS ON THE BRAZILIAN COAST

Regis St Louis takes a seaside drive from Salvador to Porto Alegre – one that showcases Brazil's astonishing diversity, from Afro-Brazilian heritage to European-style townships.

The roar of the drums fills the square. I follow the sound past palm trees, terrace cafes and pastel-hued buildings as the heavy beats echo off the cobblestones. Rounding a corner, I nearly stumble into a lineup of musicians: three rows of percussionists weaving hypnotic rhythms on oversized drums striped in red, yellow and green – the group's colors yet another obvious link to its African roots. The name on their shirts makes it clear: this is Olodum, one of many percussion-based bands playing *batucada*, a blend of African-influenced samba and Caribbean beats on the streets of the Pelourinho, the oldest district in Salvador.

There's no better place to experience the syncretic culture of Brazil than in Salvador, the coastal capital of Bahia. Disparate cultures collide – Catholicism and Candomblé (an Afro-Brazilian religion), Portuguese architecture and African street food – against the backdrop of gilded 17th-century churches and aquamarine views of the Atlantic. I'd come to the city as the departure point for a month-long drive down the coast with the hopes of encountering some of the distinct cultures that make up this complicated nation of 220 million, with ethnic roots in three different continents and a long history of immigration.

I spend the day taking in the city's historic landmarks, watching spinning martial artists against the twang of the single-stringed berimbau at a capoeria studio, and munching on *acarajé* (a fritter of black-eyed peas with dried shrimp, manioc and coconut milk), sold by street vendors. The next morning I catch the vehicle ferry across the bay to Ilha de Itaparica, and begin the long drive down the coast of Bahia. You could spend weeks exploring this sun-drenched corner of Brazil, following back lanes to tiny villages facing windswept beaches or catching ferries out to car-free

islands of sandy streets and seafood shacks just steps from the lapping waves.

In the far south of the state, I stop for a visit to the Parque Nacional de Monte Pascoal, a protected area of Atlantic rainforest, mangroves and swamplands. It was here that Portuguese ships, under the command of Pedro Álvares Cabral, sighted the broad hump of Monte Pascoal, their first glimpse of the vast continent of South America. The park is run by the Pataxó, the largest Indigenous group of Bahia. A guide named Kaxiló leads me on a forested trail to the 1759ft (536m) summit for which the park is named. Along the way he points out some of the unique species

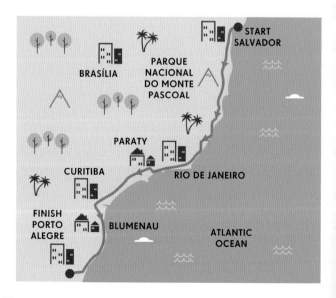

ILHA GRANDE

Thanks to its isolation, Ilha Grande (the 'Big Island') served for decades as a prison and leper colony. Spared from development by this unusual history, its jungle-clad slopes and golden beaches are some of the best preserved in all of Brazil. Days are spent hiking through lush Atlantic rainforest, snorkeling in aquamarine seas and cooling off in waterfalls. Get there by ferry from Conceição de Jacareí, a two-hour drive west of Rio.

"That strange feeling of finding myself in another place and time grows stronger in Blumenau, a city founded by German immigrants"

Clockwise, from opposite top left: colonial German architecture at Parque Vila Germânica, Blumenau; women dressed in traditional Bahian dress in a street procession; acarajé being prepared on the streets of Salvador; Pico do Papagaio on Ilha Grande. Previous page: Rio de Janeiro overlooked by Christ the Redeemer

here, like the ancient *juerana* and *jequitibá* trees as well as pau-brasil, whose bark was coveted by the Portuguese.

In Rio de Janeiro, I stop for a look at the massive murals by the São Paulo street artist known as Kobra. Entitled *Etnias* (Ethnicities), the work features large-scale portraits depicting Indigenous people from five different corners of the world and was created in the run-up to the 2016 Rio Olympics. Stretching some 560ft (171m), the vividly hued graffiti wall is among the largest in the world and played a pivotal role in the rejuvenation of Rio's derelict port district.

Speeding west and south, I drive along the aptly named Costa Verde (Green Coast), where mountains covered in thick vegetation come to the edge of the sea. Dense tree cover crowds both sides of the road, though I occasionally glimpse the islands just offshore and deep blue stretches of the Atlantic. The colonial town of Paraty, with its colorfully painted 300-year-old buildings and cobblestone lanes, has some of Brazil's most photogenic streets. Gold that was mined from the interior was brought to the port here, and vestiges from the city's 18th-century boom days live on in ornate churches and grand mansions (now cultural centers and high-end guesthouses). Nearby, the beaches are famed for their untouched stretches of sandy shoreline backed by tropical forest, and some are reachable only by boat.

The following day I skirt past the booming metropolis of São Paulo – wondering if the Costa Verde was just a figment of my imagination as heavy traffic engulfs me on a 10-lane superhighway. It's late afternoon by the time I roll into Curitiba, a city with some of Brazil's greenest credentials. Back in the 1970s, a progressive architect-mayor named Jaime Lerner transformed the downtown into a pedestrian zone, planting trees and adding parks. He also created a bus-powered rapid transit system that mimicked the speed and efficiency of an underground metro system. In the evening I ditch the car for a stroll along Rua das Flores, its flower

boxes, vintage lampposts and patio cafes reminiscent of city centers in Western Europe.

That strange feeling of finding myself in another place and time grows stronger in Blumenau, a city founded by German immigrants in the mid-19th century. I see a surprising number of fair-skinned, blue-eyed Brazilians as I wander through the neighborhood of Rua XV Novembro, home to Teutonic-style architecture – including a department store modeled on a city hall in Michelstadt, Germany. Later I find an outdoor table at Bier Vila and linger over a well-chilled Hefeweizen while waiters hurry between tables carrying plates of *eisbein* (cured ham hock), *kassler* (smoked pork chop) and wiener schnitzel. Like other German-style bars nearby, Bier Vila packs heaving crowds during the city's annual Oktoberfest, the second largest in the world after Munich's.

Further south I roll by more tantalizing coastline, zipping past mountainous Ilha de Santa Catarina off to the east, before plunging into the pastoral landscapes of Rio Grande do Sul. Brazil's southernmost state is known for its *gaúcho* (cowboy) culture, where *churrasco* (grilled steak) dominates and late-night talks are fueled by *chimarrão* – tea-like *erva maté* typically drunk from a hollowed-out gourd. After many days on the road, I have mixed feelings as I make my final stop in Porto Alegre. I've seen so many different facets of Brazil that I'll need weeks to process it all. And yet, there's much more of this country I'm longing to experience. "Don't worry, you'll be back," a Belgian expat tells me over drinks that night. "Brazil is a lifetime addiction."

DIRECTIONS

Start // Salvador
Finish // Porto Alegre
Distance // 2050 miles (3300km)
Getting there // Salvador receives direct international flights from Lisbon and Miami; most go through Rio or São Paulo.
When to drive // Peak times are December through February, when it is also hot and humid. An ideal time is March to May and October to November, when it is warm but less crowded.
Where to stay // The art-filled Pousada Baluarte (www.facebook.com/pousadabaluarte) in Salvador is run by a friendly French-Brazilian couple and has a great location off Praça de Santo Antonio.
Detours // In the south, the Ilha de Santa Catarina has 42 idyllic beaches, plus seaside villages such as Pântano do Sul serving up some outstanding seafood.

MORE LIKE THIS
BRAZILIAN DRIVES

DUNES AND LAGOONS IN THE NORTH

In Brazil's far northeast, a vast expanse of dunes stretches along the coast, extending some 30 miles (48km) inland. The terrain is like nothing on Earth, especially from May to September when rain filtered through the sand forms thousands of crystal-clear pools and lakes between the dunes. While you can't drive the Parque Nacional dos Lençóis Maranhenses on your own, you can sign up for an adventurous multiday guided 4WD and dune-buggy trip. Depart from the historic city of São Luís, then head to Barreirinhas, a large sunbaked town on the edge of the national park. From there you can take a boat excursion along the Rio Preguiças, before continuing on to Tutóia, gateway to the wildlife-filled Delta das Américas. The journey ends in Jericoacoara, a relaxing village of sandy streets and dramatic coastal scenery.

Start // São Luís
Finish // Jericoacoara
Distance // 440 miles (708km)

NATURE IN THE NORTHEAST

Palm-fringed beaches, music-filled cities and tranquil seaside villages are the big draws of this road trip across three small states in Brazil's northeast. Immerse yourself in northeastern culture in Recife, a city with vibrant arts centers and a dynamic live music scene. Nearby, historic Olinda has a historic center dotted with colonial churches and picturesque squares. You'll leave the pavement behind as you head north to picture-perfect beaches like the clothing-optional Praia de Tambaba, with petrified sandstone forming natural tide pools along the shoreline, and Praia Coqueirinho, set on a curving bay and backed with jungle-clad cliffs. Continuing to the town of Praia da Pipa, you'll find pristine sands, limpid lagoons and good surfing. End the journey in Natal, home to a 16th-century fort and boardwalks that wind beneath the branches of the world's largest cashew tree.

Start // Recife
Finish // Natal
Distance // 260 miles (418km)

AMAZON ADVENTURES

Nearly twice the size of France, Pará is a place of massive proportions, which is entirely fitting given the world's largest rainforest covers much of the state. Lying near the mouth of the mighty Amazon River, Belém is a former rubber-boom town with aging mansions, parks full of mango trees and busy waterfront markets. The roads are rough, so take it slow as you roll to the Ilha do Mosquero, which has over a dozen freshwater beaches. From there continue on rugged roads northeast to Marudá, where you'll leave the car behind and hop a ferry to the small fishing village of Algodoal on Ilha de Maiandeua. Drive back to Belém, park the car and take a riverboat to Ilha do Marajó, a large river island full of wetlands, tiny villages and roaming water buffalo.

Start // Belém
Finish // Ilha do Marajó
Distance // 315 miles (507km)

*Clockwise, from top: a scarlet ibis
preening near Belém; a sumaúma tree
on Ilha do Combú, Belém; climbing the
sand dunes of Lençóis Maranhenses*

THROUGH THE CALCHAQUÍ VALLEYS

Mark Johanson explores the multicolored mountainscapes and high-altitude vineyards of Argentina's Valles Calchaquíes, where intrepid oenophiles can find the perfect wine pairing: adventure.

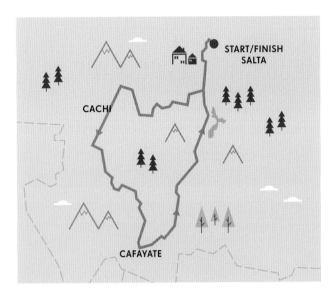

When adobe walls vibrate to the sound of trembling guitars, the air smells of sizzling steaks and your tongue tastes of greasy empanadas and jammy malbec you'll know you've finally made it to a *peña*. These music halls, famed for their *zamba* folk singers and meaty comfort foods, are the big draw luring local Argentines to Salta, a city in the northwestern corner of this triangular nation where it bumps up against the dusty frontiers of Chile and Bolivia. I found this *peña* by accident, like a foreigner entering Nashville and stumbling into a honky-tonk unawares. That's because I've come to this forgotten corner of Argentina precisely to leave this city in my rearview mirror. Yet, I'm finding that extremely hard to do.

Salta means "the beautiful one" in the language of the Indigenous Aymara people. Spanish-speaking Argentines call it *Salta la Linda*, or "Salta the beautiful." With its bubblegum-pink cathedral, soaring neoclassical architecture and lively curb-side cafes, it's not hard to see why. This time-capsule of a city sprung

up on the outer fringes of the Inca empire during the height of the Spanish conquest and would go on to become a vital cog of commerce nearly halfway between Lima and Buenos Aires.

After a long night at the *peña* and a lazy morning spent reveling in Salta's storied history at the institutions on Plaza 9 de Julio (including a treasure-filled archaeology museum), I set off on the pockmarked roads out of town. It's here my real adventure begins as I ride into the sunbaked nether regions of greater Salta Province.

The plan is to spend three days winding through the windswept Valles Calchaquíes of the Andean foothills, crossing through three vastly different ravines before looping back to Salta. The first ravine, Quebrada de Escoipe, is surely the work of Mother Nature's abstract-expressionist friend; its mountains are multicolored thanks to the oxidation of minerals such as sulfur (yellow), iron (red) and copper (green) over thousands of years.

After crossing this surreal landscape I zigzag my way to the top of Bishop's Slope, a 11,150ft- (3400m-) high overlook where visitors seek the blessing of Archangel Raphael (patron saint of travelers) at a chapel built in his honor.

At the thatched stall by the chapel I purchase road snacks (llama sausage and goat's cheese) and continue onward into the rust-red hills of Parque Nacional los Cardones. This reserve is a photographer's dream – cartoonish cacti appear on the horizon like an army of green ghosts wandering through a desert plain.

When I reach the adobe homes and time-forgotten streets of Cachi, I cut my engine for the evening and stroll through the village

"Cafayate is home to some of the highest vineyards in the world, a landscape of soaring mountains and emerald vines"

to its banana-yellow church, whose roof was hewn with cactus wood. I then watch as the sun sets over this sleepy village and the sky fades to an inky black. My eyes thicken as I gaze at the Southern Cross twinkling above and, with time, they glue shut.

The following morning I set out into the cool air of the Andean foothills and forge onward past the archaeological ruins of a pre-Inca city called La Paya into the Quebrada de las Flechas (Ravine of Arrows). It's a landscape not unlike the badlands of South Dakota, with a menagerie of misshapen rocks and beguiling formations that can make you question whether the Earth hasn't tilted just a little bit off its axis.

With massive condors soaring up above and hiking trails snaking off into the distance, it's a place I could linger for hours. But I know that on the far side of this spectacular geological rift lies an even more appetizing treat: the vineyards of Cafayate.

Cafayate is Argentina's second wine center after Mendoza, but it's a place that's much more down to earth and approachable than its ritzier neighbor to the south. While Mendoza prizes big bold bottles of malbec, Cafayate is a region dominated by the more demure torrontés, a white wine grape that grows exceptionally well

WINES WITH ALTITUDE

The high vineyards of Salta lie between 5580ft (1700m) and 10,200ft (3110m), giving the wines power, structure and minerality. Torrontés is the most common grape, but you'll also find bottles of malbec markedly different from those further south in Mendoza, where vines grow below 4920ft (1500m). The altitude creates stressful conditions – such as higher solar radiation and dramatic shifts in temperature – that give the grapes more concentrated flavors.

From opposite left: torrontés grapes on the vine and in the barrel; the altar of the Cathedral of Salta; the winding road to Cachi. Previous page: curious rock formations mark the Quebrada de las Flechas

DIRECTIONS

Start/Finish // Salta
Distance // 325 miles (523km)
Getting there // Salta's airport has direct flights from Buenos Aires and Lima. You can bus in from most big cities in Argentina, as well as San Pedro de Atacama in Chile.
When to drive // Nighttime temperatures can dip to near freezing in the dry winter months (June to August), while summer (December to March) is rainier and hotter. Heavy summer rains can make some roads impassable.
Where to stay // La Merced del Alto (lamerceddelalto. com) is an elegant adobe-built estancia just outside Cachi. Patios de Cafayate Wine Hotel (www.patiosdecafayate. com) puts you right in the middle of Cafayate's vineyards.
Detours // Explore the light installations of American artist James Turrell at his museum on the Colomé wine estate.

in these cold, windswept valleys. Torrontés has a deceptively sweet nose (like a riesling) that belies its dry finish. As such, it goes down like grape juice when you're basking in Cafayate's afternoon sun.

Cafayate is home to some of the highest-altitude vineyards in the world, so to sip and swirl your way through this quite literally breathtaking landscape of soaring mountains and emerald vines is a rare experience. The town itself – with its Andean handicraft markets and family-run bodegas – has a refreshing authenticity.

I leave the rolling vines behind on my last day in Santa Province as I enter yet another magnificent landscape: the fossil-rich Quebrada de las Conchas (Ravine of the Shells). The remnants of an ancient lakebed, it is rife with otherworldly rock formations such as the Garganta del Diablo (Devil's Throat) and Anfiteatro (Amphitheater). The latter is the site of a prehistoric waterfall with solid rock that now takes on blanket-like folds and improbable swirls. Its walls are also riddled with holes, which reveal themselves to be the homes of burrowing parrots.

My final leg skirts past a ghost town called Alemania and an artificial lake, Cabra Corral, that's become a popular weekend retreat for Salteños. Green fields of tobacco then give way to a smattering of increasingly substantial villages.

Soon the adobe walls are vibrating once again, the air is thick with sizzling steaks and my tongue is purple with malbec.

I have made it back to the city of Salta and I have stumbled – though very much on purpose this time – into the all-absorbing atmosphere of the *peña*.

Opposite, from top: the winding
road through the Serra do Rio
do Rastro, Brazil; an organic
vineyard in Maipo Valley, Chile

MORE LIKE THIS
SOUTH AMERICAN
WINE ROUTES

SERRA DO RIO DO RASTRO, BRAZIL

Built in 1903, the serpentine SC-390 winds
its way up the Serra do Rio do Rastro
mountain range in southern Brazil. The
route begins gently, weaving through lush
valleys dotted with colorful houses and
distinctly European villages, but once past
the town of Lauro Müller the incline gets
steeper, the road clinging to the side of
the valley as it passes canyons, waterfalls
and forests. The scenery is spectacular
and huge windmills generate electricity to
keep the treacherous bends lit at night, but
even by day you should drive cautiously,
as trucks and buses need the full width
of the road to get round the bends. São
Joaquim, at the end of the route, is one of
Brazil's coldest spots but a fruit-growing
region known for its sauvignon blanc and
chardonnay varietals.
Start // Tubarão
Finish // São Joaquim
Distance // 83 miles (134km)

VALLES DEL MAIPO AND DE COLCHAGUA, CHILE

Chile's 2600-mile (4200km) stretch gives
it a neat cross-section of climates, and
the middle third hits the sweet spot for
wines. The southern edge of the capital
Santiago's urban sprawl is where true wine
country begins. Concha y Toro's palatial
estate gives its name to a wine region
where cabernets star. Heading south, you
can take Ruta 5 (the Pan-American Hwy),
but you'll find more wineries if you stick
closer to the mountains. Andean peaks
are your constant companions through
the left window as you follow signs to San
Fernando, but in the Valle de Colchagua
it's time to turn toward the Pacific. Pick from
a cluster of estates open to visitors around
the colonial city of Santa Cruz, before a
grand ocean finale in the favorite surfer
spot of Pichilemu.
Start // Santiago
Finish // Pichilemu
Distance // 183 miles (294km)

LOS CAMINOS DEL VINO, URUGUAY

Uruguay's renown as a wine producer is
not as widespread as it deserves – export
bottles often add an inset map to show
where in South America the country lies.
Short answer: just across the Río de la
Plata from wine giant Argentina. Begin
your discovery of Uruguayan vintages in
the town of Carmelo. Nearby Bodega
Campotinto is a good place for possibly
your first taste of tannat, the "national
grape," which makes reds that are as much
a match for meaty grills as Argentina's
malbecs. After a detour to the Unesco-
listed town of Colonia del Sacramento,
aim for the country's primary wine region
of Canelones, where white albariños add
balance to the tannats. After backroad
loops past bodegas such as Artesana
or Bouza, strike east to toast your new
discoveries by the beach in the resort city
of Punta del Este.
Start // Carmelo
Finish // Punta del Este
Distance // 250 miles (402km)

THE COLOMBIAN CORDILLERAS

Oliver Smith's road trip through Colombia takes in hectic metropolises, sleepy colonial-era towns and coffee plantations, all flourishing in the shadow of the cordilleras.

Not so long ago, the prospect of a road trip through Colombia would have turned the blood of a travel insurer cold – fairly or unfairly, the country was synonymous with guerilla warfare and crime. For much of the past decade, however, Colombia has been the South American star in the ascendant: its safety issues are far from resolved, but highways that were once no-go zones have opened to tourists, and neighborhoods where few dared to set foot are now populated with boutique hotels and cafes selling artisanal coffee.

Beyond the traditional tourist trails of Latin America, Colombia gives a genuine opportunity to detour onto quiet lanes amid coffee plantations, cobbled streets in little towns and footpaths up cloud-capped Andean summits. Many of its greatest sights are accessible in a circuit of the Cordillera Central and Cordillera Oriental.

The blockbuster scenery begins in Bogotá: one of the most dramatically sited capitals in the Americas, poised at an ear-popping elevation of 8070ft (2460m). Reigning undisputed over the skyline here is Monserrate – an urban mountain topped by a holy sanctuary – while running to its foot is La Candelaria, the barrio of centuries-old townhouses where students gather in cafes and a statue of Simón Bolívar (leader of the campaign for Colombia's independence from Spain) grimaces at the pigeons, sword in hand.

Come Monday morning I join the four-wheeled traffic crawling northward out of town and park up in the nearby city of Zipaquirá. Below the surface lies one of South America's most peculiar sights – the Catedral de Sal, a subterranean cathedral created from a void in a salt mine, whose spectrally lit passages are a point of pilgrimage for pious Colombians.

Reemerging into the bright Andean sunshine, I veer east to find a far older sacred site: Laguna Guatavita, a lake set in a sinkhole, whose banks look out across patchwork fields. The lake was the focus of rituals by the Muisca – the Indigenous rulers of the Colombian sierras – who allegedly offered golden objects to the waters. When the Spanish conquistadors learned of this practice, they assumed that treasures were accumulating in the fathoms, which in turn gave birth to the legend of El Dorado.

The ghosts of the distant past also loom large in Villa de Leyva: a charming colonial-era settlement a short drive further north, sheltering among the mountains of Boyacá. The town was founded

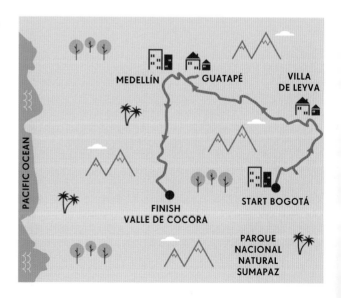

as a retreat for military officers and clergy, and today is still a popular rallying point for Bogotános on a weekend getaway. The appeal here lies in idly nosing into Old World mansions with trickling Moorish fountains, cobbled courtyards and creaky balconies – some have been reincarnated as shops and restaurants; others are museums with exhibits on the revolutionary inhabitants who fought for independence from faraway Madrid.

Departing Villa de Leyva, it's a full-day's drive out west, tracing the hairpin bends of the Cordillera Oriental downhill to reach the Magdalena River, on its slow, stately journey to the Caribbean. Crossing the river basin, the road rockets skyward again toward the Cordillera Central to reach Guatapé, a little resort town whose buildings are adorned with bright frescoes, set beside a maze of peninsulas and islets on an artificial lake. The geography makes a bit more sense once you've climbed roughly 700 steps to the top of the Peñón de Guatapé – a granite monolith with a summit that teeters high over waters where kayakers glide and pleasure boats putter.

In truth, Guatapé is a warmup act for Colombia's second city. Medellín was nicknamed the City of Eternal Spring for the cool airs

afforded by its mountain perch, but for much of the late 20th century it had a frosty reputation as the world's most dangerous city and the sometime fiefdom of drug lord Pablo Escobar. In more recent times spring has returned and Medellín is blooming once more – the most celebrated example being the metro system, a combined elevated rail and cable car network hailed as a masterstroke of urban planning. Leaving the car behind, I buy a ticket for a condor's-eye view of the city, passing the grandiose Palace of Culture and parks adorned with plump sculptures by Fernando Botero, eventually swooping up to the favela of Santo Domingo where the rooftops and satellite dishes of Medellín fall away beneath my feet.

Emerging from traffic-clogged streets, I follow the road south to the Zona Cafetera – Colombia's coffee-growing heartland. It's a landscape to stimulate the senses: sudden showers set the leaves of coffee plants glistening emerald green, vintage American Jeeps stacked with pungent sacks of beans clatter down flooded lanes, and little fincas with shady verandas and tidy gardens lie by the roadside. Despite all the caffeine here, the pace is unhurried: the Zona Cafetera is a region that rewards the idle. I stop the car to

PLAYING TEJO

If you spend time in little Colombian towns, you will eventually become accustomed to the sound of exploding gunpowder after dark – not a sign of armed insurrection, but rather a part of the wildly popular game of Tejo. The sport involves throwing a metal puck at a target around 60ft (18m) away, which is adorned with firecrackers that detonate on impact. It's often played informally, with a beer in hand.

"It's a landscape of Edenic beauty"

Clockwise, from opposite: the expansive lake system viewed from Peñón de Guatapé; a highland motmot in the cloud forest of Valle de Cocora; Casa Terracota in Villa de Leyva, an entire house made of clay. Previous page: Bogotá spread out below Monserrate

DIRECTIONS

Start // Bogotá
Finish // Valle de Cocora
Distance // 560 miles (900km)
Getting there // Bogotá's El Dorado International Airport is fairly close to the city center. Matecaña International Airport is the main hub for the Zona Cafetera, and is one hour from Salento and Valle de Cocora. It's also possible to drive here from Bogotá in a day. Both airports offer car rental.
When to drive // The Andes are at their driest from December to March; rainforest areas are wet year-round.
Hot tip // Bogotá is at its liveliest on a Sunday, when streets are closed to motorized traffic. While the capital city has become safer in recent years, avoid driving at night.
More info // See the Colombian tourism website (colombia. travel/en).

explore primary-colored streets in the pueblos of Jardin, Filandia and Salento. I drive to the edge of Los Nevados National Park, where the Andean terrain rises through a mosaic of ecosystems: from humid cloud forests to 16,000ft (5000m) summits where glaciers lurk.

For many, however, the definitive sight in the Zona Cafetera – indeed in the whole of Colombia – is the Valle de Cocora. It's a landscape of Edenic beauty: hummingbirds whir about the riverbanks, toucans flutter amid the canopy, elusive pumas and spectacled bears stalk the secret nooks of the valley. The main attraction is impossible to miss: the wax palm is the national tree of Colombia, capable of reaching a neck-craning height of 200ft (60m). To see them, I leave my car behind and hitch a ride aboard a coffee-carrying Jeep. The bumpy mountain roads churn passengers around like freshly harvested beans, and before long we reach a copse of wax palms. Their fronds are so high, they sometimes become lost in the clouds that blow in from the Pacific Ocean.

I sit at the bottom of a tree and sip from a flaskful of local coffee – every bit as robust, refreshing and addictive as the land in which it was farmed.

*Opposite: the atmospheric Old Town
neighborhood of Cartagena*

MORE LIKE THIS
COLOMBIAN ROAD TRIPS

TAYRONA NATIONAL PARK

For many, it's the Caribbean that lingers in the memory after a trip to Colombia. Start in Cartagena, founded as a 16th-century Spanish outpost. Its old town still holds a claim as the most beautiful on the continent, with stout battlements enclosing mustard-yellow townhouses and squares where dances strike up at dusk. From here, continue east past mangroves to the historic city of Santa Marta and nearby Tayrona National Park, a swathe of rainforest edging onto heavenly white sand beaches. Spend idle days in a hammock, or drive further inland to the foothills of the remote Sierra Nevada de Santa Marta. You'll need to leave the car behind to make the epic trek through the forests to Ciudad Perdida – a mini Machu Picchu built millennia ago, rediscovered only in recent decades.

Start // Cartagena
Finish // Ciudad Perdida
Distance // 280 miles (450km)

CALI AND THE SOUTH

Cali, Colombia's third-largest city, sees fewer visitors than Bogotá and Medellin, but wins fans with its rebellious spirit and unparalleled passion for salsa: expect dancing into the small hours in the barrio bars. It's also well placed for a shimmy around the little-traveled south: drive the Pan-American Hwy to Popayan, a beautiful town founded by conquistadors in the 16th century, with whitewashed homes flanking streets bustling with university students. Make a detour to the market at Silvia – where Indigenous Guambiano communities come to sell fresh produce on a Tuesday – before swerving along mountain roads to the Parque Arqueológico at Tierradentro, a mysterious complex of subterranean tombs and statues. Diverting north, a surreal interlude comes in the form of the lunar landscape of the Desierto de la Tatacoa, before following the highways up to Colombia's capital.

Start // Cali
Finish // Bogotá
Distance // 470 miles (750km)

ON THE TRAIL OF MÁRQUEZ

Most bookworms will jump at the chance to explore the fantastical landscapes of literary icon Gabriel García Márquez. Start in Barranquilla – the spirited port where Márquez first worked as a journalist – and pop into La Cueva, a bohemian restaurant where his literary circle often met. Drive south to Aracataca, the workaday river town where the author was born, which is said to be the inspiration for Macondo in *100 Years of Solitude*. For dreamers, a more likely candidate for Macondo is Mompós, a wildly beautiful town lying amid the backwaters of the Rio Magdalena, which also served as the setting for *The General in His Labyrinth*. Follow the river downstream and then veer west to arrive at the storied battlements of Cartagena: another Márquez haunt, which provided the inspiration for *Love in the Time of Cholera*.

Start // Barranquilla
Finish // Cartagena
Distance // 400 miles (650km)

PERU'S DESERTED NORTH COAST

Kevin Raub drives through a Mad Max desertscape harboring windswept beaches, upbeat surf enclaves, pre-Columbian ruins and Peruvian cities rich in ceviche and cerveza.

As anyone who has flown into Lima can attest, the length and breadth of the dust cloud that hangs over the world's second-driest capital city (after Cairo) is staggering. Flights descend across bursts of rust-hued grit swept up between modern office buildings, colonial facades, a shanty here and there, and the rowdy Pacific as it crashes into the Costa Verde cliffs around the exclusive neighborhood of Miraflores. From this vantage point, it's only fair to point out that Lima doesn't appear especially endearing – the first impression is that a down-and-dirty adventure will commence upon driving away from Jorge Chávez International Airport.

From the ground, however, the dust settles. Its impact is restricted to dry lips and a drier throat as I stroll around the city in search of the perfect ceviche, perusing Lima's fascinating museums and 16th-century architecture – and envisioning the various empires that once called the surrounding desert home.

All that changes again as I get behind the wheel and head north. I chase suburban Lima on Hwy 1N (Carretera Panamericana), the 725-mile (1666km) conduit by which I aim to take in monumental ruins, dune-backed shores, and the towns and colonial treasures of Peru's north coast all the way to the beach resort of Máncora. A windswept landscape begins to emerge, reminiscent of the backdrop to an apocalyptic film of the *Mad Max* variety. To my right, the Andes crowd the horizon like looming monoliths of granite. To my left is the Pacific coast, home to vast stretches of dunes that weave through the scenery, only to be broken up by the ramshackle coastal towns that arise from the desert.

The road-side scene is desolate but gorgeous, emitting a certain final battle serenity as the crowdedness of Lima falls

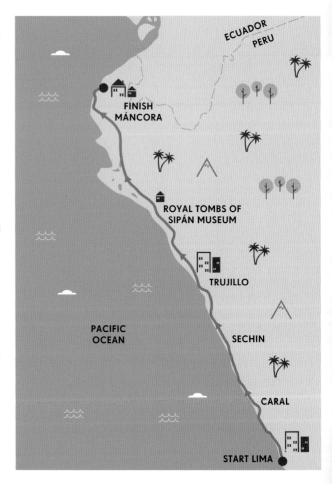

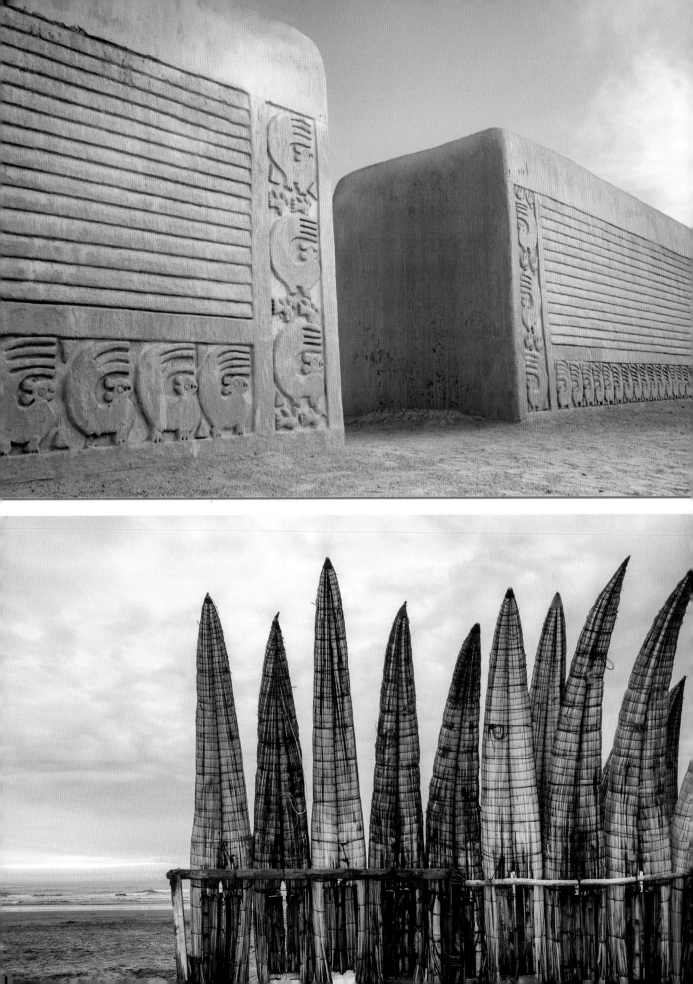

*"Just a lone driver
making a passing
acquaintance with
a landscape that
has been shaped by
dust and wind for
millennia"*

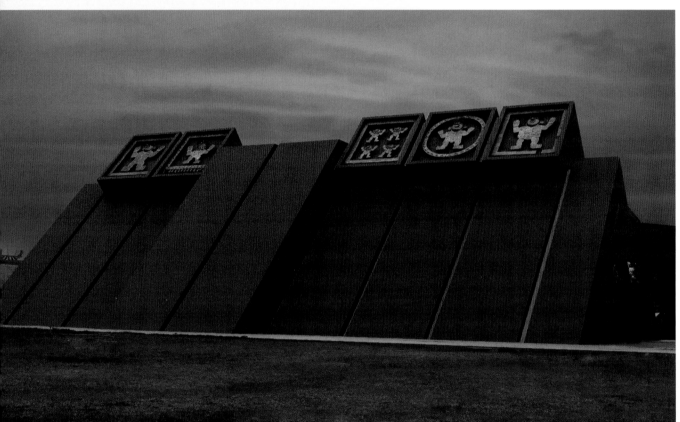

further behind in my car's rearview mirror. I develop a sense of how inconsequential I seem here – just a lone driver making a passing acquaintance with a landscape that has been shaped by dust and wind for millennia. This area was once the epicenter of numerous highly sophisticated civilizations – the Moche, Sican and Chimu kingdoms, among others. Today it feels relatively retrogressed from a standpoint of development, and generally wild and unexplored in its terrain.

After a brief detour 15.5 miles (25km) inland from the coastal city of Barranca, I approach Caral, the first of numerous sacred sites along this ride. Some 4500 to 5000 years ago, the oldest civilization in South America once called this settlement home. The Caral-Supe people were astonishingly advanced in public administration, fishing and agriculture – to the extent that some take their farming techniques and sustainable practices as a reference to this day. The Unesco World Heritage Site of Caral features temples, stone-built pyramids, amphitheaters and sunken circular plazas rising from the desert, all superbly well preserved.

Just outside Casma, 131 miles (211km) north of Caral, the archaeological site of Sechin dates to 1600 BCE. Its temple, built by a mysterious warlike people who weren't afraid to wear their violence on their sleeves, features 13ft (4m) bas-relief carvings of eviscerated captives. I mostly have Sechin to myself on this day, a realization that for me only adds to the ominous atmosphere.

Back on the highway, glimpses of the Pacific – sometimes impossibly blue, other times less so – dart in and out of view. Near Chimbote, I pass panoramas that are deserted, dry and bleak, in the most beautiful of ways.

I roll into Trujillo, aiming to spend the night in one of northern Peru's prettiest cities, a colonial gem whose bright yellow cathedral evokes the color of one of the nation's most famous dishes, *ají de gallina* (chicken stew). But because I'm on the coast, I'm certainly not thinking about chicken. Tomorrow's lunch means one thing – a pile of fresh and spicy ceviche, the grand dame of Peruvian cuisine.

If you've ever visited the Peruvian coast, you'll know what's coming. Ceviche connoisseur-ism becomes a thing here. Over time, you tell yourself you're going to order something else, only for a Pavlov's dog–like drool to immediately inhibit your ability to choose alternatives to a pile of raw fish marinated in citrus and spicy chili peppers.

I have eaten ceviche up and down the north coast, and can confirm that Trujillo's Mar Picante restaurant does it best. I order their ceviche *mixto*, a revelation that combines raw fish, crab, scallops and onions, marinated in salty lime juice, piled on top of yucca and sweet potato, and served with a side of *canchas* (toasted corn) and corn on the cob. I chase it all with a side of *rocoto* chili pepper salsa that lights me up something fantastic.

Outside Trujillo lie the ruins of the immense Chimú capital of Chan Chan, constructed around the 9th century CE and once the largest adobe city in the world. Close by are two Moche temples, over 700 years older than Chan Chan, known as the Huacas del Sol y de la Luna (the Sun and Moon Temples). All warrant extensive exploration. At Chan Chan, I'm awed by the ten walled citadels that include truncated pyramids, broad plazas and narrow passageways. Meanwhile, the Huaca del Sol stands out as the largest pre-Columbian structure in Peru.

The wonders that await up the highway in Sipán blow me away. The Museo Tumbas Reales de Sipán is located outside the city of Chiclayo, some 238 miles (383km) south of Máncora. It harbors the booty of an Indiana Jones–evoking real-life drama, complete with buried treasure, murder, looters of antiquities and, of course, archaeologists. This is a dazzling, world-class display of the immense fortune uncovered at the Moche burial site of the Lord of Sipán – detailed ceramics, ear ornaments, gold pectoral plates and other fascinating artifacts.

On approach to the surf town of Máncora, a savanna-like scrub begins to dominate the desertscape. Fugitive vegetation reminiscent of tumbleweed occasionally shakes, rattles and rolls across the highway, appearing with greater frequency than passing cars.

Once again, this feels like end-of-days stuff – and all I am is just dust in the wind.

RESERVA ECOLÓGICA CHAPARRI

Located 46.5 miles (75km) east of Chiclayo, Reserva Ecológica Chaparri delivers a radical change in scenery from the oceanhugging desert. This protected dry forest is one of the planet's few places to shelter the spectacled bear – along with over 230 bird species, including Andean condors, king vultures and numerous eagles. Chaparri Ecolodge (chaparrilodge.com) has wonderfully rustic adobe and bamboo bungalows.

Clockwise, from opposite top: the expansive beach at Máncora; a spectacled bear; the Museum of the Royal Tombs of Sipán, designed to resemble ancient Moche tombs. Previous page, from top: sculpted walls at the ancient city of Chan Chan; traditional Peruvian small reed boats

DIRECTIONS

Start // Lima
Finish // Máncora
Distance // 725 miles (1166km)
Getting there // Jorge Chávez International Airport in Lima is Peru's main gateway. Rent cars from the arrival terminal.
When to drive // Summer (December through February) brings warmth and little rainfall to Peru's north coast.
Where to eat // Big Ben (Huanchaco), Mar Picante (Trujillo), Fiesta Gourmet (Chiclayo), La Sirena d'Juan (Máncora)
Where to stay // Hotel Colonial (Trujillo), Hotel Caballito de Totora (Huanchaco), Playa Colán Lodge (Colán), Sunset Hotel (Máncora)
Tours // Moche Tours (www.mochetourschiclayo.com.pe)
More info // Peru Travel (www.peru.travel) is the official tourism website, with iPerú offices in Trujillo, Chiclayo and Piura.

MORE LIKE THIS
PERUVIAN ROAD TRIPS

THE SOUTH COAST

Peru's south coast is home to an equally intriguing (though less traveled) assortment of pit stops, thriving in this brutally dry desert. The idyllic oasis of Huacachina, beautifully depicted on Peru's 50 sol banknote, is a postcard-perfect place to lose a few days near Ica. The inexplicable Nazca Lines, a fascinating Unesco-listed group of supersized desert geoglyphs best viewed from a plane, are found 267 miles (420km) south of Lima. Birders flock to Santuario Nacional Lagunas de Mejía, 164 miles (246km) north of the Chilean border, where over 200 species of resident and migratory birds, and the coast's largest permanent lakes, are protected. The town of Lunahuaná and tiny "village" of Lagunillas are fun stops along the route.
Start // Lima
Finish // Tacna
Distance // 760 miles (1224km)

THE SACRED VALLEY

Incan ruins, ancient villages and artisanal markets await on this Andean road trip around Peru's Sacred Valley. Heading in a clockwise direction from Cusco, stop off at the immense archaeological site at Sacsaywamán, before continuing to the Incan site of Moray and Maras, home to a fascinating terraced amphitheater. Nearby, the salt pans of Salinas are worth a detour. Next up, the impressive ruins in the ancient cobblestoned village of Ollantaytambo – the best surviving examples of Incan city planning. At the charming village of Pisac, a hilltop Incan citadel awaits above and, in the streets below, the artisan market is famous across Peru for its handicrafts and other traditional wares – but be wary of mass-produced junk. And this is your chance to try guinea pig!
Start/Finish // Cusco
Distance // 114 miles (184km)

SANTUARIO NACIONAL HUAYLLAY

For a different take on Peru's distinctive landscapes, this ramble on four wheels starts at sea level in Lima and proceeds skyward to one of the highest cities in the world – Cerro de Paso. Nearly 4000ft (1219m) higher than Cusco, this city in the Andes leaves the tree line in your rearview mirror. The ride up via Hwy 20A passes by waterfalls, rarely seen Incan ruins, cerulean lakes and wayward llama herds. Radical changes in scenery appear as you ascend, from green valleys to the altiplano (Andean plains) to alpine tundra. In Obrajillo, at 8900ft (2713m) above sea level, you can dine on Chillón River trout for lunch. About 31 miles (50km) south of Cerro de Pasco, the bizarre rock formations of Santuario Nacional Huayllay emerge from a panorama that couldn't be more at odds with the Peruvian coast.
Start // Lima
Finish // Cerro de Pasco
Distance // 163 miles (262km)

Clockwise, from top: Urubamba river
and town in the Sacred Valley of the
Incas; one of the Nazca geoglyphs
viewed from a plane; the circular
terraces built by Incas at Moray

TO THE TIP OF SOUTH AMERICA

Amanda Canning drives though some of Chilean Patagonia's most dramatic landscapes to reach Torres del Paine National Park, watching for the wildlife of the far south along the way.

It's rare that a trip gets going immediately from the airport, but that's the case on the Ruta 9 from Punta Arenas. There are no traffic-snarled suburbs to inch through before hitting the open road here – within seconds of turning out of Presidente Carlos Ibáñez International Airport (a grand name for such a small operation), I'm on it. My goal is the Torres del Paine National Park, a 700-sq-mile (1813-sq-km) reserve in southern Chile that holds within its borders one of the world's most impressive mountain ranges.

I head north, leaving behind the coast and the dark waves of the Straits of Magellan. On either side is the wide, flat pampas, punctuated occasionally by small tin-roofed estancias. For many miles, the only distraction is the scruffy Patagonian sheepdogs that sit sternly in the back of the pickup trucks sharing the road and – the yin to their yang – a few straggly sheep in the fields. After about an hour, though, a line of hills appears on the horizon. As if to herald the change in tempo, a flamboyance of Chilean flamingos flap overhead, perhaps on their way to the plankton-rich waters of nearby Laguna Blanca.

By the time I trundle into Puerto Natales, some 150 miles (240km) later, those distant hills have grown into mountains, snow coating their peaks. The last settlement of any size before Torres del Paine, there's a palpable sense of excitement in town. Tourists potter in and out of adventure outfitters, trying on hiking boots and testing walking poles. Farmers pick up supplies and stop for a coffee before heading back out to the wild emptiness of the pampas.

A little way out of town, I leave the car and join a guided trek up through the hills bordering Lago Sofia. We tramp through a

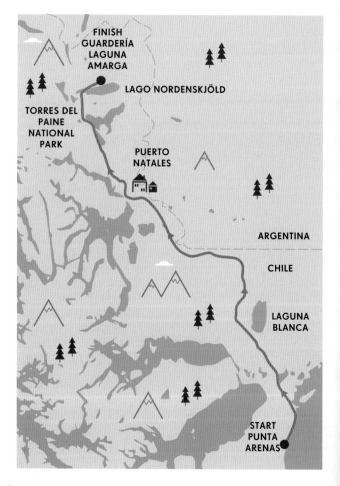

*"I sit and wonder at the chance of it all. That I could
see such a rare creature while sitting in my car."*

beech forest bedazzling in its autumn colors, and arrive on a broad
plateau above the lake. It's an area known for its sightings of
Andean condors, and our luck is in: we watch for an hour as the
birds wheel on the thermals above us and swoop down the cliff
face to unseen nests. Beyond them, on the other side of the water,
the mountains look tantalizingly close.

A series of shapely hills descends to a smattering of lakes, a
low wind ruffling their surface. As I return to the car and drive
onward, dark clouds break to better reveal the jagged, spiked
mountains of the Torres del Paine. They tower so high, I struggle to
see their peaks even when I contort my neck around the sun visor.
It's nothing short of a complete revelation as they're unveiled – as
if the curtain has risen on a spectacular theater set, or I've been
caught out by some improbable magic trick.

The cordilleras are in full view when I pass through the southern
entrance point and continue into the park on gravel roads. After a
winding drive on a narrow track that skirts the foothills of the range,
I get out to stretch my legs at Lago Pehoé. For a few minutes, the
mountains are mirrored in fantastic detail in the still water. Scarves
of mist drift around their tips and across shadowy crevasses piled

high with snow. A deep rumble reverberates across the water, likely
signifying the start of an avalanche from somewhere within. A gust
of wind announces the end of the show – the surface is disturbed,
the clouds close in and the peaks disappear.

I travel deeper into the park, and it becomes harder and harder
to keep my eyes on the road. Seemingly on every hilltop, herds of
guanaco stand sentry, the llama-like creatures alert to every sound
carried on the breeze. They occasionally trot across the track or
pour over the hills and out of view. Joining them in picking through
the grass are Darwin's rhea. Standing about 3ft (1m) tall, the
browny-gray birds resemble slightly dowdy ostriches – until they're
disturbed. At the merest suggestion of danger, they set off across
the fields at an unexpectedly brisk pace, long legs whirring beneath
them like the Road Runner. I half expect to hear a "beep beep" as
they dash away.

The creature that I and many of the park's visitors are keenest
to see is the one that we're least likely to: the Patagonian puma.
Most people leave their vehicles behind and march out across the
grassland to spot them, tracking the cats by the tufts of fur caught
on barbed-wire fences or the bloody leftovers of a meal on the

From left: a male puma, one of only 60-odd in the Torres del Paine region; the Cordillera del Paine mirrored in Lago Pehoé; a gaucho rounds up sheep on Estancia La Criollita, with the Sierra Baguales rising behind. Previous page: a long empty road heading toward the mountains of Torres del Paine

WILDLIFE CHECKLIST

Patagonia has its own Big Five, and – with a bit of luck – you can see them all in the Torres del Paine. Top of the food chain is the puma. Their main prey is the llama-like guanaco, which live in herds and are easy to spot. More elusive is the endangered south Andean deer. Two mighty bird species complete the lineup: the flightless rhea and the Andean condor, the world's largest flying bird.

DIRECTIONS

Start // Punta Arenas
Finish // Guardería Laguna Amarga
Distance // 235 miles (377km)
Getting there // Fly in and out of Presidente Carlos Ibáñez International Airport at Punta Arenas.
When to drive // The southern-hemisphere autumn (March to May) is an excellent choice; the colors of the foliage are spectacular, and the cooler temperatures are good for hiking.
Where to stay // In Puerto Natales, check into the Remota, a short walk into town (remotahotel.com). In the park, the Explora Torres del Paine has mesmerizing views of the cordilleras and rates that include a personalized program of experiences for the duration of your stay.
More info // The official tourist board (www.chile.travel) can recommend hikes in the Torres del Paine.

ground. I join a naturalist-led walk into an area where a male puma is commonly seen, finding nothing but a few guanaco, which run off into the mist on our approach.

The natural wonders of the Torres del Paine are so great that it's difficult to remain disappointed by the failure for too long. Back in the car, I drive past Lago Nordenskjöld, the jagged peaks of the Cordillera del Paine rearing up behind it. I intend to follow the Rio Paine to the Laguna Amarga further east before calling it a day. As I bump along the track, my eye is caught by movement in a calafate bush. Guessing a fox might be hiding within, I pull over and sit and watch. What emerges is not a fox... but a puma. It crouches low and creeps up the hillside toward a number of guanaco gathered on a ridge. They're soon wise to its presence, though – in a cacophony of shrieks, they're gone.

The puma turns and casts me a long look, his yellow eyes locked on mine, then pads off, slinking over the hill in half-hearted pursuit of the herd. I sit and wonder at the chance of it all. That I could see such a rare creature while sitting in my car. Then, like the puma, I turn and head away. There are a few more miles to drive and then it'll be time for my dinner, too.

Chilean Patagonia

MORE LIKE THIS
WILDLIFE-VIEWING TRIPS

BOW VALLEY PARKWAY, CANADA

You could never accuse the Rockies of being short of epic scenery – a road trip here means encountering towering mountain after towering mountain, the forests along their flanks breaking only to make way for vast lakes. With so much vying for your attention, wildlife gets a little less fanfare, but there is plenty to ogle here, too. Drive slow along the Bow Valley Parkway from Banff to Lake Louise, and keep your eyes peeled for Alberta's four-legged residents. Grizzly and black bears are a frequent sight, while enormous elk, weighing over half a ton, appear en masse for the September rut. Bighorn sheep, with their magnificently curled horns, are even more common – you might need to stop to let a herd finish picking grass out of the cracks in the road.

Start // **Banff**
Finish // **Lake Louise**
Distance // 30 miles (48km)

THEODORE ROOSEVELT NATIONAL PARK, NORTH DAKOTA

North Dakota is flat. Really flat. Theodore Roosevelt National Park comes, then, as something of a surprise, with the endless plains giving way to soft green hills and the distinctive, crenelated rock formations known as badlands. Take the Scenic Drive Loop to appreciate some of these natural highlights, and to get an eye-full of the park's inhabitants, from herds of shaggy, hulking bison to elk and wild horses. Come early for the best chance of seeing the elk, and ask rangers for help pinpointing the horses. You'll need no assistance tracking down the park's smaller critters – you'll see prairie dogs bobbing up and down in the grasslands all along the loop. The route can be completed in under an hour, but it's best to budget half a day.

Start/Finish // **South Unit entrance, Medora**
Distance // 36 miles (58km)

WEST COAST OF MAUI, HAWAI'I

A coastal trip around Maui is a delight any time of year, with each bend in the road revealing another curve of golden sand. Come between January and April, though, and your eyes will be drawn further out to sea. This is whale-watching season, with pods of humpbacks arriving to birth and rear their calves in the shallow waters offshore. Meandering south from Kapalua to Makena, there are plenty of viewpoints from which to spy them. Be sure to stop at McGregor Point Lookout; it's a prime viewing spot and there's usually a naturalist from the Pacific Whale Foundation on hand to share info. Allow plenty of time for the drive; it's likely you'll want to jump in the water at some point and join the whales.

Start // **Kapalua beach**
Finish // **Makena beach**
Distance // 41 miles (66km)

*Clockwise, from top: a breaching humpback
whale in the sea near Maui, Hawai'i; a bull
elk at Bow Valley Parkway in Banff National
Park, Canada; sunrise over the hills of Theodore
Roosevelt National Park, North Dakota*

CENTRAL AMERICA

COSTA RICA'S HIDDEN BEACHES

Anna Kaminski drives along Península Nicoya in northwest Costa Rica, searching for secret coves in jungle nature reserves and wave-battered surfer havens.

My sister Genie and I nearly come to grief on our first day in Nicoya, on the spectacularly rutted shortcut from Sardinal to Potrero. We're hoping to find Potrero's wild sugar-white beaches, but beyond the settlement of Nuevo Colón, the unpaved road – locally known as the "monkey trail" – deteriorates into a muddy mess. There is much wheel-spinning before the well-guarded shores are revealed.

Pressing on toward that night's destination of Playa Grande, we take the more accessible track to palm-fringed Playa Conchal. The coarse white sand, made up of millions of crushed small shells, crunches under our bare feet as we look for a good place to snorkel. We spot tiny white faces peering down at us from the overhanging foliage along the beach – they belong to a troop of a dozen capuchin monkeys, foraging for fruit. Unlike many of Nicoya's surfing beaches, Conchal's sheltered waters are calm and clear. After donning our snorkeling masks, we watch shoals of reef fish darting through the shallows.

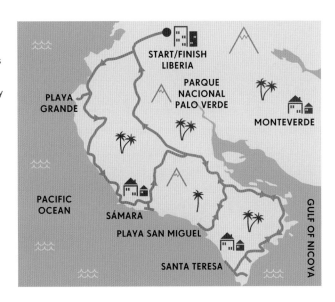

*"It's just us
and the
rolling surf"*

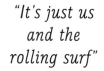

Since Nicoya has some of the world's most important nesting grounds for the critically endangered leatherback turtle, I have made plans for us to go turtle-spotting at Playa Grande. Come evening, we wander down a dirt road toward the beach, breathing in the mulchy smells of the jungle. Our guide Jhonathan is waiting for us on the wide sweep of sand, his walkie-talkie keeping him in crackling contact with his colleague Pablo, who is out on the beach, searching for turtles. "Keep completely silent," he tells us. Costa Rica takes conservation extremely seriously, and there is a strict procedure to turtle-watching. As the nesting turtles emerge from the ocean in the dark to lay their eggs in nests carved from the sand, they must remain completely undisturbed. In the dim light of our infra-red flashlights, we see movement up ahead – a huge leatherback turtle is laboriously digging a hole in the sand. We hold our breath and watch a spectacle driven by ancient instincts.

Chastened by our first day's experience, we plan to pass through the dusty inland settlements of Santa Cruz and Nicoya before day-tripping to Nosara over coast-hugging hills. We acquaint ourselves with rehabilitated howler monkeys at the Sibu Sanctuary and Refuge for Wildlife, and watch Tico (Costa Rican) fishermen haul in their catch at the brown-sand Playa Garza. Playa Sámara – a chilled-out beach town that feels like a metropolis after the tiny places we've just been through – lures us in and we end up picnicking with weekending Ticos on the palm-backed crescent of Playa Carrillo, as merengue tunes blare from parked cars. We go on to explore the hidden, wild beaches north of town, where it's just us and the rolling surf.

Following a tip from José, the owner of a restaurant in Sámara, we detour to practically deserted Playa San Miguel, which is bookended by a granite headland, and Playa Coyote, a remote silver-gray beach with a few guesthouses dotting the nearby hillsides. We choose to stay at the bougainvillea-bedecked B&B Arca de Noe, where we while away our time in hammocks, venturing down to the sea to eat the freshest ceviche, prepared by José's friend Henner from within an old shipping container.

Eventually, we leave San Miguel behind, and follow a largely paved main road. It hugs the coast as we drive along the Gulf of Nicoya, breezing through the port town of Playa Naranjo and turning sharply south. We're beginning to feel some trepidation, as we've been warned that the road to Santa Teresa is a challenge. The potholed track climbs steeply up the hillside, but the descent toward Pochote and Playa Tambor proves to be gentle. We park in a clearing south of the tiny beachfront town of Montezuma, where a park ranger points us to another mud-clogged trail, leading into the jungle. Cicadas shriek in the undergrowth as we make our way to a couple of waterfalls. By the time we reach the cascades and plunge into the deep swimming hole below, our beach clothes are soaked with sweat.

Our final destination is Santa Teresa, and as we pull in that evening, we're immediately enchanted. Actually, three small settlements come together here – Santa Teresa, Malpaís and Playa del Carmen – strung along a single dirt track running parallel to the beach. We slowly drive past fruit juice shacks, yoga studios and guesthouses peeking out of riotous vegetation. Surfers emerge from the water and pad along the sand as a blood-red sun drops.

Early the following morning, we are out on the long white sweep of Santa Teresa's beach. The surfers are already back, bobbing on the waves, as the owner of our guesthouse and surfing instructor, Pierre, lifts surfboards from the rack of his 4WD. Out in the shallows, we practice paddling on our bellies then standing up in one smooth motion after catching waves, until we become stiff with exhaustion. My sister proves to be the better surfer, staying on her board for more than a few seconds – and even attempting some turns – before collapsing into the water.

As twilight descends, our last night finds us pensively sipping cocktails at a bar high on the hill overlooking the bay. Earlier that day, we had taken an excursion to the nearby Reserva Natural Absoluta Cabo Blanco, Costa Rica's oldest protected area, at the southernmost tip of Nicoya. We hiked for hours through evergreen forest to a couple of wild white-sand beaches, then Genie decided to go for one last swim in the ocean. Dismissing my recommendation not to swim in fading light among all the surfers trying to catch the last waves of the day, she chose to carry on regardless.

Drinks finished, we now slowly pick our way back to our guesthouse through the darkness, amid an atmosphere fragrant with sea breeze, decomposing jungle and orchid flowers. My sister's voice emerges from behind me: "It all worked out in the end, didn't it?" Facing the journey back to tomorrow's starting point, I admit that, yes, it really did.

DIVING NICOYA

The Península Nicoya offers some of Costa Rica's best diving, with scuba outfitters based in Playas del Coco. Highlight locations include Isla Santa Catalina and Isla Murciélago, both of which attract migrating manta rays between December and April, while turtles and sharks are spotted year-round. During the January-to-March calving season, you might spot (or hear) humpback whales. Beginner divers can swim amid vast shoals of tropical fish around Punta Gorda.

Opposite, clockwise from top left: a squirrel monkey peeks between the leaves; a surf shop sign in Nosara; a leatherback turtle digs a nest. Previous pages: one of Nosara's beautiful beaches

DIRECTIONS

Start/Finish // Liberia
Distance // 400 miles (650km)
Getting there // Fly into San José, then take a shuttle service north to Liberia (128 miles/206km).
When to drive // Driving around Nicoya is possible year-round. Hot, sunny days are typical during the January to April high season, while May brings the rainy season. September and October are the rainiest months, when the peninsula is lush but many unpaved coastal tracks become impassable.
Car rental // A 4WD is not essential for getting to the main destinations around Nicoya, but it is highly advisable, since some unpaved roads are pretty rough. A 4WD is essential for driving certain coastal tracks between beach towns.
Best beaches // Playa Carrillo, Playa Cocolito, Playa Conchal, Playa Junquillal

Costa Rica

Opposite: Laughing Bird Caye, Belize;
the island is named after a population
of laughing gulls that once bred here

MORE LIKE THIS
CENTRAL AMERICAN
COASTAL DRIVES

PLACENCIA, BELIZE

Unlike the majority of Belize's many offshore cays, Placencia has long been known as "the cay you can drive to." Scuba divers come here between March and June to dive with migrating whale sharks, and the village's diving outfits run boat trips to Laughing Bird Caye, Glover's Reef and Belize's fabled Blue Hole – a giant marine sinkhole made famous by pioneering diver and marine biologist Jacques Cousteau. From Belize City, Western Hwy leads toward Belmopan; turn south along the Coastal Hwy that merges with the Southern Hwy, before a paved road peels off toward the coast through a sea of green. The final stretch winds its way along a narrow, sandy peninsula, with watery vistas on one or both sides, and heads through the Garifuna community of Seine Bight, with its colorfully painted wooden shacks and resident artist studios.
Start/Finish // Belize City
Distance // 228 miles (367km)

POPOYO, NICARAGUA

San Juan del Sur is Nicaragua's prime party town, where scores of surfers compete for the same breaks. In contrast, the miles of empty shoreline in Playa Popoyo – punctuated by dramatic rock formations – come as a relief to serious wave-chasers. This spread-out community comprises a single beachside track dotted with a few guesthouses, bare-bones surf camps and a couple of beach bars. From San Juan del Sur, a decent paved road passes through the urban sprawl of Rivas, getting you as far as the unassuming agricultural town of Tola, before it turns into a dirt-and-gravel track – a 4WD is needed during the rainy months of April to October (surfing season). Rugged tracks branch off Rte 62 toward the fishing and surfing communities of Playa Amarilla, Playa Gigante and Playa Jiquelite, before you reach the Popoyo turnoff.
Start // San Juan del Sur
Finish // Popoyo
Distance // 47 miles (76km)

PLAYA VENAO, PANAMA

With guesthouses and rustic surf camps peeking out of the dense tropical vegetation that extends almost to the shoreline, this horseshoe of dark volcanic sand is a surfing destination par excellence. Venao's laidback, barefoot surfing community is on the south coast of the Península de Azuero, a farming and ranching hub with a strong Spanish colonial influence; it's known for having the most traditional festivals in the country. From Panama City, drive west along Hwy 1 to Hwy 2, which takes you through the colonial town of Chitre and on to Las Tablas, where revelers throng during Carnaval – and the *seco* (sugarcane firewater) flows freely. Beyond, the paved road narrows and pushes between borders of dense foliage until you catch your first glimpse of the sea at El Ciruelo, just short of Venao.
Start/Finish // Panama City
Distance // 446 miles (718km)

VOLCANIC NICARAGUA

Oliver Smith drives between the volcanoes that continue to shape the geography of Nicaragua, from mystical islands to cinder cones that can be slid down like ski slopes.

Nicaragua has some truly heart-stopping geography – vast jungles, immense inland lakes, a wave-pummeled Pacific coast and paradisiacal Caribbean islands. But tilt your head up a little, and the defining feature of the country becomes apparent – mighty volcanoes lord over the horizons here, forming a short, smoldering episode in the Pacific Ring of Fire.

Nicaraguan volcanoes come in all shapes and sizes. Some are slumped, sulfurous and sleeping soundly. Others are wide awake and angrily spew lava over the landscape.

Fortunately, volcanic Armageddon seems far away in easy-going San Juan del Sur. This surfers' enclave on the Pacific Coast is where I start my journey. Here, a fiberglass statue of Christ looks down from a cliff to a sweep of bronze sand, and the streets beyond stir with ramshackle bars playing reggaeton after the sun sinks into the sea. It's a half-hour drive through coastal hills from San Juan to the shores of Lake Nicaragua.

The lake is strewn with islands, none more peculiar looking than Ometepe, which is crowned by twin black volcanoes, Concepción and Maderas, and eternally fogged by clouds. A rusty ferry transports my car from San Jorge on the mainland to the island. From the deck, the approaching shore looks like the sort of forbidding place where Godzilla lives in banishment. Upon disembarking, Ometepe is more appealing: driving its country lanes reveals gardens sprouting from fertile volcanic soil and forests noisy with the mischief of howler monkeys. Here and there are statues left by the island's pre-Hispanic inhabitants, for whom the island was said to represent a promised land. Today, Ometepe promises respite from days at the wheel: a place where you might

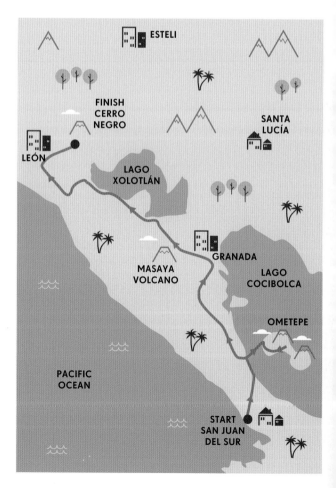

linger in hammocks in eco-lodges, or set out to kayak the butterfly-haunted backwaters of the lake.

Back on the mainland, I follow roads along the shore of Lake Nicaragua – beneath the cloud forests and orchid-swathed slopes of the Mombacho volcano – to the colonial city of Granada, a central character in Nicaragua's national story. Allegedly the first European-founded city on the mainland of the Americas, it was named by Spanish conquistadors in 1524. To drive into its centuries-old grid of streets is to put time into reverse gear – I pass tumbledown colonial-era bungalows and aristocratic mansions, parks and promenades, and churches built to match the Moorish majesty of Granada's Andalusian namesake.

After a night or two here, all travelers find themselves irresistibly drawn to Nicaragua's most famous volcano, Masaya, whose gray mass looms just beyond the rooftops and laundry lines of Granada. Masaya is not a tidy, symmetrical pyramid like the volcanoes of Ometepe, but rather a muddled mishmash of craters referred to as "the gates of hell" by the first Spaniards to set eyes upon them. After driving through the lunar wastes, I reach a parking lot right at the rim of the Santiago crater, where crowds peer through stinking, sulfurous mists to witness magma stewing below.

Somewhat less dramatic (but more pleasant smelling) is the capital of Managua – a modern metropolis cooled by the offshore breezes of Lake Xolotlán. Many travelers to the country pass it by, but in doing so they skip the best place to measure the pulse of contemporary Nicaragua. The Plaza de la Revolucion has been the site of protests and parades through the decades, presided over by a hollowed-out cathedral that was the victim of a 1972 earthquake. Managua is also a good base for day trips to the surrounding landscapes, notably the Reserva Natural Chocoyero-El Brujo, a fragment of rainforest where waterfalls tumble down cliff faces studded with parakeets' nests.

I drive north along the shore of Lake Xolotlán, past the hulking peak of Momotombo, which stands sentinel over the north shore. This counts as one of the more recent Nicaraguan volcanoes to erupt: during my visit an exclusion zone is in place, and peering through a telescope early one evening I can see a luminous red river of lava ebbing down its slopes.

Eventually the electric lights of León emerge from the dusk. This was once Granada's rival: a proud city that considers itself the cultural and intellectual heart of Nicaragua. Come morning its streets throng with students at one of Central America's oldest universities, while within its mighty whitewashed cathedral lies

THE NICARAGUAN CANAL

A proposed Nicaraguan Canal, which would rival the one in Panama, has been batted around since the 19th century. The concept centers on using Lake Nicaragua as a shipping corridor, and a Chinese-backed plan was set to be completed by 2019, before being shelved indefinitely. Lake Nicaragua is Central America's largest fresh water reservoir, and environmentalists say such development would devastate both wildlife and local communities.

From opposite left: Ojo de Agua, a natural water hole on Isla de Ometepe; Our Lady of the Assumption Cathedral in Granada; volcano boarding down Cerro Negro. Previous page, from top: Volcán Mombacho seen from the viewpoint at Catarina Mirador; fiery Volcán Masaya

"They give and take like gods, and were once revered as such"

literary titan and national poet Rubén Darío, entombed beneath a stone lion. There's an aura of antiquity among the trickling fountains and wrought-iron lamp posts of León – but in fact this is León 2.0: the first incarnation had to be abandoned in the 17th century due to seismic activity triggered by volcanic rumblings.

From the roof of León's cathedral you get a panorama of the volcanoes that might have authored the destruction of the original. Beyond the bell towers and palms of old León are the grassy meadows of Volcan del Hoyo and the humpbacked Las Pilas. Squinting hard I can make out the black blot of Cerro Negro: the youngest and strangest volcano in Central America, formed after an eruption in the 19th century.

This is where you can try... volcano boarding. Participants clad in boiler suits climb past sulfur vents to the top of the trail, before sliding down cinders on a wooden board a bit like a toboggan. It sounds easier than it is – when I attempt it my board gets wedged in a heap of cinders and I am briefly marooned at the top of the volcano. But while other boarders have their eyes fixed on the plummeting ground before them, I have some time to look around. To the north I see the great volcano of San Cristobal and to the south, Momotombo – both part of a family of volcanic giants whose cousins are as far away as Japan and Java, Alaska and Argentina. Their eruptions have taken lives and uprooted landscapes; their nutrients feed the green forests. They give and take like gods, and were once revered as such.

Eventually the board comes loose, and I continue hurtling down the slope – again following the path of bygone eruptions.

DIRECTIONS

Start // San Juan del Sur
Finish // Cerro Negro
Distance // 220 miles (350km)
Getting there // San Juan del Sur is roughly equidistant from the international airports at Managua and Liberia (Costa Rica). Cerro Negro lies at the terminus of a dead-end road 15 miles (25km) from Leon; the nearest international airport is Managua.
Where to stay // Jicaro Island Lodge, on Lake Nicaragua and a short boat ride from Granada, has nine comfortable *casitas* and arranges guided nature tours (www.jicarolodge.com).
Car rental // If you rent a car in Costa Rica, note that few if any companies will allow you to drive a car across the border, but they will arrange for another car in Nicaragua.
More info // www.visitnicaragua.us

MORE LIKE THIS
CENTRAL AMERICAN VOLCANOES

GUATEMALA

Many visitors avoid the country's sprawling capital, Guatemala City, but it's a good starting point for a road trip through the southwest. The first stop is Pacaya: an ash-raining leviathan that counts as one of the most active volcanoes in Central America. In peaceful times, guided groups trek to the summit – but in 2021, lava flows cascaded ominously down the southern slopes. Much more sedate is the former capital, Antigua, a colonial-era town of pastel-hued streets set beneath the coffee-swathed foothills of the Agua volcano. A drive northwest brings you to Lago de Atitlan, a highland lake of ethereal beauty, where yet more sullen volcanoes loom in mirror-like waters. Take the time to get acquainted with contemporary Maya culture in the villages that line the shore before returning to Guatemala City.

Start/Finish // Guatemala City
Distance // 190 miles (305km)

EL SALVADOR

El Salvador may be the smallest country in Central America, but it sure has its quota of supersized geological drama. Heading east from the Guatemalan border, the Ruta de las Flores meanders happily through El Salvador's coffee country. Further along, scale the concentric craters of the Santa Ana volcano, whose rim commands godlike views. Don't miss the Maya village Joya de Cerén, known as the Pompeii of the Americas, which was buried in volcanic ash around 600 CE and paints an intimate picture of pre-Hispanic life. Then it's on to the capital San Salvador: not instantly loveable, but helpfully sited for day trips to the attractive little town of Suchitoto. The final leg sees you strike east on the Pan-American Hwy to the city of San Miguel and the border with Honduras.

Start // Ahuachapan
Finish // San Miguel
Distance // 175 miles (280km)

HONDURAS

Honduras is unhappily synonymous with violent crime. Behind the grim headlines, however, lies a gem of a destination, from the luminous blue waters of the Caribbean to the immense cloud forests of the interior. Arriving from Guatemala, the first stop is the Copán ruins – a Maya city that ruled the surrounding hills millennia ago. Driving east, you reach the lively highland town and hot springs of Gracias, the perfect antidote after long days on the road. Magnificently wiggly roads usher you to Lago de Yojoa, a lake set in a volcanic depression that's become a hub for kayakers, stand-up paddleboarders and beer lovers on a pilgrimage to its much-loved brewery. Then drive southeast to Tegucigalpa, perhaps Central America's most spectacularly sited capital, with a fine crop of museums and restaurants awaiting to dispel its forbidding reputation.

Start // Copán
Finish // Tegucigalpa
Distance // 340 miles (550km)

Clockwise, from top: decorative horses
as props for family photos at Lago de
Atitlan, Guatemala; Maya carvings at
Copán, Honduras; climbing the Santa
Ana volcano, El Salvador

THE MAYA MYSTERIES OF CARACOL

Anna Kaminski takes a rugged, jungle-shrouded drive to Belize's greatest Maya ruins, escaping the crowds of equivalent sites across Central America.

"It says here that we shouldn't be driving to Caracol by ourselves," says Nazeem. He's flicking through an old guidebook as I steer our rented, dun-colored 4WD past the Green Iguana Conservation Project and turn off Belize's main highway.

"Oh, why is that?" I ask.

"Apparently, there have been attacks on tourists by Guatemalan bandits. Something about territorial disputes. Although I don't see what tourists have to do with it," he says. And frowns.

Now that Nazeem mentions it, I vaguely recall reading about an armed robbery, but the report was dated. I do my best to reassure him. "When José rented us our car and I told him we were headed for Caracol, he didn't mention any recent incidents."

"Well, we're going to pass an army checkpoint on the way. Let's ask them. I mean, tour minibuses head along here every day, so..." Nazeem returns to perusing his guidebook.

While visiting the Maya ruins of Tikal in Guatemala recently, we had joined a morning stampede of minibuses. During that trip, we were unable to find a corner of the jungle without scores of other travelers posing for a selfie in the same spot. Having then crossed the border from Flores, Guatemala, to San Ignacio, Belize, we are now keen to experience Caracol by ourselves – hence the early start.

Like Tikal, Caracol was once a powerful Maya city and strategic trading post along the trade routes between the Caribbean Sea and the Southern Maya Lowlands. Caracol predates the rival Maya kingdom of Tikal by around 500 years, having originally been settled in 1200 BCE. However, Tikal overtook it in prominence in the mid-4th century CE, when Chak Tok Ich'aak (King Great Jaguar Paw) adopted the effective and deadly form of "aerial" warfare

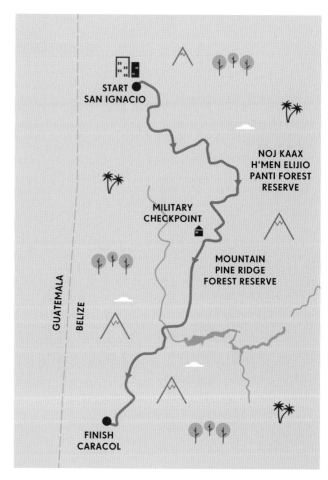

Clockwise, from left: young iguanas; a muddy track leads into the Mountain Pine Ridge Forest Reserve; Maya ruins in the jungle. Previous page: the Temple of the Wooden Lintel at Caracol

GREEN IGUANA CONSERVATION PROJECT

If you wish to acquaint yourself more closely with local wildlife, this excellent program located in the grounds of the San Ignacio Resort Hotel helps to ensure the survival of the green iguana here. Resident biologists collect, incubate and hatch iguana eggs, then release the large-growing lizards into the wild once they're past the most vulnerable stage in their growth. Visitors are taught about the iguanas' life cycle and can encounter them up close.

practiced by the rulers of Teotihuacán in central Mexico – his warriors encircled the enemy and threw spears from a distance, rather than engaging in hand-to-hand combat.

Caracol then became a tributary state of Tikal, until Yajaw Te' K'inich II (Lord Water) emerged as the ruler of Caracol in 553 CE. Within a decade, the balance of power had shifted again. Yajaw Te' K'inich II overran Tikal, after which it languished for over a century while Caracol grew in prominence and size, even forming an alliance with the Maya kingdom of Calakmul (in Mexico) in 619 CE.

The first part of our drive has taken us through the tiny settlements of Cristo Rey and San Antonio, with signposted turnoffs toward remote lodges on the Macal River and the Belize Botanic Gardens. South of San Antonio, beyond the turnoff toward the Barton Creek Cave Reserve, the level dirt road snakes south through the pine forest (an unexpected sight in the tropics) of the Mountain Pine Ridge Forest Reserve, established in 1944 to protect dense stands of Honduras pine.

> ## "The pine forest road turns into a narrow muddy track, with a tangle of jungle foliage creating a green tunnel around us"

"Do we want a military escort?" Nazeem asks. He's got his nose in the guidebook again.

"Apparently, members of the Belize Defence Force depart from the Douglas D'Silva Forest Station every morning at 9am, and return from Caracol at 2pm."

The mist of early morning still hangs over the pines. As we're not far from the military checkpoint where travelers passing through are required to register, and it's barely 7am, I suggest proceeding to the ruins by ourselves if told it's safe to do so. I'm not keen on arriving as part of a convoy and wandering around Caracol alongside men with machine guns, and the whole point of our early start was to beat everyone else there.

We have time for a quick breather so wander just off the road, following a sign toward a river known as the On. This leads us to a couple of small waterfalls, surrounded by dense vegetation, that trickle down to an inviting swimming hole. "I wonder why the Maya built Caracol where they did," I muse, dipping my feet into the cool water. Caracol's development as a powerful Maya kingdom is all the more remarkable given that it didn't have a natural water source. Its residents dug artificial reservoirs, capturing the rainwater needed to quench the thirst of their ancient metropolis and to water its agricultural terraces – all testimony to Maya resourcefulness.

At the military checkpoint, a bored and sleepy BDF soldier gets us to scribble our names in his dog-eared ledger. He informs us that the last armed robbery took place in 2006, and waves us on.

The pine forest road turns into a narrow muddy track, with a tangle of jungle foliage creating a green tunnel around us. The air becomes scented with mulch and tropical flowers. An eerie whooping roar echoes around us – somewhere at a great height up in the canopy is a howler monkey. I concentrate on the track as we are confronted by some enormous potholes, and slow down to narrowly avoid a washed-out section, barely marked by a stretch of flagging tape.

Finally, we pass through a rust-colored metal gate that welcomes us to Caracol. Aside from a snoozing caretaker beside a small wooden hut, there is no one else here yet. A system of trails connect the visitor center to the excavated heart of this Maya kingdom – two central plazas, a ball court, a multitude of stelae, tombs with hieroglyphic inscriptions, carvings of forgotten deities, and pyramids hemmed in from three sides by the tangle of vines, trees and undergrowth that still cover most of the ancient metropolis.

We climb the steps of the Caana (Sky Place) pyramid – still Belize's tallest building – and look out over the sea of green. Many centuries ago, during its heyday, Caracol and its complex agricultural systems supported around 150,000 people – almost triple the population of Belize City, the nation's largest city, today. In the late 800s CE, for reasons unknown, Caracol fell into decline. By the 10th century, it was abandoned to the jungle. From the stillness and silence of our vantage point, we contemplate how readily the demise of such a mighty city – and the civilization that built it – could come about.

DIRECTIONS

Start // San Ignacio
Finish // Caracol
Distance // 102 miles (164km)
Getting there // Fly into Belize City, then take a bus to San Ignacio (71 miles/114km).
When to drive // Driving to Caracol is only possible during the drier months (January to June), since the unpaved section of the road that runs thought the jungle becomes a largely impassable mudslide during the rainy season.
Car rental // Rent a car at Belize Airport or in San Ignacio. While a 4WD is not strictly necessary, a high clearance vehicle is essential. Take local advice seriously.
Hot tip // Get to Caracol early in the morning to have the ruins to yourself, since tour minibuses from San Ignacio are unlikely to arrive until late morning.

*Opposite: the El Mundo Perdido
(Lost World) complex and Templo
IV at Tikal, Guatemala*

MORE LIKE THIS
MAYA MYSTERY DRIVES

TIKAL, GUATEMALA

Tikal's edifices were constructed in waves from 700 BCE to around 100 CE. The steep-sided stone towers rising above the dense jungle canopy and numerous plazas – most cleared of riotous vegetation and some sensitively restored – hint at the past importance of Guatemala's largest and most powerful Maya kingdom. Highlights include the Gran Plaza, surrounded by impressive structures such as Templo de Gran Jaguar, and Templo I – the final resting place of Ah Cacao, a ruler who conquered the rival Maya state of Calakmul in Mexico. The road from Flores is mostly paved and generally well-maintained. The drive takes you across the causeway from the island in Lake Petén Itzá and skirts Mundo Maya International Airport, before hugging the east shore of the lake. As you duck into the jungle, slow down – you may well spot coatis, monkeys and agoutis in the undergrowth.
Start/Finish // Flores
Distance // 54 miles (87km)

CHICHÉN ITZÁ, MEXICO

Visit the most famous Maya ruins in Mexico on the spring or fall equinox and you'll get to witness the play of light and shadow that mimics the creep of a mighty serpent down the northern staircase of the Pyramid of Kukulcán. The ancient city of Chichén Itzá rose and fell between 400 and 900 CE. Its main highlights include the "time pyramids" important to the Maya astronomical calendar, carvings of Quetzalcóatl (the Plumed Serpent), carved eagles tearing open the chests of men to feed on their hearts on the Platform of Skulls, and the Gran Huego de Pelota (ancient ballgame court). You can drive almost up to the ruins along a paved access road branching off Hwy 180 just east of the colonial town of Pisté, itself a straightforward journey along Hwy 180, a greenery-fringed toll road, from Mérida.
Start/Finish // Mérida
Distance // 148 miles (238km)

CALAKMUL, MEXICO

Reaching the remotest of Mexico's Maya ruins – the ancient city at the heart of vast Reserva de la Biosfera Calakmul in the southern reaches of the Yucatán Peninsula – is well worth the effort. Comparable in size and importance to the rival Maya kingdom of Tikal in Guatemala, the Kingdom of the Snake flourished between 400 BCE and 900 CE; during its heyday, it was home to 50,000 people. The central part of the ruins has been cleared of vegetation and you can wander among the giant stepped pyramids and other stone constructions rising out of greenery, but much remains to be reclaimed from the jungle. From Campeche, follow the coastal Hwy 180 south, turn inland toward Encárcega, then follow Hwy 186 east. Just past Nuevo Conhuás, take a signposted turn south down a paved, single-track road encroached on both sides by the jungle.
Start/Finish // Campeche
Distance // 376 miles (605km)

THE CARIBBEAN

COASTAL DOMINICAN REPUBLIC, BEYOND THE CROWDS

Kevin Raub drives north of Punta Cana to the Dominican Republic's Samaná Peninsula, where remote sands, off-the-beaten-path dining and isolated sleeps present an idyll unspoiled.

The most stressful part of a road trip to the idyllic Samaná Peninsula is finding the highway entrance to set you on your way. In fact, the on-ramp lies exactly 4.6 miles (7.5km) west of Las Américas International Airport, outside the Dominican Republic's capital, Santo Domingo. I would know, as I've already missed it twice.

The DR-7 toll highway to the peninsula opened in 2009 and is one of the island's most modern roads, yet it seems to be operating under a shroud of secrecy. I know it's up ahead, but where are the signs? Determined to avoid the nerve-wracking fate of accidentally heading into the Caribbean's largest city, I grip the steering wheel tightly and focus on the road. At the last possible moment, I make out a lonely orange sign for "Samaná" that pops up out of nowhere. I gun the gas and exit right onto the DR-7.

"Not today," I mumble to myself.

As the diesel fumes and dust of Santo Domingo are slowly reduced to a speck in the rearview mirror, I sigh in relief. Hwy DR-7 picturesquely combs through the coconut tree–peppered hills of the Dominican Republic's heart without so much as a hint of heavy traffic, leading to a portion of promised land most visitors to the country never get to see. Of the DR's 8 million or so visitors in 2019, over half spent their time in all-inclusive buffet lines in heavily touristed Punta Cana. Samaná is different.

Markedly uncrowded by comparison, the Samaná Peninsula favors nature lovers, holiday isolationists and sun worshippers less than willing to share their personal space on the sands. It is the domain of secluded cays, mangrove reserves and end-of-the-world viewpoints. Only 5 percent of the island's hotel rooms are here – almost none of them in all-inclusive resorts. I'm traversing the

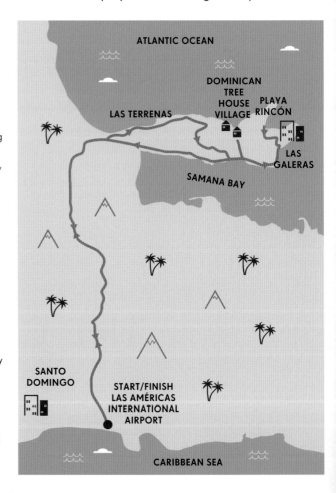

HUMPBACK SPOTTING

The Samaná Peninsula is one of the world's top destinations for observing humpback whales, which turn the Samaná Bay into their personal breeding and calving grounds from mid-January to late March. This annual song and dance of the most demonstrably active whale species in the North Atlantic – male courting songs, flippering, tail lobbing and breaching – is the one time of year the peninsula becomes a beaten path, with an estimated 45,000 tourists arriving.

Clockwise, from top: El Valle beach; swimming with humpbacks is possible at Silver Bank Sanctuary; the thatched cabins at Dominican Tree House Village; bathing in the jungle at Casa El Paraíso. Previous page: a motor scooter ride in Las Terrenas

EPIC ROAD TRIPS OF THE AMERICAS

peninsula's entirety to the end of the road, some 124 miles (200km) northeast of Santo Domingo. Destination: Las Galeras, the kind of remote village that obscure indie movies are set in.

But my first overnight stop is the Dominican Tree House Village, which can be reached either via the DR-5, which hugs the southern coast of the peninsula, or the DR-133 and the secondary Carretera Las Terrenas, a slightly longer route that rides the northern coast before turning inland and meeting DR-5 at Samaná town (officially Santa Barbera de Samaná). The decision is easy – I'm in need of a caffeine jolt, so I choose the latter, in order to fuel up with a double espresso in the lovely town of Las Terrenas.

Once a rustic fishing village, nowadays Las Terrenas is an exception to the typical off-the-grid Samaná ethos, and is easily the peninsula's best bet for finding knowledgeable baristas. It's also a wonderful spot to grab a French baguette, stock up on sundries and otherwise embrace a vaguely cosmopolitan seaside hamlet before heading deeper into the peninsula's verdant interior, where services are few and far between. Thanks to Boulangerie Française, I'm properly caffeinated and head onward, trading the town's turquoise seas for more jungly backdrops.

The remarkable Dominican Tree House Village leaves little to unravel from its name. Set in a tropical valley in appropriately named El Valle, it has 22 thatched-roofed treehouse cabins that are stocked with just enough comforts (electricity, ceiling fans, hammock chairs) to keep you sane, but limited enough that it feels more Amazonian than Dominican (no WiFi, cold-water showers). The treehouses and common areas were constructed from 98 percent organic materials and are supported by a twisted climbing-root system known as *bejuco*. Waking up here to the sounds of nature couldn't be further removed from the bustle of the breakfast buffet in Punta Cana. Remote and isolated El Valle beach is just 1.8 miles (2.9km) away. In two words: pure magic.

Next day, back on the road toward Las Galeras, the route turns wilder east of Samaná town. There is a shift from the forested countryside inland to the rich swatches of malachite-hued cliffsides along the coast, which give way to the crashing Caribbean Sea beyond. It's the perfect stretch to get lost in the hypnotizing rhythms of *bachata*, the local soundtrack, and watch the fertile hills fly by. About 4.4 miles (7km) south of Las Galeras, a fork in the road beckons a detour – Playa Rincón, one of Samaná's pitch-perfect beaches, awaits 7.4 miles (12km) northwest.

Playa Rincón's long stretch of sun-toasted sands means it's easy to carve out a patch for myself between picnicking Dominican families and day-trippers who've arrived by boat. Services are limited but a few restaurants dish up freshly grilled lobster and rent beach chairs, affording me the opportunity to kick back for a while. In fact, the only thought that tears me away is the certainty that tonight's accommodation will deliver a sea view without parallel, right from the bedsheets.

Initially, Casa El Paraíso seems a distinctly rustic B&B in an otherwise unremarkable location, just off the main highway in

La Guázuma, 2.7 miles (4.5km) south of Las Galeras. And though I've been here before and know exactly what lies beyond the modest entrance, it matters not. The open-sided rooms practically rest on a bed of tree canopy, framing one of the world's most outrageous bedroom sea views, a museum-worthy portrait of dense green jungle tumbling down the mountainside into a never-ending blue. There's an in-house Milanese gourmet chef and an incredible pool, too, but who cares?

> *"It's the perfect stretch to get lost in the hypnotizing rhythms of bachata, the local soundtrack, and watch the fertile hills fly by"*

It is from here that I base myself for adventures into laid-back Las Galeras, where the highway ends at a shack on the beach – as I said, the stuff of movies. I will eat at restaurants like El Monte Azul, which serves up some of the island's best French-leaning Thai food and most dramatic views. And I will generally get lost from the world at large.

I dig my toes into the sand and push the troublesome notion of driving back to the big city as far from my mind as possible. "Not today," I mumble to myself.

DIRECTIONS

Start/Finish // Santo Domingo
Distance // 270 miles (434km)
Getting there // El Catey International Airport is on the Samaná Peninsula, but you're far more likely to arrive at Santo Domingo's Las Américas International Airport. Car rental is easy to arrange at either airport.
When to drive // The Dominican Republic is lovely year-round, though the months of May, September and October are rainier than the rest of the year.
Hot tip // To ensure you don't miss the turnoff for Samaná Peninsula, merge right off Autopista Las Américas (Hwy DR-3) onto Marginal Avenida Las Américas immediately after the autopista toll booth when heading west from the airport.
Local tours // For whale-watching tours, join naturalist Kim Beddall at Whale Samaná (www.whalesamana.com).

Dominican Republic

*From top: snorkeling at low tide at
Taipu de Fora beach, Brazil; coastal
dwellings near Osorno, Chile*

MORE LIKE THIS
REMOTE COASTS

DOMINICAN REPUBLIC'S WILD SOUTHWEST

A wealth of nature awaits in the Dominican Republic's remote southwest. From Santo Domingo, follow the sunset into the foothills of the Cordillera Central on Hwy DR-2, and you'll encounter some of the country's most dramatic landscapes alongside its most beautiful beach. As you make your way west to the Pedernales Peninsula, the cactus-studded desert landscape is more evocative of the American Southwest than the tropical Caribbean. From Barahona, head southwest along Hwy DR-44 toward the Haiti-hugging Peninsula Pedernales for highlights deep, wide, and tall: intensely cerulean seaviews around the pleasant villages of Paraíso and Los Patos; the hypersalinic Laguna Oviedo, the Dominican's second-largest lake, flush with flamingos and leatherback sea turtles; and pristine Bahía de Las Águilas, reachable by boat or hardcore 4WD from Las Cuevas.
Start // Santo Domingo
Finish // Bahía de Las Águilas
Distance // 194 miles (312km)

BRAZIL'S MARAÚ PENÍNSULA

Brazil is no stranger to tropical hyperbole and the northeastern state of Bahia often commandeers the lot of it. It's not without reason. Located 79 miles (127km) north of the nearest airport (Ilhéus), Bahia's Maraú Peninsula is an idyllic stretch of coast harboring natural tide pools, deserted beaches, serene fishing villages and intense sunsets – all against a panorama colored by the state's famed coconut palms. The Rio da Serra begins to carve the peninsula from the mainland around 60 miles (100km) north of Ilhéus; Hwy BR-030 leans east toward Praia de Algodões, a long, quiet marriage of golden sands and transparent sea. Further north via Estrada Barra Grande, the peninsula's most photogenic beach, Taipu de Fora, beckons with tide pools so translucent, snorkeling equipment seems unnecessary. The road ends at Ponta do Mutá on Camamu Bay, known for vivid sunsets and celestial twilights.
Start/Finish // Ilhéus
Distance // 163 miles (263km)

CHILE'S OSORNO COAST

It doesn't occur to most folks to head west from Osorno, a working-class transport hub in Chile's otherwise outstanding Lakes District, but this stretch of coast 40 miles (60km) away in San Juan de la Costa is a wonderfully off-the-beaten-path assembly of remote coastal villages that feel distinctly different from the surrounding region – and the rest of Chile. Indigenous Huilluiche communities are centered on a series of spectacular *caletas* (bays) – Pucatrihue, Maicolpué, Bahia Mansa and Tril-Tril. As you travel north to south from Pucatrihue to Tril-Tril against a backdrop of lush Valdivian forest, each *caleta* emerges along the coastal road before rows of colorful fishermen's homes riding up the hillside. Everything culminates here in a side trip to Caleta Condor, an isolated, difficult to reach Eden, accessed by a rough and wild 1½-hour boat trip from Bahia Mansa.
Start/Finish // Osorno
Distance // 92 miles (148km)

HAVANA TO VIÑALES

Cruising west from Havana in a classic car, Christa Larwood discovers the tobacco plantations and incredible limestone landscape of Cuba's Valle de Viñales.

The Malecon comes alive at sunset. This broad ribbon of cement curves around Havana's waterfront, and as the sun wanes, the sky turns pink and the road is washed in coppery gold light. Orderly rows of fishermen perch on the sea wall, chatting as they cast their lines and hoping for a haul of bonito tuna or red snapper. Locals sit in pairs, laughing and occasionally canoodling, while the sea breeze brings with it the sound of a three-piece jazz ensemble that's just started up along the way.

This stretch is considered the classic drive of Havana, tracing over 4 miles (7km) along the coast from the colonial center of the Old Town to the business district of Vedado via a stately lineup of weather-faded houses from the 19th century and brutish Russian-style architecture.

It's here that the city meets the surging ocean. When a strong cold front hits this coast as it often does, waves hurl themselves against the sea wall and over, spraying dozens of feet in the air and flooding the road, but today the sea is calm and mild, lapping innocently at the dark rocks of the shore.

Unlike most great drives, where the highlight of the journey is glorious scenery passing by the windows, the best sights on the Malecon are on the road itself. Vintage 1950s American cars of all colors and kinds parade along its length. One second there is a dreamy round-nosed Buick in duck-egg blue; the next, a Chevrolet Bel Air convertible in brilliant red with silver fins followed by a royal purple Cadillac. They are so numerous and so perfect-looking, it could be a city-wide classic car rally.

The truth is, these vintage cars are not always a dream to drive. As I make my way along the waterfront behind the wheel of a 1955 Chevy – royal red and gold in color – the gears show flashes of temperament, sticking and occasionally slipping, and the steering has so much give, each turn of the wheel is little more than a gentle suggestion. But there is an indefinable joy in driving one of these vehicles, and it's not just the warm, fusty smell that evokes the old girl's decades on the road or her soft leather bench-seats, so broad and comfortable it's like driving a sofa.

I make my way down the Malecon and turn onto the cobbled streets of Habana Vieja, Havana's Old Town. Left to crumble after the 1959 revolution, Havana is a time capsule, its formerly grand buildings broken and pocked with neglect. The Old Town dates back to the 16th century, and retains vestiges of its former glory.

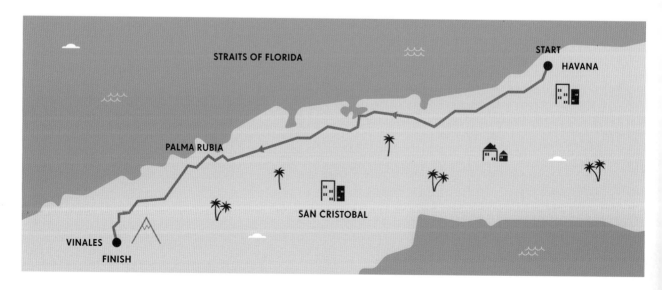

"By the roadside, coffee plantations and fields of yuccas and sweet potatoes give way to rows of young green tobacco plants"

Grand palm-filled squares are surrounded by streets with imposing churches, houses painted in cheery pastel colors and tiny kiosks selling freshly butchered meat or piles of fruits warmed by the sun.

Overhead, neighbors call to one another as they hang out washing in colorful strings from balconies; others gather on doorsteps to shoot the breeze, as often as not with fat Cuban cigars dangling from their fingers.

I wind my way through the Old Town, carefully avoiding street-sellers with their handcarts filled with peanuts or flowers or bread, and I tap my fingers on the wheel in time with the bursts of salsa music that float in through the windows.

From here, I head west into Havana's quieter, more residential suburbs, with wider streets and pretty, detached 1930s houses, and out onto the open road. My destination is Viñales, Cuba's agricultural heartland, around 110 miles (180km) from the city.

Havana disappears from the rearview mirror and the roadside spaces grow greener and more open until the landscape is filled to the horizon with broad fields and groves of waving palm trees. As the scenery changes, so do the cars.

In Havana, many of the vehicles are beautifully maintained – often convertibles, they're buffed, perfected and primed to ferry visitors around the Old Town's sun-dappled streets. Out here on the highway are Cuba's real vintage cars – many of them old bangers, put to work transporting families or hauling trailers stacked with goods.

At the turnoff for Viñales, the road changes abruptly from smooth pavement to coarse packed dirt, with corrugations and basin-sized potholes that make for a lurching, thumping drive. Out the window, pretty farm houses begin to dot the landscape, many with troupes of scratching, curious hens guarding front gardens.

The principal means of transport changes, too. In amongst the mix of old cars, juddering bicycles and carts filled with fresh local tomatoes and eggplants, are horses. Some have single riders on their backs; others are hauling goods on wooden carts that could have been in use a century ago, and *guarijos* (local farmers) all around sport wide-brimmed ponderosa cowboy hats woven from dried palm leaves.

Viñales is in the Pinar del Rio region, the western center of Cuban agriculture, where much of the country's best fresh produce is grown in the fertile soil. By the roadside, coffee plantations and fields of yuccas and sweet potatoes give way to rows of young green tobacco plants, whose leaves will soon be dried and expertly rolled into the world's best cigars.

I pull up on the roadside at a viewpoint overlooking the Valle de Viñales. An expanse of red soil and waving crops stretches ahead, bordered with palms and backed by a rugged shelf of green-fringed limestone. In the middle distance, a farmer drives his ox through a field, turning over clumps of iron-rich clay, in a scene that's three hours' drive and a hundred years away from the modern bustle of Havana.

CAYO LEVISA

This Cuban cay is a 35-minute journey by boat from Palma Rubia. It's a worthwhile trip: sugar-white sand and sapphire waters earmark Cayo Levisa as Pinar del Río's best beach. American writer Ernest Hemingway frequented the area in the early 1940s. These days Levisa attracts up to 100 visitors daily. While you won't feel like an errant Robinson Crusoe here, you should find time (and space) for plenty of rest and relaxation.

Opposite, clockwise from top left: in-car decoration; roadside companions; the limestone cliffs of the Valle de Viñales overlook tobacco plantations. Previous page: driving Havana's Malecon

DIRECTIONS

Start // Havana
Finish // Viñales
Distance // 112 miles (180km)
Getting there // Havana receives direct international flights from Europe, Canada, Latin America and several US cities, including Miami.
Car rental // Hiring a car in Cuba is fraught with pitfalls. There are state-owned rental companies at the airport but cars will need to be booked long in advance: prices are high, maintenance standards low. Seek up-to-date advice from Lonely Planet's Cuba guidebook. It's also possible to hire a private car and driver in Havana.
When to go // Peak times are Christmas, Easter, July and August – when it is also hot. An ideal time is from January to May, when it is warm but less crowded.

Opposite: San Miguel de Allende, Mexico, is Unesco-listed for its historical architecture

MORE LIKE THIS
CULTURE CRUISES

LINCOLN HIGHWAY, PENNSYLVANIA

Running from New York to San Francisco, the Lincoln Highway was established in 1913, a decade before it was superseded by Rte 30. In Pennsylvania, it's still a highway steeped in history, hugging the north side of the Mason-Dixon Line. To the west, Pittsburgh ranks as one of America's most livable cities, with its steel wealth translated into many museums. One detour from Rte 30 leads to Fallingwater: architect Frank Lloyd Wright's design-changing house in the wooded hills. Rejoining the route east, you're reminded of epochal moments in US history, passing the Flight 93 Memorial and the Gettysburg battlefield. The small cities of York and Lancaster are home to colonial-era architecture and one of America's oldest working theaters. And journey's end in Philadelphia is where the story of US nationhood began at Independence Hall.

Start // Pittsburgh
Finish // Philadelphia
Distance // 333 miles (536km)

CAMINO REAL DE TIERRA ADENTRO, MEXICO

Long before Mexico's Carretera Federal system, there was the Camino Real de Tierra Adentro. This highway ran inland for some 870 miles (1400km) between Mexico City and Santa Fe, New Mexico, transporting mining wealth to fund the Spanish Empire. To retrace the Camino Real in manageable fashion, and avoid driving in Mexico City's sprawl, try a three-stop tour between the beautifully preserved historic centers of Santiago de Querétaro, San Miguel de Allende and Guanajuato City. Highlights in the last, besides the paintbox-raiding cityscape, include the birthplace of artist Diego Rivera, and a museum of mummies for a very Mexican approach to mortality. As a final detour and historic postscript, take the road over forested mountains from Guanajuato to Dolores Hidalgo, where the famous cry that launched the fight for Mexican independence was made in 1810.

Start // Santiago de Querétaro
Finish // Dolores Hidalgo
Distance // 121 miles (195km)

DENVER TO SAN FRANCISCO

Friday night, Denver. Delivery driver Kowalski receives the keys to a 1970 Dodge Challenger R/T 440 Magnum and vows to deliver it to an address in San Francisco on Monday morning. It's a drive of 1200 miles (1900km) across Colorado, Utah, Nevada and California. The film is *Vanishing Point*, a cult classic from 1971 and while we're not suggesting readers self-medicate or break speed limits like Kowalski in order to attempt it in two days, it is a great route across the West that has become something of a pilgrimage. The film itself is not much assistance in planning a road trip – many of the scenes are shot in wildly different locations – but it is possible to plot a route that shares some of the movie's huge horizons. Kowalski heads west on I-70; stop in the ghost town of Cisco in Utah to discover one of the few filming locations along the route. You should also try to find a soul radio station on the dial to add to the atmosphere for an accurate recreation of Kowalski's epic drive.

Start // Denver
Finish // San Francisco
Distance // 1200 miles (1900km)

NUTMEG BY THE ROADSIDE

One of the smallest Caribbean nations has all the ingredients for adventure, as Rory Goulding discovers on a drive around the spice island of Grenada.

Nowhere in Grenada should be more than an hour and a half's drive from anywhere else – that is, if you haven't been waylaid by spice-tinged aromas drifting from a roadside barbecue or brought to a halt by a goat that's ambled over from the shoulder. This is the second-smallest independent nation in the Americas; Grenada's main island is just over 20 miles (32km) from end to end, and most visitors only ever stay at one of those extremities. Though the time I have here is far too short, just two nights of a longer Caribbean trip, I want to see how much of the country I can get to know in a day.

With a road map spread out, Grenada looks a bit like a comma with a tiny tail, or perhaps some small sea creature drifting through a coral reef offshore. This four-mile "tail" is where you'll find Maurice Bishop International Airport, and almost all of the island's resort hotels. There's a good reason for this: most of Grenada's finest golden-sand beaches are concentrated on this point of this land, including the longest of all, Grand Anse.

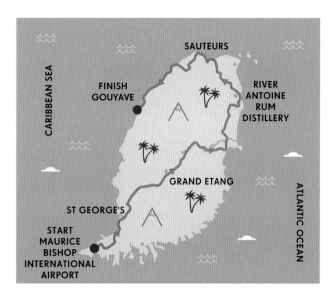

"The culmination is a nutmeg ice cream that makes me appreciate why wars have been fought over this spice"

Following the coast road from here through Grenadian suburbia – houses in ice-cream colors, tropical plants bursting from behind balustrades – I don't have long to adjust to local driving rhythms before I reach the inner harbor of St George's, one of the most appealing capitals in the Caribbean. The name of the city, like its surviving red telephone boxes, is a legacy of two centuries of British rule. But the harbor's oldest quayside is known as the Carenage, where sailing ships were once beached for maintenance: one of many other island place names left over from the previous colonizers, the French. The big cruise ships now mostly dock on the other side of the spit of land occupied by St George's old town. Its buildings hold on doggedly against hurricanes – the worst of recent years being Ivan in 2004.

I stop at a white-and-pink cottage, with a covered terrace by the road out front. If you're looking to learn as much as you can about Grenada in the space of a lunchbreak, Patrick's Local Homestyle Restaurant more than does the job. The small plates, well over a dozen, keep coming: spinach-like callaloo soup with a touch of Scotch bonnet chili, cinnamon plantains, snapper with pineapple Creole sauce. The culmination is a nutmeg ice cream that makes me appreciate why wars have been fought over this spice.

Originally from Indonesia, where its source was jealously guarded by Dutch traders, it was brought to Grenada in the 1840s soon after the end of slavery, and became the island's biggest export. When Grenada gained full independence in 1974, it adopted a flag with a little nutmeg symbol upon it. It's the default national spice, but far from the only one in this boundlessly fertile country, where it feels quicker to list the things that *don't* grow. Chef Karen Hall, taking a bow at the end of the meal, explains: "Many people have a ginger plant in their garden, and also grow their own cinnamon or cloves."

The road from St George's up into the mountains snakes past many houses built out on stilts for lack of level ground. One of the last settlements before the inland forest takes over bears the name Snug Corner. It isn't just here that drivers must navigate steep bends with only inches of passing room, between a deep drainage ditch and a panoramic drop. The road reaches almost 2000ft (600m) on its way to Grand Etang, a lake filling the crater of an extinct volcano, now the wildest and most forested part of the island. Stepping out, the air is cooler and more humid. Behind the lake, the summit of Mount Qua Qua is hidden in cloud. It was here that French-speaking rebels against British rule and slavery made their last stand in 1796.

My mid-afternoon aim is an enterprise that was already a decade old at that point, and whose infrastructure seems frozen in the early Victorian era. A water wheel powers the original machinery to crush sugar cane at River Antoine Rum Distillery. The spirit produced here is fiery: it can be 80 percent alcohol by volume, although since most airlines won't let you bring anything above 70 percent on board, River Antoine makes a 69 percent version for tourists to take home. As gloriously unreformed as the set-up is here, I need a few minutes after the tour to clear my head of rummy vapors before joining the road again.

The island's north end brings barely developed beaches such as Bathway and Levera, and the fishing town of Sauteurs ("Jumpers") where the last of Grenada's Indigenous Carib people are said to have leapt into the sea rather than submit to the French. Looking out from the beach here, past the undersea volcano of Kick 'em Jenny bubbling away somewhere five miles out, I can see the next small islands in a chain that stretches in a great arc all the way to Cuba.

Friday evening is approaching. I follow the coast round to the west, past chocolate plantations with cocoa beans drying in big trays in the sun, and into the hills where nutmeg trees left half-abandoned after Hurricane Ivan drop their fruit by the roadside. The glossy, dark seed inside is covered with a vivid red web, the source of a more rarefied spice, mace. The nutmeg is processed in the west-coast town of Gouyave, but one night a week the big draw here is Fish Friday. A dozen food stalls are lined up along two streets under an old church steeple, with mellow calypso playing from speakers. Around 9pm, drummers start up, and the balance of the crowd shifts from tourists to locals. I know that across the Caribbean at this moment, other islands are dining out on comfort food and music, but Grenada is like the spices it proudly produces: even a small pinch goes a long way.

GRENADA IN ONE POT

The name is something of a tough sell, but "oil down" is Grenada's beloved national dish: beef, salt pork, and sometimes chicken or salt fish, thrown in with dumplings, breadfruit, callaloo leaves and turmeric (or "saffron" as it's called here), all cooked in coconut milk. If boiled down, just the coconut oil will be left at the bottom of the pot. An oil down party is a highlight of many Grenadian weekends.

Clockwise, from opposite left: a vendor carries fruit and spices on her head; a freshly picked nutmeg pod; street food stalls at Gouyave's Fish Friday. Previous pages: colorful rooftops in the city of St George's

DIRECTIONS

Start // Maurice Bishop International Airport
Finish // Gouyave
Distance // 41 miles (66km)
Getting there // Grenada has direct flights from New York, Miami, Atlanta, Toronto and London, plus neighboring Caribbean islands. The island is a regular stop for cruise ships.
Best time of year // Most visitors avoid the wettest period, roughly June to November, though August sees the Spicemas carnival. May can be less busy with tourism, but still sunny.
Car rental // Although you don't actually need 4WD if you're sticking to Grenada's main roads, it's not a bad idea – but don't get something too big to maneuver in narrow spaces. Drive on the left, and watch for fast drivers, slow drivers, pedestrians, animals and potholes.
More info // www.puregrenada.com

MORE LIKE THIS
EASTERN CARIBBEAN ISLAND DRIVES

FIG TREE DRIVE, ANTIGUA AND BARBUDA

The rainforest that once covered Antigua now survives in the mountains of its southwest corner. Fig Tree Drive is the only road to pass through this tract, and is named after the banana plants (or "figs") that thrive here. Start in the small town of Swetes, next to the candy-pink church of Our Lady of Perpetual Help, and the first of several fruit stalls along the narrow, undulating road. After about a mile, you pass a cricket ground and the houses begin to peter out. Around the halfway point, Fig Tree Studio is a good place to stop and browse local paintings and crafts. The second part of the drive is wilder, and for a few minutes you're in a world of tropical forest growing unrestrained, before you reach the sea at beautiful Carlisle Bay Beach.

Start // Swetes
Finish // Old Road
Distance // 5 miles (8km)

THE WILD EAST, BARBADOS

The west side of Barbados, with its many desirable beaches, is among the most built-up corners of the Caribbean. Head east and you may not be able to swim, but you'll be far from golf courses and luxury developments. Tall coconut palms make Bottom Bay a winning first stop. Follow wiggly roads to reach Bathsheba, a tranquil town with mushroom-shaped boulders on a beach that's legendary with pro surfers. The hilly and semi-deserted coast road turns inland just ahead of Walkers Beach. Before you cut back west again across the top of the island toward old-world Speightstown, you'll pass several sights that stand as testament to Bajan history, of sugar cane industry built upon slavery up to the 1830s, including the Morgan Lewis Windmill and the plantation house of St Nicholas Abbey, dating from 1658.

Start // Oistins
Finish // Speightstown
Distance // 34 miles (55km)

THE PITONS, ST LUCIA

The twin cone-shaped coastal peaks of Gros Piton and Petit Piton are a Unesco World Heritage Site, honored on St Lucia's flag (and by the island's Piton beer). In other words, you can't come here and not pay them a visit. If you are staying in one of the hotels at the top of the island, north of the capital Castries, prepare for zigzags and luscious scenery on the drive south, where you'll catch your first sight of the Pitons shortly before the descent to the photogenic town of Soufrière, named after the sulfurous volcanic vents just inland. Many people turn back once they've seen the Pitons from all vantage points, but why not cover new ground on the return? Stop at Sandy Beach just past Hewanorra Airport, and loop back past east-coast villages away from the resorts.

Start/Finish // Castries
Distance // 80 miles (129km)

Clockwise, from top: a hiker looking toward Gros Piton, St Lucia; directions to surf schools and shops on the east coast of Barbados; secluded Harrismith Beach, Barbados

BAHAMIAN BEAUTY ON ELEUTHERA'S BUMPY ROAD

The sole road on this skinny Bahamian island straddles the ridge between dark Atlantic and turquoise Caribbean waters, where Emily Matchar finds pink-sand beaches and eerie sinkholes.

I thought my biggest problem driving on Eleuthera would be remembering to keep left. As it turns out, getting my rental car unstuck from a rock is a lot more of a challenge.

"Try again," calls my husband of two weeks, standing on the side of what would only generously be called a road.

I try. There's a terrible grinding sound. The late-model sedan, already not in the best of shape, doesn't move an inch.

This situation is no one's fault but my own. When we decided to drive to Lighthouse Beach, at the very southern tip of rural Eleuthera, I figured the road would be paved. When I realized it wasn't, I decided to press on anyway. A sedan can handle a few bumps, right?

After a white-knuckle half-hour of steering the car between increasingly large boulders, we finally did make it to Lighthouse Beach. It was nine in the morning on a breezy November day, and the wide stretch of pink sand was completely deserted.

Pink sand? Yes. This is one of Eleuthera's claims to fame – beaches tinted in shades of coral and peach by the shells of microscopic creatures called benthic foraminifera. It's as magical as it sounds; along with the glittering aquamarine water, you practically expect a unicorn to come wandering along.

We strolled, barefooted in the foamy surf, until we came to the old lighthouse on a limestone outcrop for which the beach is named. We swam in the Caribbean waters, then lay directly in the warm pink sand and dozed off. Looking up and down the empty beach, I thought, "This is what a honeymoon should be." Eventually, growing hungry, we got back in the car and tried to go back the way we came.

And now we are stuck. Why didn't I get a four-wheel drive?

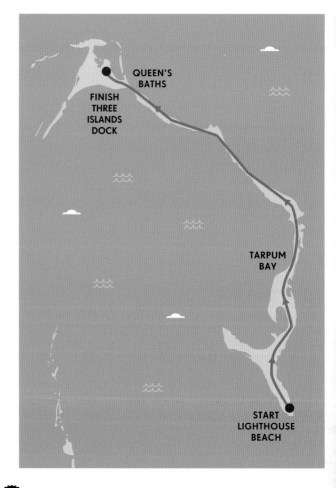

But then my husband gives the rear bumper a light push and, miraculously, the car slides forward. I silently promise myself to stick to paved roads from now on.

On Eleuthera, a 110-mile (177km) boomerang-shaped island with a sparse population and only a handful of major resorts, there's just one main road: the Queen's Highway. Our plan for today is to drive its entire length, then hop the ferry to adjacent Harbour Island for the night.

Once we return to the Queen's Highway from the rocky beach road, I drive slowly (on the left!) north. Though it's late fall, the weather is perfect: balmy but not stifling, the sky brilliant with a few shredded white clouds. And though we're starving by now, we're so curious about signs pointing to "Ocean Hole" that we make a short diversion. We find ourselves staring into the navy depths of a blue hole – one of many limestone sinkholes that dot the Bahamas, both onshore and off. I stand amid the shrubbery at the edge of a cliff and peer at the fish swimming just below the surface.

A few minutes north, we stop at the settlement of Tarpum Bay, where my husband spots a small wooden food stand. The proprietor leans out the window and, smiling, asks us how we like our conch.

> ## "At the top we stand and look down on the crashing Atlantic, navy blue and swirling with eddies and whitecaps"

Conch, a large sea snail native to the Caribbean, is the Bahamas' de facto official food. Locals cook and eat it every which way – "cracked" (fried), in fritters, in soup, marinated with tomatoes and onions. My husband and I share a plate of cracked conch and a bowl of citrusy conch salad. The cracked conch is hot and salty and delightfully chewy, while the salad is sharp and bright and spicy, a perfect contrast.

After eating, we continue on as the Queen's Highway hugs the Caribbean coast. On the right are rows of droopy palms and stands of yellow elder, punctuated with the occasional small wooden house. We stop at Ten Bay Beach and admire the casuarina-fringed sands. Hugged by the gentle curve of the island, the water is absolutely clear and flat as window glass.

The island bends west at James Point, and becomes so narrow I can see water on both sides. We pass beach after beach, all almost deserted – the big resorts haven't gotten here yet, though they're coming. In Gregory Town, an itty-bitty hamlet that hosts the annual Eleuthera Pineapple Festival, we poke around a local gift shop and emerge with pineapple cookies, pineapple-pepper hot sauce and several jars of pineapple jam.

A few minutes further north we spot a small sign reading "Queen's Baths," and pull over along the side of the road.

ELEUTHERA'S HISTORY

The island was settled in 1647 by English religious pilgrims, who named it after the Greek word for "freedom." During the mid-20th century, Eleuthera enjoyed a brief moment of glamor, with several resorts catering to global jet setters. This was followed by decades of sleepiness, at least on the mainland – adjacent Harbour Island continued to attract celebs. Now Eleuthera is changing yet again, as Disney develops the island's southern tip into a cruise resort and park.

Clockwise, from top: Princess Cays beach; the Queen's Baths rock pools; cracked conch dinner. Previous page, from top: the Glass Window Bridge; a waterside church at Tarpum Bay

On the right, a small footpath winds up a limestone cliff. We follow it, picking our way carefully through the dusty rocks. At the top we stand and look down on the crashing Atlantic, navy blue and swirling with eddies and whitecaps. Before us, on the cliff tops, are a series of small pools formed by the spray of waves at high tide. Locals call these the Queen's Baths or the hot tubs. I dip my hand in one and see why – warmed by the sun all day, they're the temperature of bathwater. If I wasn't fully dressed, I'd take a soak. Instead, I peer forward, watching small crabs and minnows dart around the pool's rocky bottom.

Nearly to the end of our drive, we climb down and walk along the road for a few minutes to see what we've been told is the island's most impressive sight: the Glass Window Bridge. Climbing up a rocky bank, we see why. The one-lane bridge spans the island's narrowest point, showcasing a marvelous quirk of geology. On the right side is the dark, fierce Atlantic. On the left, the clear, aquamarine Caribbean Sea. The contrast is astonishing.

"It hardly seems real," my husband says. "If I wasn't standing right here, I'd think it was Photoshopped."

We take pictures – so many pictures. One of them, years and many miles later, will wind up on our nightstand, a reminder of that wild honeymoon drive and of that extraordinary place that was almost too beautiful to be real.

DIRECTIONS

Start // Lighthouse Beach
Finish // Three Islands Dock (ferry to Harbour Island)
Distance // 91 miles (146km)
Getting there // There are daily flights from Nassau and Florida to the North Eleuthera and Governor's Harbour airports, as well as a ferry from Nassau.
When to drive // Hurricane season is June through November, though it's generally worse in August and September. Temps are balmy even in winter.
Car rental // There are a handful of local car rental agencies near the airports and around the settlements of Governor's Harbour and Tarpum Bay.
Where to stay // There are a growing number of luxury resorts, as well as plenty of lower-key family-run hotels and cottage rentals.

Opposite, clockwise from top: Hwy 5 heads south like an arrow through the desert, Mexico; Dames Point cable-stayed bridge over the St Johns River in Jacksonville, Florida; Boneyard Beach on Big Talbot Island, Florida

MORE LIKE THIS
HIDDEN BEACH DRIVES

JACKSONVILLE TO BONEYARD BEACH, FLORIDA

Heading north out of Jacksonville's suburban sprawl, you'll cross the cable-stayed Dames Point Bridge, which spans the St Johns River like an enormous harp. On the north side, you'll pass through rural Floridian landscapes of cabbage palmetto and sawgrass, following the wide, flat river as it bends east. On your left is the Timucuan Ecological and Historical Preserve, a protected stretch of salt marshes, dunes and hardwood hammocks (small islands of trees). This is old-school angler's country, dotted with fish camps, bait shops and rough-looking floating docks. Cross the bridge to Little Talbot Island, one of the last remaining undeveloped barrier islands. On adjacent Big Talbot, Boneyard Beach sits on Nassau Sound. Its name comes from the driftwood trees that make eerie silhouettes against the Florida sky, an extraordinary (and extraordinarily photogenic) sight

Start // Jacksonville
Finish // Boneyard Beach
Distance // 30 miles (48km)

BAR HARBOR TO ROQUE BLUFFS BEACH, MAINE

Many people visiting Bar Harbor stay put. After all, the charming seaport and its adjacent landscapes – including Acadia National Park – are glorious enough for a lifetime's worth of summers. But a short day trip northeast along Maine's famously scenic Rte 1 takes you to a much less traveled part of the state. Directly south of the old sawmill town of Machias, Roque Bluffs Rd cuts through forest and farmland – stop at Welch Farm, a century-old working blueberry farm complete with a desperately charming red barn. Then keep going south until the road terminates in Roque Bluffs State Park on the shores of Englishman Bay. On the bay side of the road is a cold, sandy saltwater beach, while on the other side are the warmer waters of Simpson's Pond.

Start // Bar Harbor
Finish // Roque Bay Beach
Distance // 82 miles (132km)

MEXICALI TO SAN FELIPE, MEXICO

Begin in the California–Mexico border town of Mexicali, a tangle of duty-free shops and dentists' offices. Drive south along Hwy 5 through the sun-blasted Sonoran Desert, one of the hottest places in Mexico. Tangles of chaparral blow in the hot winds, while giant cardón cactuses stretch skyward like the fingers of an enormous hand. Faint paths lead to settlements deep in the desert. To your left is the Reserva de la Biosfera del Alto Golfo de California, a protected area where fringe-toed lizards and Gila monsters roam amid salt pans and ancient cinder cones. The road eventually curves east toward the Gulf of California. Here, the drowsy little beach town of San Felipe has one of the largest tidal bores in the world – come at low tide and find that the sea has retreated by half a mile!

Start // Mexicali
Finish // San Felipe
Distance // 122 miles (197km)

INDEX

Epic Road Trips of the Americas
September 2022
Published by Lonely Planet Global Limited
CRN 554153
www.lonelyplanet.com
10 9 8 7 6 5 4 3 2 1

Printed in China
ISBN 978 1 8386 9533 0
Text & maps © Lonely Planet 2022
Photos © as indicated 2022

General Manager, Publishing Piers Pickard
Associate Publisher Robin Barton
Commissioning Editor Peter Grunert
Designer Kristina Juodenas
Picture Research Claire Guest
Editor Christopher Pitts
Index Polly Thomas
Print Production Nigel Longuet

Lonely Planet Global Limited
Digital Depot, Roe Lane (off Thomas St),
Digital Hub, Dublin 8,
D08 TCV4
Ireland

STAY IN TOUCH lonelyplanet.com/contact

Authors Amy Balfour; Joel Balsam; Oliver Berry; Joe Bindloss; Greg Bloom; Amanda Canning; Garth Cartwright; Elaine Glusac; Rory Goulding; Carolyn B Heller; Anita Isalska; Mark Johanson; Anna Kaminski; Adam Karlin; Christa Larwood; Emily Matchar; Hugh McNaughtan; Tim Moore; Simon Moya-Smith; Etain O'Carroll; Becky Ohlsen; Kevin Raub; Andrea Sachs; Oliver Smith; Regis St Louis; Marcel Theroux; Orla Thomas; Ryan Ver Berkmoes; Adam Weymouth; Clifton Wilkinson.

Cover illustration by Ross Murray (www.rossmurray.com)